W9-DFP-729

Bloom's Literary Themes

Alienation
The American Dream
Death and Dying
The Grotesque
The Hero's Journey
Human Sexuality
The Labyrinth
Rebirth and Renewal

ALIENATION

Bloom's Literary Themes

ALIENATION

Edited and with an introduction by
Harold Bloom
Sterling Professor of the Humanities
Yale University

Volume Editor
Blake Hobby

BLOOM'S
LITERARY CRITICISM
An imprint of Infobase Publishing

Bloom's Literary Themes: Alienation

Copyright ©2009 by Infobase Publishing
Introduction ©2009 by Harold Bloom

Bloom's Literary Criticism
An imprint of Infobase Publishing
132 West 31st Street
New York NY 10001

Library of Congress Cataloging-in-Publication Data
Alienation / edited and with an introduction by Harold Bloom ; volume editor, Blake Hobby.
   p. cm. — (Bloom's literary themes)
  Includes bibliographical references and index.
  ISBN 978-0-7910-9798-4 (acid-free paper) 1. Alienation (Social psychology) in literature. I. Bloom, Harold. II. Hobby, Blake.
  PN56.A45A45 2009
  809'.93353—dc22   2008042982

Text design by Kerry Casey
Cover design by Takeshi Takahashi

Printed in the United States of America

IBT EJB 10 9 8 7 6 5 4 3 2

This book is printed on acid-free paper and contains 30 percent postconsumer recycled content.

~ *Contents* ~

Series Introduction by Harold Bloom: Themes and Metaphors

1. Topos and Trope

What we now call a theme or topic or subject initially was named a *topos*, ancient Greek for "place." Literary *topoi* are commonplaces, but also arguments or assertions. A topos can be regarded as literal when opposed to a trope or turning which is figurative and which can be a metaphor or some related departure from the literal: ironies, synecdoches (part for whole), metonymies (representations by contiguity) or hyperboles (overstatements). Themes and metaphors engender one another in all significant literary compositions.

As a theoretician of the relation between the matter and the rhetoric of high literature, I tend to define metaphor as a figure of desire rather than a figure of knowledge. We welcome literary metaphor because it enables fictions to persuade us of beautiful untrue things, as Oscar Wilde phrased it. Literary *topoi* can be regarded as places where we store information, in order to amplify the themes that interest us.

This series of volumes, *Bloom's Literary Themes*, offers students and general readers helpful essays on such perpetually crucial topics as the Hero's Journey, the Labyrinth, the Sublime, Death and Dying, the Taboo, the Trickster and many more. These subjects are chosen for their prevalence yet also for their centrality. They express the whole concern of human existence now in the twenty-first century of the Common Era. Some of the topics would have seemed odd at another time, another land: the American Dream, Enslavement and Emancipation, Civil Disobedience.

I suspect though that our current preoccupations would have existed always and everywhere, under other names. Tropes change across the centuries: the irony of one age is rarely the irony of another. But the themes of great literature, though immensely varied, undergo transmemberment and show up barely disguised in different contexts. The power of imaginative literature relies upon three constants: aesthetic splendor, cognitive power, wisdom. These are not bound by societal constraints or resentments, and ultimately are universals, and so not culture-bound. Shakespeare, except for the world's scriptures, is the one universal author, whether he is read and played in Bulgaria or Indonesia or wherever. His supremacy at creating human beings breaks through even the barrier of language and puts everyone on his stage. This means that the matter of his work has migrated everywhere, reinforcing the common places we all inhabit in his themes.

2. Contest as both Theme and Trope

Great writing or the Sublime rarely emanates directly from themes since all authors are mediated by forerunners and by contemporary rivals. Nietzsche enhanced our awareness of the agonistic foundations of ancient Greek literature and culture, from Hesiod's contest with Homer on to the Hellenistic critic Longinus in his treatise *On the Sublime*. Even Shakespeare had to begin by overcoming Christopher Marlowe, only a few months his senior. William Faulkner stemmed from the Polish-English novelist Joseph Conrad and our best living author of prose fiction, Philip Roth, is inconceivable without his descent from the major Jewish literary phenomenon of the twentieth century, Franz Kafka of Prague, who wrote the most lucid German since Goethe.

The contest with past achievement is the hidden theme of all major canonical literature in Western tradition. Literary influence is both an overwhelming metaphor for literature itself, and a common topic for all criticism, whether or not the critic knows her immersion in the incessant flood.

Every theme in this series touches upon a contest with anteriority, whether with the presence of death, the hero's quest, the overcoming of taboos, or all of the other concerns, volume by volume. From Monteverdi through Bach to Stravinsky, or from the Italian Renaissance through the agon of Matisse and Picasso, the history of all the arts demonstrates the same patterns as literature's thematic struggle with itself. Our country's great original art, jazz, is illuminated by what the great creators called "cutting contests," from Louis Armstrong and

Duke Ellington on to the emergence of Charlie Parker's Bop or revisionist jazz.

A literary theme, however authentic, would come to nothing without rhetorical eloquence or mastery of metaphor. But to experience the study of the common places of invention is an apt training in the apprehension of aesthetic value in poetry and in prose.

Volume Introduction by Harold Bloom

The supreme literary portrait of "alienation" necessarily is Hamlet, though some might argue for Achilles in *The Iliad*. Both heroes figure in this volume, joined by protagonists created by Melville, Joyce, Woolf, Dostoevsky, Stevenson, Kafka, Beckett, T. S. Eliot, and Hawthorne, among others. These all are extraordinary writers, but even Joyce, Dostoevsky, and Kafka have to yield precedence to Shakespeare and Homer. Obsessed with Hamlet, I will center upon him here, but will be free to cite other instances of "alienation," a word I wish to revise in this introduction.

"Alienation" originally meant *estrangement*, in the sense Celia applies it in *As You Like It* when she takes on the name of Aliena, "the stranger," for her sojourn in Arden with Rosalind, whose assumed name is Ganymede. But alienation in the Age of Kafka took on the meaning of existential dread. Camus, influenced by Kierkegaard and Sartre, as well as by Kafka, shifted alienation to a category reflecting a dishonored post-war France still suffering under the stigma of the Nazi occupation.

I desire to restore alienation to the literary sense it possessed before the abominable Martin Heidegger, Nazi philosopher of *Dasein* ("Being"), whose persuasive influence produced both existentialists and deconstructionists, and also gave us Jacques Lacan, creator of "French Freud." I prefer the as-it-were original, Viennese-Jewish Freud, the Montaigne of the twentieth century. In Freud, alienation essentially is the estrangement he termed the "Uncanny" (*Unheimlich*), which, as I have argued elsewhere, is our modern version of the Sublime.

The Sublime always has been a kind of alienation-effect, an uncanny detachment in which we experience Homer, Dante, Shakespeare, Milton but come to believe that in them we recognize our own rejected thoughts, coming back to us luminous with a certain alienated majesty, as Emerson phrased it.

I give two instances, Hamlet and Franz Kafka as grand aphorists, with Nietzsche as the link between them. In *Twilight of the Idols*, Nietzsche taught us a certain kind of a contempt for the very act of speaking, since that for which we can find words is something already dead in our hearts. Nietzsche is remembering Hamlet, who says he despises himself for unpacking, like a whore, his heart with words. Kafka, his own Hamlet, tells himself that there is a True Way but it is a rope extended above the ground, not for the believer to walk upon but rather to trip over.

It may be that someday Samuel Beckett and Kafka will seem the greatest modern writers, rather than Joyce and Proust, whose formal achievements were much larger. Like Freud, Kafka and Beckett were masters of the comic grotesque rather than the warmer, more commodious comedy of Proust and Joyce. An Age of Alienation demanded a self-wounding act.

"Bartleby, the Scrivener" (Herman Melville)

"Reading the Original: Alienation, Writing, and Labor in 'Bartleby, the Scrivener'"
by Robert T. Tally, Jr.,
Texas State University

In a key section of *The Confidence-Man*, the last novel he published during his lifetime, Herman Melville allows the narrator to ruminate on the notion of an "original" character. The term is used too frequently, he says, and few characters are truly original. He names only three: Hamlet, Don Quixote, and Milton's Satan. To be sure, there are plenty of odd, quirky, or unique characters, but Melville insists that they are unlikely to be original.

> [W]hat is popularly held to entitle characters in fiction to be deemed original, is but something personal—confined to itself. The character sheds not its characteristic on its surroundings, whereas, the original character, essentially such, is like a revolving Drummond light, raying away from itself all round it—everything is lit by it, everything starts up to it (mark how it is with Hamlet), so that, in certain minds, there follows upon the adequate conception of such a character, an effect, in its way, akin to that which in Genesis attends upon the beginning of things. (*The Confidence-Man* 205)

Bartleby, the curious scrivener in Melville's first short story, seems to fit the description of the original character, except that the characteristic he radiates is darkness rather than light, a deep and troubling sense of alienation that affects all other characters in the tale as well as the reader.

The term *alienation* has its simple meaning—a condition of being estranged from someone or something—but it also has technical meanings. For instance, in law, alienation refers to a conveyance of property; something is said to be "alienable" if it can be sold. Alternately, Thomas Jefferson's famous rights to life, liberty, and the pursuit of happiness are so tied to the essence of mankind as to be "inalienable" rights; no quantity of gold or silver can make a person relinquish them. In social psychology, alienation refers to a person's psychological withdrawal from society. In this sense, the alienated individual is isolated from other people; taken to an extreme, such psychological isolation expresses itself in neurosis. In critical social theory, alienation has an additional sense of separating the individual from his or her self, a fragmenting of one's self through work. Karl Marx explained in his study of "alienated" or "estranged labor" (in German, *die entfremdete Arbeit*) that, under the capitalist mode of production, workers are alienated from the products of their labor (i.e., they do not own the things they make) and from their own labor power (which they sell for a wage), but they are also alienated from their human essence, effectively becoming machines in the mechanical system of production. Marx's materialist or economic view of alienated labor comports with the psychological view, because the process that causes the psychological isolation of the individual from society also causes the economic separation of man from his fellow man. In literature, the theme of alienation most often appears as the psychological isolation of an individual from the community or society. "Bartleby, the Scrivener" presents a perfect example of alienation in a literary text, because all senses of the term are present at once.

An unnamed Wall Street lawyer whose business is property law narrates "Bartleby." Although very different from literary art, a lawyer's work is largely devoted to writing—drafting and revising contracts, court documents, wills, memoranda, and letters. In an era before photocopiers, all documents had to be copied and recopied, and law clerks or scriveners did this work. The lawyer's tale, subtitled "A Story of Wall

Street," provides a sketch of Bartleby, "one of the strangest [scriveners] I ever saw, or heard of" (13). The lawyer concedes that little is known of Bartleby's life, other than the brief portion of it witnessed in the tale; the overall mood of the unknown casts its shadow on the story. "Bartleby was one of those beings of whom nothing is ascertainable, except from original sources, and, in his case, those are very few" (13). The mystery of Bartleby is a feature of the overall alienation depicted in the tale. Estranged from society and from himself, Bartleby is a mystery without a solution.

The narrator—generally referred to in Melville studies simply as "the lawyer"—begins by detailing what *is* known, namely, his own personality and those of his other employees. The lawyer reveals himself as a leisurely, unambitious, "eminently safe" (14) man who never goes to trial court but does "a snug business among rich men's bonds, and mortgages, and title-deeds." Many readers have also seen the lawyer as superficial or fatuous, especially because he admits craving and relishing the good opinion of the rich and famous, particularly John Jacob Astor, "a name which, I admit, I love to repeat; for it hath a rounded and orbicular sound to it, and rings like unto bullion" (14). Nevertheless, there can be little doubt of the lawyer's overall affability and good nature.

Before hiring Bartleby, the lawyer had three employees, known only by their colorful, almost Dickensian nicknames—Turkey, Nippers, and Ginger Nut—who are quirkily eccentric, though inoffensively so. Turkey, a shabbily dressed Englishman about sixty years old, is a perfect copyist in the morning but makes many mistakes after noon; the lawyer suspects that Turkey drinks during his lunch hour. Nippers, well dressed though "whiskered, sallow, and, upon the whole, a rather piratical-looking young man" (16), is sorely afflicted with ambition and indigestion. Despite being a capable scrivener, his ambition leads him to overstep his bounds. He frequently wants to draft original legal documents, which only a lawyer is qualified to do, rather than merely copy them. His indigestion, usually experienced after breakfast, makes Nippers ill tempered, and he grinds his teeth and utters maledictions throughout the morning. Fortunately for the lawyer, an afternoon transformation in Nippers compensates for Turkey's midday deterioration. Just when Turkey becomes less reliable, Nippers's indigestion (and consequent irritability) wears off, and Nippers becomes an excellent copyist. "Their fits relieved each other, like guards" (18). Ginger Nut was not a scrivener but a twelve-year-old errand boy, whose father, a cart driver, sent him to the lawyer to apprentice in hopes of "seeing his son on the bench instead of a cart" (18). Ginger Nut was named for the little cakes that Turkey and Nippers sent him off to buy throughout the day. Thus, the lawyer portrays his odd but effective office.

The lawyer's recent political appointment as master in chancery dramatically increases his "original business—that of a conveyancer and title hunter, and drawer-up of recondite documents of all sorts" (19)—and requires him to hire another clerk. Bartleby at first seems too normal to be cast among the office eccentrics, but the story shows how Melville's distinction between the merely odd and the truly original character plays out. The lawyer, happy to find such a calm, sedate person who might "operate beneficially on the flighty temper of Turkey, and the fiery one of Nippers" (19), decides to keep Bartleby close by, assigning him a desk in his own office by a window with no view. Bartleby seems a model scrivener, doing "an extraordinary quantity of writing," but he does his job "silently, palely, mechanically" (20). Often a scrivener must check the accuracy of the duplicates, a task called "reading the copies," which is accomplished by having two or more people read the copy aloud, word for word, while another reads the original. It is a dull task, the lawyer concedes, one "that mettlesome poet, Byron" certainly would not wish to do. The first time the lawyer asks Bartleby to examine a copy with him, Bartleby responds with the famous phrase for which the character and story are best known: "I would prefer not to" (20). This phrase is repeated, in response to similar requests, twenty-two times in the story, and some critics view it as the great refusal to work and to live in society. I would argue that this "refusal" significantly is phrased as a preference.

The lawyer notes with curiosity and consternation that Bartleby never seems to leave the office, apparently surviving on Ginger Nut's pastries. The lawyer later learns that Bartleby is living at the office, as he is discovered there on a Sunday morning. The lawyer feels "stinging melancholy" (28) when he thinks of Bartleby's utter friendlessness and loneliness, and he surmises that Bartleby must be afflicted with some spiritual or mental illness. The lawyer asks Bartleby about his past, but Bartleby "prefers not to" tell him anything. After preferring not to verify the copies on several occasions, Bartleby eventually stops writing altogether.

Whereas he had earlier tolerated Bartleby's peculiar refusals, appreciating his exceptional productivity, the lawyer can no longer suffer this inexplicable behavior; as delicately and considerately as possible, he fires Bartleby. Bartleby, however, prefers not to leave, and for several days the lawyer is distracted by his perplexing trespasser. Finally, the lawyer moves his offices, leaving Bartleby behind. The lawyer later learns from the space's new tenant that Bartleby remains immovable, preferring not to leave the premises. After having Bartleby physically removed from the office, the tenant finds him lingering in the building, along the banister or in the doorway. The lawyer offers to help Bartleby find lodging and a job, but Bartleby "would prefer not to make any change at all" (41). Finally, he is arrested as a vagrant and consigned to the Tombs, New York City's jail. Preferring not to eat, Bartleby dies a few days later. In a brief epilogue, the lawyer hears a rumor that Bartleby had previously worked for the postal service in the Dead Letter Office; the lawyer concludes that handling letters intended for dead recipients must have had a profoundly deleterious effect on Bartleby, sapping him of his will to live. In the tale's final line, the lawyer extends his surmises about his strange former scrivener to the human race: "Ah Bartleby! Ah humanity!" (45).

The tale of Bartleby affords multiple points of entry for a discussion of alienation in literature. Bartleby is clearly alienated from society in numerous ways, and the story's final line suggests the degree to which such alienation is part of the human condition. Leo Marx, in "Melville's Parable of the Walls," famously argues that "Bartleby" is an allegory of the role of the literary writer in a society that seems to have no place for his art. Marx notes that Melville by 1853 had experienced only limited success with *Moby-Dick* and had suffered a critical and financial disaster with his latest book, *Pierre*, just before writing "Bartleby." In Marx's view, the tale expresses Melville's dismal view of the social condition of the writer in America, and the alienation of Bartleby is an apt depiction of the writer's estrangement from other people.

The numerous "walls" in this "Story of Wall Street" underscore the isolation of Bartleby, or the writer, from other people. Bartleby sits in the lawyer's office at a desk near a window with no view;

because of a subsequently erected building, this second-floor window opens to a blank brick wall. Even inside the office, the lawyer has walled Bartleby off with a partition, "a high green folding screen, which might entirely isolate Bartleby from my sight, though not from my voice" (19). Even before voicing his preference not to read the copies, Bartleby is physically and, by extension, emotionally isolated from those around him. After he stops working, Bartleby spends his days staring at the blank wall.

For Leo Marx, Bartleby's condition is analogous to Melville's own in a society that does not value his creative, *original* writing. Melville's refusal to write, or preference not to write, the sorts of books that the public desired amounted to a refusal to copy or imitate popular forms of fiction. In two letters, Melville indicates his frustration with his life as a writer. In an 1849 note to his father-in-law, he refers to his recently completed *Redburn* and *White-Jacket*, the two books written just before *Moby-Dick*:

> [N]o reputation that is gratifying to me, can possibly be achieved by either of these books. They are two *jobs*, which I have done for the money—being forced to it, as other men are to sawing wood. [...] Being books, then, written in this way, my only desire for their "success" (as it is called) springs from my pocket, & not from my heart. So far as I am individually concerned, & independent of my pocket, it is my earnest desire to write those sort of books which are said to "fail" (*Correspondence* 138-39).

Then, in a famous letter to Nathaniel Hawthorne in 1851, as he was completing *Moby-Dick*, Melville wrote, "Dollars damn me. [...] What I feel most moved to write, that is banned—it will not pay. Yet, altogether, write the *other* way I cannot. So the product is a final hash, and all my books are botches" (*Correspondence* 191). The relative failure of *Moby-Dick* and the absolute failure of *Pierre* led Melville to magazine writing as a way to earn a living, and "Bartleby, the Scrivener" is the first story he published, in 1853. The allegorical Bartleby represents Melville's "deep hopelessness" as a writer of literary fiction, and Bartleby's silence reflects the alienation of Melville and of the literary artist in general (L. Marx 602). The alienation of the writer cuts both ways: The artist is estranged from his fellow man by being unpopular, and artists estrange themselves from society by writing works that cannot be easily digested by the masses. Melville is not merely being ironic or elitist when he says he wishes to write works that "fail"; he is also acknowledging his position as an outsider.

For Melville and for Bartleby, writing is situated in a marketplace, and the alienation experienced is, in part at least, a form of alienation caused by the capitalist mode of production. In his letters, Melville laments that the sort of writing he values would inevitably "fail" in the marketplace. The literary market has little use for original writing but rewards familiar or derivative work—copies—that Melville cannot bring himself to produce. Bartleby, who begins as a prolific copyist, nevertheless would "prefer not to" read those copies. Eventually, he would "prefer not to" write anymore, and by the end he would "prefer not to" do anything. As James C. Wilson notes, "With his 'dead wall' reveries, Bartleby provides a classic example of alienated man, though the exact nature of his alienation remains a mystery to the lawyer and thus to the reader. However, it would seem probable that his alien-ation results from the dehumanizing experience of Wall Street, from the prison of his socioeconomic system" (Wilson 338). From a socio-logical perspective, Bartleby is alienated from society by the economic forces that separate people as individuals. Marxist critics have viewed Bartleby as revolutionary in his refusal to work or as tragic in becoming an obsolete commodity. For example, Louise Barnett has called Bartleby a "victim of and protest against the numbing world of capitalistic profit and alienated labor" (Barnett 379). His alienation represents the alienation of all workers in a system that regards their labor as merely one more commodity among many to be traded in the marketplace.

Yet it is not clear that Bartleby's behavior constitutes a refusal to work or rebellion against the capitalist system in that sense. Bartleby does not say no to the lawyer, and the careful language is important for understanding Bartleby's alienation. Gilles Deleuze has shown that the phrase Bartleby uses is quite distinct from an outright refusal.

> The formula, I PREFER NOT TO, excludes all alternatives, and devours what it claims to conserve no less than it distances itself from everything else. [. . .] If Bartleby had refused, he could still be seen as a rebel or insurrectionary, and as such would still have a social role. But the formula stymies all speech acts, and at the same time, it makes Bartleby a pure

> outsider to whom no social position can be attributed. This is
> what the attorney glimpses with dread: all his hopes of bringing
> Bartleby back to reason are dashed because they rest on a *logic
> of presuppositions* according to which an employer "expects" to
> be obeyed, or a kind friend listened to, whereas Bartleby has
> invented a new logic, a *logic of preference*, which is enough to
> undermine the presuppositions of language as a whole (73).

This is key to understanding the distinction between Bartleby's "preference" and a "refusal" and also to understanding Bartleby's intense alienation. He is not a rebel fighting a crass, commercial, unpoetic society.
Contrary to Leo Marx's claim that Bartleby embodies Melville's
refusal as a writer to produce bad literature for a society that will not
accept good literature, Bartleby is even more of an outsider than the
poète maudit celebrated by artists and critics from Charles Baudelaire
onward. Bartleby is completely outside the system of language itself.
He does not wish, like Nippers, to produce original documents instead
of copies. Rather, he *prefers* not to do anything at all. Alienated from
society, from his coworkers, from social conventions of behavior, and
from language itself, Bartleby literally does not make sense.

Bartleby is truly an *original*. He does not fit into the prefabricated
mold of the typical scrivener, and neither is he the odd or quirky
type who is sometimes considered original (wrongly, according to
Melville). By having Bartleby's story told by a narrator who admits
that he really does not know the man, Melville accentuates the originality of the character. An omniscient, third-person narrator might
be able to reveal more about Bartleby, and any "original source"
might add useful information, but the lawyer is clearly attempting
to understand Bartleby along with the reader. Bartleby's "logic of
preference" that the lawyer finds so confounding becomes a linguistic
contagion in the office. The lawyer finds himself "involuntarily using
this word 'prefer' upon all sorts of not exactly suitable occasions,"
and—although they seem unconscious of it—the other scriveners
have begun using the word as well. "I thought to myself, surely I must
get rid of this demented man, who has already in some degree turned
the tongues, if not the heads, of myself and clerks" (31). Throughout
the tale, the perplexed lawyer searches not only his own extensive
personal experience in working with copyists but also literature and
philosophy in hopes of finding a clue to Bartleby's queer "preference."

The lawyer realizes that Bartleby does not *actively* refuse to "read the copies," but (as Deleuze suggests) he cannot understand the logic of Bartleby's formula. For instance, when he asks Bartleby to go to the post office and Bartleby responds with "I would prefer not to," the lawyer presses him: "You *will* not?" Bartleby responds, "I *prefer* not" (25). Melville's italics emphasize the distinction. The lawyer is so puzzled that he consults "Edwards on the Will" and "Priestly on Necessity," works by two theologians who believe in predestination and adamantly deny the existence of free will. This philosophy does not help him understand Bartleby better, but it helps put his own condition in terms he can understand. "Gradually I slid into the persuasion that these troubles of mine, touching the scrivener, had been predestinated from eternity, and Bartleby was billeted upon me for some mysterious purpose of an all-wise Providence, which it was not for a mere mortal like me to fathom" (37). Instead of reaching an understanding that would make Bartleby less alien, the lawyer tries to be content with his limited grasp.

The epilogue, disclosing a rumor about Bartleby's previous life in the Dead Letter Office, is a final attempt to make sense of the inscrutable man. The lawyer, and perhaps the reader, thinks he has stumbled upon the clue to understanding Bartleby's demeanor. But disposing of "dead letters" does not really explain Bartleby; it merely adds to the overall picture of alienation that Bartleby personifies. At the Dead Letter Office, Bartleby presumably handled words whose intended recipients were dead. In working as a scrivener, he too was handling "dead" letters, copies of copies, having no direct intercourse with the original. As Cathy Davidson has rather caustically pointed out, "The narrator rhetorically assesses how much clerking in a Dead Letter Office would have damaged Bartleby's psyche and all the while he overlooks the equally unfortunate consequences his own business copying the dead letter of the law might have had" (Davidson 58). At the Tombs, the "grub-man" mistakes Bartleby for "a gentleman forger," which he is in a sense; a scrivener, like a forger, makes copies of originals. But the lawyer says he "was never socially acquainted with any forgers" (44) and does not know such people. Indeed, Bartleby's alienation—from society, from his work, from his fellow man, and, at the end, from himself—makes him profoundly *unknowable* and *unreadable*. As a person, a worker, and a writer, Bartleby is an *original* character, and as such he is utterly alien and alienated. Early in the tale, Bartleby prefers not to "read the copies," but the overall effect of "Bartleby, the Scrivener" is that the lawyer and the reader are unable to "read the original."

BIBLIOGRAPHY

Barnett, Louise K. "Bartleby as Alienated Worker." *Studies in Short Fiction* 11 (1974): 379-385.

Davidson, Cathy. "Courting God and Mammon: The Biographer's Impasse in Melville's 'Bartleby, the Scrivener.'" *Delta* 6 (1978): 47-59.

Deleuze, Gilles. "Bartleby, or the Formula." *Essays Critical and Clinical.* Trans. Daniel W. Smith and Michael A. Greco. Minneapolis: U of Minnesota P, 1997. 68-90.

Marx, Karl. "Estranged Labor." *The Economic and Philosophic Manuscripts of 1844.* Trans. Martin Milligan. New York: International Publishers, 1964. 106-119.

Marx, Leo. "Melville's Parable of the Walls." *The Sewanee Review* 61 (October 1953): 602-627.

Melville, Herman. "Bartleby, the Scrivener." *The Piazza Tales.* Ed. Harrison Hayford et al. Evanston: Northwestern UP, 1996. 13-45.

_____. *Correspondence.* Ed. Harrison Hayford, Alma A. MacDougall, G. Thomas Tanselle, et al. Evanston: Northwestern UP.

_____. *The Confidence-Man.* Ed. Hershel Parker. New York: Norton, 1971.

Wilson, James C. "'Bartleby': The Walls of Wall Street." *Arizona Quarterly* 37 (Winter 1981): 335-346.

THE BELL JAR
(SYLVIA PLATH)

"Alienation and Renewal
in Sylvia Plath's *The Bell Jar*"
by Steven Gould Axelrod,
University of California at Riverside

Sylvia Plath's novel, *The Bell Jar* (1963), is a story of alienation and renewal. The protagonist's alienation is complicated by her latent wish for reconnection, and her eventual renewal is clouded over by the possibility of future estrangement. Written in the first person, as were so many post–World War II novels, *The Bell Jar* focuses on the struggles of Esther Greenwood in her rite of passage from adolescence to adulthood without any rules to guide her. Images of repulsion and aspiration suffuse her prose, and thus the novel's figurative texture becomes as crucial as the plot to its literary meaning. Beyond being Esther's personal story, the novel posits a dynamic of alienation, reconnection, and renewal at the core of American life, especially in the 1950s. *The Bell Jar* thus concerns an individual, her confrontation with society, her style of self-expression, and, more generally, the difficult crossing from juvenile subordination to adult autonomy.

Esther Greenwood initially tries to adapt herself to the strange world of status and power she encounters on her first extended time away from home or school. The nineteen-year-old college junior has won a summer guest editorship at a fashion magazine called *Ladies' Day*, modeled on such actual magazines as *Ladies' Home Journal* and *Mademoiselle*. Plath did serve as guest editor at *Mademoiselle* one

11

summer while a student at Smith College, and she based much of the detail in this autobiographical novel on her experiences (Wagner-Martin 96-111, 185-87). Although Esther tries to conform to the sophisticated, urban world of New York City, she remains essentially withdrawn from it and, more significantly, from herself. She becomes increasingly apathetic about the writing and editing career she thought she wanted and distant from the life of success and privilege she thought she was pursuing. Isolated from the professional world around her and from the mainstream of American life, she is also exiled from her own feelings and desires. She went to New York behaving as what David Riesman called an "other-directed" person (19-22), a conformist who sees through the eyes of others and whose highest goal is to fit in. But she discovers a contrary wish to become an "autonomous" person (Riesman 242) capable of seeing through her own eyes even while relating to others. This inner division ultimately leads to a fissuring of her identity, a diversion from normal functioning to mental derangement. The novel depicts her progressive fragmentation and partial recovery.

Despite Esther's superficial attempts to adapt to society's success ethic, she initially views everything she encounters with a reflexive contempt and suspicion. Alienating as well as alienated, this worldview makes her seem unlikable to many readers; yet it also convinces many, especially those going through a similar evolution, that her way of seeing and feeling corresponds to their own at some private, vulnerable level. Like some of Jane Austen's most memorable protagonists, Esther invites in the reader an uneasy mixture of dislike and sympathy, distance and identification.

Through Esther's inability to coexist harmoniously with the people and scenes around her, she constructs a landscape of radical alienation that we can understand in two different ways. First, the world of competition, conformity, consumerism, and commodification deserves derision. As in J.D. Salinger's *The Catcher in the Rye* (1951), which is *The Bell Jar*'s most immediate precursor, post–World War II American society is shown as phony and bewildering. Second, Esther herself is out of kilter, able to see only what is false because she is false to herself. Her inner estrangement parallels that of *Catcher*'s Holden Caulfield. Whereas Holden's derangement only becomes clear at the end of that novel, Esther's is apparent from the beginning—and her efforts at a cure are delineated, whereas his are not. Moreover, Esther must combat the additional alienation of being an aspiring woman in an era of strict limitations for women. Although *The Bell Jar* echoes the alienated ethos of *The Catcher in the Rye* and such other Cold War–era narratives as Ralph Ellison's *Invisible Man* (1952), Saul Bellow's *Seize the Day* (1956), and Jack Kerouac's *On the Road* (1957), it swerves from them in focusing on female experience and detailing the renewal of the alienated soul.

On the surface, Esther is an unlikely and unlikable heroine. She is "jealous" (*Bell Jar* 4), snobbish, and hostile—the kind of person who steps on as many feet as she can while leaving a theater (43). She incessantly complains about others in a way that implies she is morally superior. Much of the time she lacks empathy. Yet Esther is also sensitive, intelligent, and honest (even about her own negative qualities). Like her early progenitor, Huck Finn in Mark Twain's *The Adventures of Huckleberry Finn* (1885), she is obsessed with telling the truth, even though she inhabits a culture shot through with lies. The social world makes contradictory demands on her but provides no useful guidance or helpful mentors. She is lonely, unloved, and at a loss.

In the opening chapters, Esther repeatedly reveals her alienation from herself and society. She writes that "I knew something was wrong with me that summer, because all I could think about was the Rosenbergs" (2). Esther identifies with Julius and Ethel Rosenberg, who were sentenced to death in the electric chair for passing American nuclear secrets to the Soviets—a crime that Julius almost certainly committed but his wife Ethel possibly did not. Esther here empathizes with people excluded and sacrificed by American law. Although the Rosenbergs' executions are meant to strengthen the bonds connecting mainstream Americans, they have the opposite effect on Esther, who identifies with the couple's transgression and pain. Esther will later undergo electroshock treatment as a result of her own inability to adapt to societal norms—a pale echo of the Rosenbergs' electrocutions.

Socially estranged, Esther is self-estranged as well. She admits that "all the little successes I'd totted up so happily at college fizzled to nothing outside the slick marble and plate-glass fronts along Madison Avenue" (2); her own achievements seem trivial when compared to the glossy professionalism of Madison Avenue. If the prospect of a high-powered career suddenly seems implausible, the alternative of marriage and motherhood seems dull. Observing young women on the marriage track, Esther thinks they look "awfully bored" (4). Later, she asks of herself, "Why was I so unmaternal and apart?" (222). Esther has been pursuing external goals—a prestigious career or an advantageous marriage—while ignoring her internal needs. Given an opportunity to face herself in New York, she questions both goals. In pursuing them unthinkingly, she had simply internalized society's norms for women. She now evaluates those norms critically and becomes a stranger in society and to herself. Her guest editorship in New York, which was intended to integrate her into adult society, has instead disintegrated her.

Esther feels split between a fabricated public self and a truer and more elusive hidden self. When Jay Cee, an editor at *Ladies' Day*, asks her what she intends to do after graduation, she says she does not know. Although she immediately attempts to recover her "old, bright salesmanship" (33), Esther realizes that her admission of uncertainty was true. It is ironic that Esther stops believing in her self-promotion in the center of American advertising, Madison Avenue. She uses her time in New York as what Erik Erikson would call a "psychosocial moratorium" between late adolescence and adulthood (Erikson 199-200). She expresses her inner division by inventing alter egos such as "Elly Higginbottom" (11) and a fictional heroine named "Elaine" (120)—just as Plath invented a fictional double of herself in Esther (Axelrod 10-13, 121-24). Esther feels as if she has "a split personality or something" (21). She also projects her interior split onto others: She thinks of Betsy and Doreen, her new acquaintances, as opposed aspects of herself. Doreen embodies Esther's dark side—satirical, cynical, wild—and everything Doreen says is "like a secret voice speaking straight out of my own bones" (7), but Betsy is a "Pollyanna Cowgirl" (6). Pretty, conformist, and inauthentic, Betsy corresponds to Esther's "bright salesmanship." Although Esther regards Doreen as "testimony to my own dirty nature" (23), she decides that "deep down, I would be loyal to Betsy" (19). She tries to convince herself that "it was Betsy I resembled at heart" (19).

Another, more important "double" emerges for Esther later in the novel in her old friend Joan Gilling (205). Each young woman has had a suicidal breakdown, and they are recovering in the same mental institution. Fascinated by Joan's similar crisis but naïvely shocked by her same-sex desire, Esther asks Dr. Nolan, her female psychiatrist,

"What does a woman see in a woman that she can't see in a man?" (219). Dr. Nolan responds, "Tenderness." "That shut me up," Esther reports.

Esther regards Joan with a mixture of rejection and identification. Although she frequently scorns her friend, she also admits, "I would always treasure Joan. It was as if we had been forced together by some overwhelming circumstance, like war or plague, and shared a world of our own" (215). Perhaps Joan represents the excluded margin of Esther herself, the road not taken. Soon after the conversation with her psychiatrist, Esther initiates her first heterosexual encounter with a mathematician she barely knows and experiences the opposite of tenderness. While Esther loses her virginity to become "my own woman" (223), Joan's despair deepens and she commits suicide. At the funeral, Esther wonders "what I thought I was burying" (242). The reader may wonder the same thing. Is it her own suicidal urge or the tenderness of same-sex desire?

Esther's alienation has multiple causes, including Cold War tensions and the era's restrictions on women. Esther's domineering boyfriend, Buddy Willard, tells her that "what a man wants is a mate and what a woman wants is infinite security" and "what a man is is an arrow into the future and what a woman is is the place the arrow shoots off from" (72). Esther rejects such gender clichés: "The last thing I wanted was infinite security and to be the place an arrow shoots off from. I wanted change and excitement and to shoot off in all directions myself, like the colored arrows from a Fourth of July rocket" (83). Buddy learned his clichés from his mother, who once spent weeks braiding a beautiful, multicolored rug but then used it as a kitchen mat, "and in a few days it was soiled and dull" (85). Esther comes to believe that, despite the romantic thrill of courtship, a man secretly wanted his wife "to flatten out underneath his feet like Mrs. Willard's kitchen mat" (85). She recalls Buddy saying "in a sinister, knowing way" that after she had children she "wouldn't want to write poems any more" (85). Such a marriage would doom her creative desires. She begins to fear that "when you were married and had children it was like being brainwashed and afterward you went about numb as a slave in some private, totalitarian state" (85).

Another cause of Esther's alienation is her relationship with her parents. Her mother, though superficially caring and picture perfect, is controlling and reproachful. She resembles the domineering mother in *Now, Voyager* (1941), a popular novel written by Plath's mentor, Olive Higgins Prouty. Esther's mother insists that her daughter channel herself in socially acceptable directions without paying attention to her own needs. As a result, Esther makes a point of "never living in the same house with my mother for more than a week" (118). When she lives with her mother after returning from New York, she adopts a "hollow voice" that becomes a "zombie voice" as her crisis worsens (118-19). Esther overdoses on sleeping pills and hides in a basement crawl space to die. Yet she survives, with only a scar on her face to mark her suicide attempt. Recovering in a mental hospital with the help of Dr. Nolan, Esther makes a startling admission about her mother: "'I hate her,' I said, and waited for the blow to fall" (203). But Dr. Nolan only smiles; she recognizes that Esther has identified a root cause of her alienation.

Esther's memories of her father are equally vexed. Her father died when Esther was nine, and she was forbidden to grieve. Short-circuited, her ambivalent grief went underground and contaminated every other relationship Esther had. As her mental crisis intensifies, Esther confronts this loss for the first time. In her yearning to "pay my father back for all the years of neglect" (165), one detects mixed feelings toward this remote, intimidating man. On the one hand, she feels guilty for not mourning his death; on the other, she wants revenge for his neglect of *her*—both while he was alive and by his premature death. Visiting his grave just before her suicide attempt, she howls her loss, and nature matches her grief with a "cold salt rain" (167).

In the chapters leading up to and including Esther's suicide attempt (Chapters 1-15), Plath composes a fabric of alienation that matches the narrator's worldview. Instead of feeling harmony with the observed world—as Huck Finn does when watching dawn break over the Mississippi—she draws back in repulsion. Alone and apart, Esther experiences her landscape as menacing rather than sheltering. At the outset, she describes New York as a "sultry," unhealthful jungle" (1), much as it is in Bellow's similarly anguished *The Victim* (1947). The "tropical, stale heat" hits Esther in the face "like a last insult" (17), while occasional raindrops, like ones "they must have in Brazil," strike the hot sidewalks "with a hiss" (41). Even Esther's hotel is called "the Amazon" (4). A variety of grotesque body images supplement the metaphor of a jungle-like city. On the first pages, Esther refers to the "fusty, peanut-smelling mouth of every subway" (1); the Rosenbergs "being burned alive" all along their nerves (1); the "dry, cindery dust" (like that of Eliot's *The Waste Land*) blowing down her throat (1); the memory of a cadaver that resembled "some black, noseless balloon stinking of vinegar" (2); and the sight of her new clothes "hanging limp as fish in my closet" (2).

Thus, *The Bell Jar* evokes a fearful world of yawning monsters and overwhelming ugliness. As the novel progresses, Esther encounters more disturbing sights, ranging from Doreen's "brown vomit" (22) to Buddy's genitals, which make her think of "turkey neck and turkey gizzards" (69). Esther's self-images suggest an abiding sense of otherness: She describes herself as a "smudgy-eyed Chinese woman" (18), "the blade of a knife" (98), a "sick Indian" (112), and an "orphan" from Chicago (132). Such portrayals suggest her blurred self-image (a weeping or sick woman, a dangerous weapon) and her identification with cultural margins (a woman of Chinese ancestry, a Native American, a parentless child).

Esther's anguished imagination transforms the outside world, other people, and Esther herself. The novel is stylistically brilliant, creating a vivid, figurative reality cut off from stable referents. This world of words provides an arena of experimental self-reflexivity within the novel's frame of realist conventions, with the trope of the bell jar holding this verbal wildness together. A bell jar is a bell-shaped glass laboratory vessel designed to cover objects or to contain gases or a vacuum. The image neatly condenses Esther's feelings about her condition: She sees herself as a specimen in a jar—distorted from view, preserved against her will, acted upon by others. The metaphor suggests suffocation, immobility, and separation. Trapped in her social and psychological crisis, Esther is "stewing" in her own "sour air" (185). She reflects that "to the person in the bell jar, blank and stopped as a dead baby, the world itself is the bad dream" (193).

As Esther recovers from her paralyzing depression, the bell jar lifts. As she regains access to "the circulating air" (215), the alienated imagery of her narrative yields to a more humanized imagery, in which self and other achieve a reciprocal—rather than hostile—relationship. Expressions of affection appear for the first time: "I liked Dr. Nolan, I loved her" (211). Images of freedom and autonomy appear as well: "I am climbing to freedom, freedom from fear, freedom from marrying the wrong person" (223). Although the universe no longer terrifies Esther, it remains a confusing place of "question marks" (243). She cannot know if "the bell jar, with its stifling distortions" will someday descend again (241). Indeed, there are indications that it may do so.

Although Esther has said she would "go mad" if she had to "wait on a baby all day" (222), she also reveals that the week before beginning to write her book she was caring for "the baby" (3). She thereby hints that after the narrative ends she might break under the weight of maternal conventions, in the manner of Edna Pontellier, the doomed protagonist of Kate Chopin's *The Awakening* (1899). Nevertheless, at the end of *The Bell Jar*, a renewed Esther pictures herself as a "patched, retreaded" tire (244) and a child taking her first steps into an "anxious and unsettling world" (222). Vacillating between the objectified self-image of a used wheel rolling through space and the humanized self-image of a child learning to walk, she guides herself into her final interview (244), her verb suggesting a measure of agency and autonomy that she previously lacked.

The Bell Jar has roots in a handful of traditional novelistic forms: the picaresque (the movement of a rogue or innocent through geographical space, exposing the follies of the individuals and groups he meets); the *Bildungsroman* (the social education of a young initiate); and the *Künstlerroman* (the development of an artist). The novel adapts these male-centered forms to a female protagonist who discovers and creates herself as both a woman and a writer. Thus several plots proceed simultaneously in this book: the ostensible plot of Esther's breakdown and recovery; the verbal plot of alienated imagery yielding to rehumanized images; and the compositional plot of a young woman telling her story and thereby proving herself a writer. All of these plots involve a complicated rite of passage.

Esther Greenwood, as her last name implies, is young and green. She suffers from her culture's lack of initiation rituals to sustain her in her transformation from child to adult. Esther experiences discordant pressures, both internal and external, but lacks communal structures to help her move safely through them. Her suicide attempt is a result of this lack of support. Paradoxically, her attempt becomes an ad-hoc ritual of symbolic death (of the frustrated child) and rebirth (of an independent, creative adult). This "ritual of being born twice" (244) is consolidated by the creative act of narrating it. The transition to sexually active adulthood appears to be successful, in that Esther has ultimately married and had a child (3), though given the troubled way the novel represents marriage and motherhood, we cannot be sure if they indicate a turn to normality or a return to crisis. The creative, vocational achievement seems more assured in that Esther has fictively written *The Bell Jar*, an enduring work of art.

Esther's passage resembles those in such contemporaneous novels as Ellison's *Invisible Man* (1952), Bellow's *Seize the Day* (1956), and Joyce Carol Oates's *Them* (1969), in which the protagonists, unable to make the leap to adult autonomy and intimacy, attempt a symbolic death and rebirth. Bellow's Tommy Wilhelm, however, is not depicted as reborn, and Oates's Maureen Wendall is reborn into a false consciousness or pseudo-adulthood. The reemergence of Ellison's Invisible Man is intimated, as he appears to us as a writer—as do Melville's Ishmael (in *Moby-Dick*), Dickens's Pip (in *Great Expectations*), Twain's Huck Finn, and Fitzgerald's Nick Carraway (in *The Great Gatsby*). *The Bell Jar*, particularly if we divorce it from our knowledge of Plath's suicide, aligns itself with the more hopeful of these analogous texts. Like the stories spun by Ishmael, Huck, and the Invisible Man, her tale suggests her enduring position on the social margins (her identification with orphans, minorities, and children taking baby steps). Yet her marginality is precisely what gives her insight into the condition of others—all those who sit "under bell jars of a sort" (238). Like the Invisible Man, Esther tries to speak "on the lower frequencies" for us (Ellison 581).

Why does Esther Greenwood construct her self-narrative in *The Bell Jar*, a narrative so poignantly similar to Plath's own? Is Esther seeking to relive her estrangement in order to reexperience her cure? Is Esther's narrative a way for her to ward off pain in her present married life? The alienation that sets the novel in motion is manifest, but the renewal that concludes it remains tentative. Although Esther can finally say, "I am, I am, I am" (243), she also knows that "somewhere, anywhere" the bell jar might "descend again" (241).

WORKS CITED

Axelrod, Steven Gould. *Sylvia Plath: The Wound and the Cure of Words.* Baltimore: Johns Hopkins UP, 1990.

Ellison, Ralph. *Invisible Man.* 1952. New York: Vintage, 1995.

Erikson, Erik. *Life History and the Historical Moment.* New York: Norton, 1975.

Plath, Sylvia. *The Bell Jar.* 1963. New York: HarperCollins, 2006.

Riesman, David, with Nathan Glazer and Reuel Denney. *The Lonely Crowd: A Study of the Changing American Character*. 1950. New Haven: Yale UP, reissued 1969.

Wagner-Martin, Linda W. *Sylvia Plath: A Biography*. New York: Simon and Schuster, 1987.

BLACK BOY
(RICHARD WRIGHT)

"Richard Wright's Blues"
by Ralph Ellison,
in *Shadow and Act* (1964)

INTRODUCTION

In this essay from *Shadow and Act*, Ralph Ellison outlines how Richard Wright's *Black Boy* borrows from the musical form of the blues to "keep the painful details and episodes of a brutal experience alive in one's aching consciousness, to finger its jagged grain, and to transcend it, not by the consolation of philosophy but by squeezing from it a near-tragic, near-comic lyricism. As a form, the blues is an autobiographical chronicle of personal catastrophe expressed lyrically." Thus, Ellison explores how Wright's work captures the alienation of black Americans and how art allows for the understanding, processing, and witnessing of human suffering. For Ellison, *Black Boy*, like the blues, expresses "both the agony of life and the possibility of conquering it through sheer toughness of spirit." In depicting the modern alienated black American struggling with a racist past and a violent present, Ellison finds Wright's most important achievement: "He has converted

---

Ellison, Ralph. "Richard Wright's Blues." *Shadow and Act*. New York: Random House, 1964. 77–94. (First published in *The Antioch Review* 5.2 [June 1945]: (198–212)

the American Negro impulse toward self-annihilation and
'going-underground' into a will to confront the world, to evaluate his experience honestly and throw his findings unashamedly into the guilty conscience of America."

༄

If anybody ask you
who sing this song,
Say it was ole [Black Boy]
done been here and gone.[1]

As a writer, Richard Wright has outlined for himself a dual role: to
discover and depict the meaning of Negro experience and to reveal
to both Negroes and whites those problems of a psychological and
emotional nature which arise between them when they strive for
mutual understanding.

Now, in *Black Boy*, he has used his own life to probe what qualities
of will, imagination, and intellect are required of a Southern Negro in
order to possess the meaning of his life in the United States. Wright
is an important writer, perhaps the most articulate Negro American,
and what he has to say is highly perceptive. Imagine Bigger Thomas
projecting his own life in lucid prose, guided, say, by the insights of
Marx and Freud, and you have an idea of this autobiography.

Published at a time when any sharply critical approach to Negro
life has been dropped as a wartime expendable, it should do much
to redefine the problem of the Negro and American democracy. Its
power can be observed in the shrill manner with which some professional "friends of the Negro people" have attempted to strangle the
work in a noose of newsprint.

What in the tradition of literary autobiography is it like, this
work described as a "great American autobiography"? As a nonwhite
intellectual's statement of his relationship to Western culture, *Black
Boy* recalls the conflicting pattern of identification and rejection
found in Nehru's *Toward Freedom*. In its use of fictional techniques,
its concern with criminality (sin) and the artistic sensibility, and in its
author's judgment and rejection of the narrow world of his origin, it
recalls Joyce's rejection of Dublin in *A Portrait of the Artist*. And as a
psychological document of life under oppressive conditions, it recalls

The House of the Dead, Dostoyevsky's profound study of the humanity of Russian criminals.

Such works were perhaps Wright's literary guides, aiding him to endow his life's incidents with communicable significance, providing him with ways of seeing, feeling, and describing his environment. These influences, however, were encountered only after these first years of Wright's life were past and were not part of the immediate folk culture into which he was born. In that culture the specific folk-art form that helped shape the writer's attitude toward his life and that embodied the impulse that contributes much to the quality and tone of his autobiography was the Negro blues. This would bear a word of explanation:

The blues is an impulse to keep the painful details and episodes of a brutal experience alive in one's aching consciousness, to finger its jagged grain, and to transcend it, not by the consolation of philosophy, but by squeezing from it a near-tragic, near-comic lyricism. As a form, the blues is an autobiographical chronicle of personal catastrophe expressed lyrically. And certainly Wright's early childhood was crammed with catastrophic incidents. In a few short years his father deserted his mother, he knew intense hunger, he became a drunkard begging drinks from black stevedores in Memphis saloons; he had to flee Arkansas where an uncle was lynched; he was forced to live with a fanatically religious grand-mother in an atmosphere of constant bickering; he was lodged in an orphan asylum; he observed the suffering of his mother who became a permanent invalid, while fighting off the blows of the poverty-stricken relatives with whom he had to live; he was cheated, beaten, and kicked off jobs by white employees who disliked his eagerness to learn a trade; and to these objective circumstances must be added the subjective fact that Wright, with his sensitivity, extreme shyness, and intelligence, was a problem child who rejected his family and was by them rejected.

Thus along with the themes, equivalent descriptions of milieu, and the perspectives to be found in Joyce, Nehru, Dostoyevsky, George Moore, and Rousseau, *Black Boy* is filled with blues-tempered echoes of railroad trains, the names of Southern towns and cities, estrange-ments, fights and flights, deaths and disappointments, charged with physical and spiritual hungers and pain. And like a blues sung by such an artist as Bessie Smith, its lyrical prose evokes the paradoxical, almost surreal image of a black boy singing lustily as he probes his own grievous wound.

In *Black Boy*, two worlds have fused, two cultures merged, two impulses of Western man become coalesced. By discussing some of its cultural sources I hope to answer those critics who would make of the book a miracle and of its author a mystery. And while making no attempt to probe the mystery of the artist (who Hemingway says is "forged in injustice as a sword is forged"), I do hold that basically the prerequisites to the writing of *Black Boy* were, on the one hand, the microscopic degree of cultural freedom that Wright found in the South's stony injustice and, on the other, the existence of a personality agitated to a state of almost manic restlessness. There were, of course, other factors, chiefly ideological; but these came later.

Wright speaks of his journey north as

> ... taking a part of the South to transplant in alien soil, to see if
> it could grow differently, if it could drink of new and cool rains,
> bend in strange winds, respond to the warmth of other suns,
> and perhaps, to bloom. ...

And just as Wright, the man, represents the blooming of the delinquent child of the autobiography, just so does *Black Boy* represent the flowering—cross-fertilized by pollen blown by the winds of strange cultures—of the humble blues lyric. There is, as in all acts of creation, a world of mystery in this, but there is also enough that is comprehensible for Americans to create the social atmosphere in which other black boys might freely bloom.

For certainly, in the historical sense, Wright is no exception. Born on a Mississippi plantation, he was subjected to all those blasting pressures which, in a scant eighty years, have sent the Negro people hurtling, without clearly defined trajectory, from slavery to emancipation, from log cabin to city tenement, from the white folks' fields and kitchens to factory assembly lines; and which, between two wars, have shattered the wholeness of its folk consciousness into a thousand writhing pieces.

Black Boy describes this process in the personal terms of *one* Negro childhood. Nevertheless, several critics have complained that it does not "explain" Richard Wright. Which, aside from the notion of art involved, serves to remind us that the prevailing mood of American criticism has so thoroughly excluded the Negro that it fails to recognize some of the most basic tenets of Western democratic thought when encountering them in a black skin. They forget that human life possesses an innate dignity and mankind an innate sense of nobility; that all men possess the tendency to dream and the compulsion to make their dreams reality; that the need to be ever dissatisfied and the urge ever to seek satisfaction is implicit in the human organism; and that all men are the victims and the beneficiaries of the goading, tormenting, commanding, and informing activity of that imperious process known as the Mind—the Mind, as Valéry describes it, "armed with its inexhaustible questions."

Perhaps all this (in which lies the very essence of the human, and which Wright takes for granted) has been forgotten because the critics recognize neither Negro humanity nor the full extent to which the Southern community renders the fulfillment of human destiny impossible. And while it is true that *Black Boy* presents an almost unrelieved picture of a personality corrupted by brutal environment, it also presents those fresh human responses brought to its world by the sensitive child:

> There was the *wonder* I felt when I first saw a brace of mountainlike, spotted, black-and-white horses clopping down a dusty road ... the *delight* I caught in seeing long straight rows of red and green vegetables stretching away in the sun ... the faint, cool kiss of *sensuality* when dew came on to my cheeks ... the vague *sense of the infinite* as I looked down upon the yellow, dreaming waters of the Mississippi ... the echoes of *nostalgia* I heard in the crying strings of wild geese ... the *love* I had for the mute regality of tall, moss-clad oaks ... the hint of *cosmic cruelty* that I *felt* when I saw the curved timbers of a wooden shack that had been warped in the summer sun ... and there was the *quiet terror* that suffused my senses when vast hazes of gold washed earthward from star-heavy skies on silent nights. . . .[2]

And a bit later, his reactions to religion:

> Many of the religious symbols appealed to my sensibilities and I responded to the dramatic vision of life held by the church,

feeling that to live day by day with death as one's sole thought
was to be so compassionately sensitive toward all life as to view
all men as slowly dying, and the trembling sense of fate that
welled up, sweet and melancholy, from the hymns blended with
the sense of fate that I had already caught from life.

There was also the influence of his mother—so closely linked to
his hysteria and sense of suffering—who (though he only implies it
here) taught him, in the words of the dedication prefacing *Native Son*,
"to revere the fanciful and the imaginative." There were also those
white men—the one who allowed Wright to use his library privileges
and the other who advised him to leave the South, and still others
whose offers of friendship he was too frightened to accept.

Wright assumed that the nucleus of plastic sensibility is a human
heritage: the right and the opportunity to dilate, deepen, and enrich
sensibility—democracy. Thus the drama of *Black Boy* lies in its depiction of what occurs when Negro sensibility attempts to fulfill itself
in the undemocratic South. Here it is not the individual that is the
immediate focus, as in Joyce's *Stephen Hero*, but that upon which his
sensibility was nourished.

Those critics who complain that Wright has omitted the development of his own sensibility hold that the work thus fails as art.
Others, because it presents too little of what they consider attractive
in Negro life, charge that it distorts reality. Both groups miss a very
obvious point: that whatever else the environment contained, it had
as little chance of prevailing against the overwhelming weight of the
child's unpleasant experiences as Beethoven's Quartets would have of
destroying the stench of a Nazi prison.

We come, then, to the question of art. The function, the psychology,
of artistic selectivity is to eliminate from art form all those elements of
experience that contain no compelling significance. Life is as the sea,
art a ship in which man conquers life's crushing formlessness, reducing
it to a course, a series of swells, tides, and wind currents inscribed on
a chart. Though drawn from the world, "the organized significance of
art," writes Malraux, "is stronger than all the multiplicity of the world;
. . . that significance alone enables man to conquer chaos and to master
destiny."

Wright saw his destiny—that combination of forces before which
man feels powerless—in terms of a quick and casual violence inflicted

upon him by both family and community. His response was likewise violent, and it has been his need to give that violence significance that has shaped his writings.

[...]

It is only when the individual, whether white or black, *rejects* the pattern that he awakens to the nightmare of his life. Perhaps much of the South's regressive character springs from the fact that many, jarred by some casual crisis into wakefulness, flee hysterically into the sleep of violence or the coma of apathy again. For the penalty of wakefulness is to encounter even more violence and horror than the sensibilities can sustain unless translated into some form of social action. Perhaps the impassioned character so noticeable among those white Southern liberals active in the Negro's cause is due to their sense of accumulated horror; their passion—like the violence in Faulkner's novels—is evidence of a profound spiritual vomiting.

This compulsion is even more active in Wright and the increasing number of Negroes who have said an irrevocable "no" to the Southern pattern. Wright learned that it is not enough merely to reject the white South, but that he had also to reject that part of the South which lay within. As a rebel he formulated that rejection negatively, because it was the negative face of the Negro community upon which he looked most often as a child. It is this he is contemplating when he writes:

> Whenever I thought of the essential bleakness of black life in America, I knew that Negroes had never been allowed to catch the full spirit of Western civilization, that they lived somehow in it but not of it. And when I brooded upon the cultural barrenness of black life, I wondered if clean, positive tenderness, love, honor, loyalty, and the capacity to remember were native to man. I asked myself if these human qualities were not fostered, won, struggled and suffered for, preserved in ritual from one generation to another.

But far from implying that Negroes have no capacity for culture, as one critic interprets it, this is the strongest affirmation that they have. Wright is pointing out what should be obvious (especially to his Marxist critics): that Negro sensibility is socially and historically conditioned; that Western culture must be won, confronted like the animal in a Spanish bullfight, dominated by the red shawl of codified experience, and brought heaving to its knees.

Wright knows perfectly well that Negro life is a by-product of Western civilization, and that in it, if only one possesses the humanity and humility to see, are to be discovered all those impulses, tendencies, life, and cultural forms to be found elsewhere in Western society.

The problem arises because the special condition of Negroes in the United States, including the defensive character of Negro life itself (the "will toward organization" noted in the Western capitalist appears in the Negro as a will to camouflage, to dissimulate), so distorts these forms as to render their recognition as difficult as finding a wounded quail against the brown and yellow leaves of a Mississippi thicket—even the spilled blood blends with the background. Having himself been in the position of the quail—to expand the metaphor—Wright's wounds have told him both the question and the answer that every successful hunter must discover for himself: "Where would I hide if *I* were a wounded quail?" But perhaps that requires more sympathy with one's quarry than most hunters possess. Certainly it requires such a sensitivity to the shifting guises of humanity under pressure as to allow them to identify themselves with the human content, whatever its outer form; and even with those Southern Negroes to whom Paul Robeson's name is only a rolling sound in the fear-charged air.

Let us close with one final word about the blues: Their attraction lies in this, that they at once express both the agony of life and the possibility of conquering it through sheer toughness of spirit. They fall short of tragedy only in that they provide no solution, offer no scapegoat but the self. Nowhere in America today is there social or political action based upon the solid realities of Negro life depicted in *Black Boy*; perhaps that is why, with its refusal to offer solutions, it is like the blues. Yet, in it thousands of Negroes will for the first time see their destiny in public print. Freed here of fear and the threat of violence, their lives have at last been organized, scaled down to possessable proportions. And in this lies Wright's most important achievement: He has converted the American Negro impulse toward self-annihilation and "going-underground" into a will to confront the world, to evaluate his experience honestly and throw his findings unashamedly into the guilty conscience of America.

NOTES

1. Signature formula used by blues singers at conclusion of song.
2. Italics mine.

BRAVE NEW WORLD
(ALDOUS HUXLEY)

"Alienation in Aldous Huxley's
Brave New World"
by Josephine A. McQuail,
Tennessee Technological University

Critics greeted the publication of Aldous Huxley's *Brave New World* with nearly universal disapproval. Some said that Huxley was nothing but a "clever misanthrope" (Watt 1), and luminaries like H.G. Wells charged that Huxley's novel attacked and betrayed science (Watt 16). Today, *Brave New World* is Huxley's best-known novel and widely considered his finest. In some ways, though, perhaps his critics were right: He wrote it in only three months and later criticized the novel's structure, saying he wished he had offered a third alternative to the dystopian Brave New World—also called the World State—and the Savage Reservation. A later novel, *Island*, presents that third alternative for independent-minded exiles from the World State.

The quandary of Huxley's message in *Brave New World* is that only the alienated individual—or at least the person aware of being alienated—can achieve true human consciousness, if not happiness. In some ways, the society of "After Ford" *is* a utopia: No one (except Bernard Marx) is unhappy or troubled with uncomfortable emotions; soma, the perfect pharmaceutical, soothes any pain. The mantra of his novel is not "*everything* belongs to everyone else" but "*everyone* belongs to everyone else."

Huxley treats the theme of alienation on several fronts: psychological, sociological, sexual, biological, and even aesthetic. The way Huxley's dystopia treats humanity's estrangement from an inner life is what makes his vision truly disturbing. Where Karl Marx proposes the abolition of private property as a means to end economic and religious estrangement and bring about "the return of man from religion, family, state, etc., to his *human*, i.e., *social* existence" (Marx 22), Huxley's dystopic vision is based on a *distortion* of the ideas of Marx and Sigmund Freud.

The World State's members are conditioned to shun nature and crave consumer goods. Huxley seems to have anticipated contemporary culture, although even in his own time print advertising and broadcast media were forces for consumer propaganda:

> ... A love of nature keeps no factories busy. It was decided to abolish the love of nature, at any rate among the lower classes; to abolish the love of nature, but not the tendency to consume transport. For of course it was essential to keep on going to the country, even though they hated it. The problem was to find an economically sounder reason for consuming transport than a mere affection for primroses and landscapes. It was duly found.
>
> "We condition the masses to hate the country," concluded the Director. "But simultaneously we condition them to love all country sports. At the same time, we see to it that all country sports shall entail the use of elaborate apparatus. So that they consume manufactured articles as well as transport. Hence those electric shocks" (*BNW* 22).

Many intellectuals of Huxley's time interpreted the book as an attack on science, yet Huxley only decries science's manipulation by economic theory and its service to the greatest number of people in the World State. *Brave New World* demonstrates that the philosophy of the greatest happiness for the greatest number may not lead to happiness at all. As Mustapha Mond, Resident World Controller of Western Europe, states, "What fun it would be ... if one didn't have to think about happiness!" (180-1). This was prescient for 1932, before consumer society rebounded from the deprivations of World War II and before the rise of psychiatric drugs to treat depression, anxiety, alienation, and other threats to mental well-being.

Huxley's ideas about alienation are radical twists on Marxist and Freudian notions. The word *alien* dates to Old French, with the first recorded use in English in 1340, according to the *Oxford English Dictionary*. At that time, it meant "belonging to another person, place or family; strange, foreign, not of one's own." According to Horowitz in "On Alienation and the Social Order," "At its source, the word 'alienation' implies an intense separation first from objects in a world, second from other people, third from ideas about the world held by other people. It might be said that the synonym of alienation is separation, while the precise antonym of the word is integration" (231). The psychological sense of alienation is probably more modern, but Arnold Hauser asserts that the modern meaning of alienation originated in the Renaissance as new mechanical processes alienated people from their work (394). This is a key concept of Marxism: The worker is alienated from the product of work in the modern, industrial world; for Marx, abolishing class differences and private property would abolish alienation. According to Horowitz, "It was Marx himself who made the clear and decisive break with the philosophical tradition of explaining alienation. No longer was alienation a property of man or of reason, but it became a specific property of select classes of men in factory conditions who were, as a result of these conditions, deprived of their reasons . . ." (Horowitz 231). Marx himself explains it:

> What then, constitutes the alienation of labor? First, the fact that labor is external to the worker, i.e., it does not belong to his essential being; that in his work, therefore, he does not affirm himself but denies himself, does not feel content but unhappy, does not develop freely his physical and mental energy but mortifies his body and ruins his mind. The worker therefore only feels himself outside of his work, and in his work feels outside himself. He is at home when he is not working, and when he is working he is not at home. His labor is therefore not voluntary, but coerced; it is *forced labor* (quoted in Horowitz 234).

In *Brave New World*, all of the members of the society, from Alpha to Epsilon, are tailored specifically for the work they will do. Through *in vitro* fertilization and the fictional Bokanovsky's cloning process, multiple identical twins are bred in Huxley's dystopian world. Because individuals born into the lower classes are genetically tailored to do their assigned jobs, the labor force is *not* alienated. In Huxley's novel, the techniques of mass production are applied to human reproduction, creating social classes perfectly fitted to the work they perform. Inane work is done by mindless Epsilon-Minus Semi-Morons:

> "Roof!" called a creaking voice.
>
> The liftman was a small simian creature, dressed in the black tunic of an Epsilon-Minus Semi-Moron.
>
> "Roof!"
>
> He flung open the gates. The warm glory of afternoon sunlight made him start and blink his eyes. "Oh, roof!" he repeated in a voice of rapture. He was as though suddenly and joyfully awakened from a dark annihilating stupor. "Roof!"
>
> He smiled up with a kind of doggily expectant adoration into the faces of his passengers. Talking and laughing together, they stepped out into the light. The liftman looked after them.
>
> "Roof?" he said once more questioningly (*BNW* 59).

Bernard Marx, from the beginning of the novel, is described as a social misfit. When Lenina Crowne tells her friend Fanny that she is considering "having" Bernard, they have the following conversation:

> Fanny looked startled. "You don't mean to say . . . ?"
>
> "Why not? Bernard's an Alpha Plus. Besides, he asked me to go to one of the Savage Reservations with him. I've always wanted to see a Savage Reservation."
>
> "But his reputation?"
>
> "What do I care about his reputation?"
>
> "They say he doesn't like Obstacle Golf."
>
> "They say, they say," mocked Lenina.
>
> "And then he spends most of his time by himself—*alone*." There was horror in Fanny's voice.
>
> "Well, he won't be alone when he's with me. And anyhow, why are people so beastly to him? I think he's rather sweet" (*BNW* 44-45).

Horowitz points out that "Alienation is the driveshaft of revolution" (232). Predictably then, Bernard Marx and his friend Helmholtz, who secretly scribbles poetry, become nodes of resistance against the enforced conformity of the Brave New World. Helmholtz, like Bernard, is afflicted by a crippling self-consciousness:

> A mental excess had produced in Helmholtz Watson effects very similar to those which, in Bernard Marx, were the result of a physical defect. Too little bone and brawn had isolated Bernard from his fellow men, and the sense of this apartness, being, by all the current standards, a mental excess, became in its turn a cause of wider separation. That which had made Helmholtz so uncomfortably aware of being himself and all alone was too much ability. What the two men shared was the knowledge that they were individuals (*BNW* 67).

A convincing aspect of the novel, which some readers see as a flaw in its structure, is that Bernard, given the chance, revels in the quest for social advantages he did not enjoy when he was considered an outsider because of his behavior and physical defectiveness (his small stature makes him resemble a Delta rather than an Alpha Plus, and it's rumored that alcohol was accidentally introduced in his blood-surrogate during gestation). He becomes a conformist when he brings John the Savage and John's mother, Linda, from the Savage Reservation to the World State.

Linda had been accidentally impregnated by Thomas, director of the London Hatchery and Conditioning Center (D.H.C.) and Bernard's hated boss, on their own trip to the Savage Reservation nearly two decades earlier. In the World State, where natural impregnation and birth are studiously avoided in favor of test-tube babies, Linda and her son are considered obscene artifacts. Indeed, the words *mother* and *father* are unknown in the Brave New World, and aging has been slowed and dread of death conditioned away. Linda, an inadvertent exile from the Brave New World, looks old to its inhabitants.

As Thomas prepares to fire Bernard and send him into exile, Bernard triumphantly presents Linda to her old lover Tomakin, and John meets his father in a scene that publicly humiliates the director. Bernard, who once mocked the enforced promiscuity of the Brave New World and pitied Lenina for her many sexual partners, exploits his sudden popularity by sleeping with as many young women as he can.

If Henry Ford and the idea of assembly-line production are bedrocks of the World State, Huxley introduces the concomitant philosophical principle of Freudian theory with the Savage. One of the ironies of *Brave New World* is that even though "Ford" is an oath (as in "Our Ford!" for "By Jove!"), sometimes "Our Ford" is spoken as "Our Freud": "Our Freud had been the first to reveal the appalling dangers of family life. The world was full of fathers—was therefore full of misery; full of mothers—therefore of every kind of perversion from sadism to chastity; full of brothers, sisters, uncles, aunts—full of madness and suicide" (*BNW* 38).

As with the manipulation of Marxist theory to produce the unalienated worker, Freudian theory becomes a means in *Brave New World* to avoid alienating experiences that might cause separation and pain. As Freud showed how psychological conflicts are caused by the nuclear family and sexual repression, the dystopian society in Huxley's novel averts them by eliminating the family altogether. Thus, there are no Oedipal complexes, and sexuality is indulged rather than repressed. Huxley elaborates on this further in his foreword to the 1946 edition of the novel: "As political freedom diminishes, sexual freedom tends compensatingly to increase. And the dictator (unless he needs cannon fodder and families with which to colonize empty or conquered territories) will do well to encourage that freedom. In conjunction with the freedom to daydream under the influence of dope and movies and the radio, it will help to reconcile his subjects to the servitude which is their fate" (xvii). Therefore, children are encouraged to engage in erotic play from a young age, and promiscuity is enforced.

John the Savage, as a true outsider to the Brave New World, embodies the alienation caused by "Freudian" complexes. His mother's conditioned promiscuity conflicts with the reservation's values, and John is an outsider in Savage and Brave New World cultures. John displaces Bernard Marx as the hero of the novel in its second portion.

Many have commented on Huxley's friendship with writer D.H. Lawrence, who died two years before the publication of *Brave New World*. Despite Lawrence's frank treatment of sexuality, he did not condone promiscuity, and Brad Buchanan in "Oedipus in Dystopia" suggests that the Savage resembles Lawrence (86-88). John is the most "civilized" character in the book and, in keeping with Freudian theory as expressed in essays like *Civilization and Its Discontents*, is thus the most neurotic. As a fatherless child, he is abnormally close to his mother and jealous of her Native American lover, Popé. John's reading of Shakespeare has shaped his thinking (perhaps an allusion to the way Freud used works by Sophocles, Shakespeare, and other fiction writers to form many of his ideas about human nature). Raised among Savages who reject sexual promiscuity in general, John dislikes the Brave New World's loose sexual mores and most other aspects of this supposedly ideal society.

After Linda dies in the Park Lane Hospital for the Dying, John turns on the grown-up Deltas who run the hospital and tries to awaken them by throwing their soma away:

> "... Don't you want to be free and men? Don't you even understand what manhood and freedom are?" Rage was making him fluent; the words came easily, in a rush. "Don't you?" he repeated, but got no answer to his question. "Very well, then," he went on grimly. "I'll teach you; I'll make you be free whether you want to or not." And pushing open a window that looked on to the inner court of the Hospital, he began to throw the little pill-boxes of *soma* tablets in handfuls out into the area (*BNW* 218-9).

But the soma-stupefied Deltas want none of this "freedom," and John's refusal to take the escapist path leads ultimately to his death. It is impossible to imagine John being happy in the Brave New World.

Far from being a nihilist, as some of his detractors claimed, Huxley is very much a humanist. Through John the Savage he expresses the human need for God; through Mustapha Mond, he affirms the values of science and life. Putting aside "A New Theory of Biology," a work reminiscent of a nineteenth-century treatise on evolutionary biology, Mond thinks:

> ... It was a masterly piece of work. But once you began admitting explanations in terms of purpose—well, you didn't know what the result might be. It was the sort of idea that might easily decondition the more unsettled minds among the higher castes—make them lose their faith in happiness as the Sovereign Good and take to believing, instead, that the goal was somewhere beyond, somewhere outside the present human

sphere; that the purpose of life was not the maintenance of well-being, but some intensification and refining of consciousness, some enlargement of knowledge (*BNW* 180).

Likewise, the goal in writing is to express oneself in a manner that affects others. As Helmholtz says: "Words can be like X-rays, if you use them properly—they'll go through anything. You read and you're pierced" (*BNW* 70). Talking to John the Savage about Shakespeare, Helmholtz says, "Why was that old fellow such a marvelous propaganda technician? Because he had so many insane, excruciating things to get excited about. You've got to be hurt and upset, otherwise you can't think of the really good, penetrating, X-rayish phrases" (*BNW* 188). Helmholtz and John the Savage in *Brave New World* show that the artist is the ultimate exile in a world lacking introspection and seeking immediate gratification. Huxley argues successfully that a society without great art is one that's not worth living in, even if it means sacrificing happiness for pain, suffering, and alienation.

BIBLIOGRAPHY

"Alien." *Oxford English Dictionary*, Compact Edition, 1982.

Bedford, Sybille. *Aldous Huxley*. New York: Carroll and Graf, 1974.

Buchanan, Brad. "Oedipus in Dystopia: Freud and Lawrence in Aldous Huxley's *Brave New World.*" *Journal of Modern Literature* 25.3 (2002). 75–89.

Hauser, Arnold. "Alienation as the Key to Mannerism." *Marxism and Art*. Ed. Berel Lang and Forrest Williams. New York: McKay, 1972. 393–414.

Higdon, David Leon. "The Provocation of Lenina in Huxley's *Brave New World.*" *The International Fiction Review* 29 (2002). 78–83.

Horowitz, Irving Louis. "On Alienation and the Social Order. *Philosophy and Phenomenological Research* 27.2 (1966). 230–237. J-Stor. 27 February 2008.

Huxley, Aldous. *Brave New World*. New York: Harper and Row, 1946.

Krakauer, Jon. *Into the Wild*. New York: Anchor, 1996.

Lang, Berel, and Forrest Williams, eds. *Marxism and Art*. New York: McKay, 1972.

Marx, Karl. "Property and Alienation." *Marxism and Art*. Ed. Berel Lang and Forrest Williams. New York: McKay, 1972. 21–30.

Sartre, Jean-Paul. *Nausea*. New York: New Direction, 1964.

Trotsky, Leon. "Proletarian Culture and Proletarian Art." *Marxism and Art*. Ed. Berel Lang and Forrest Williams. New York: McKay, 1972. 60–79.

Watt, Donald, ed. *Aldous Huxley: The Critical Heritage*. London: Routledge & Kegan Paul, 1975.

THE CATCHER IN THE RYE
(J.D. SALINGER)

"Alienation, Materialism, and Religion in J.D. Salinger's *The Catcher in the Rye*"
by Robert C. Evans,
Auburn University at Montgomery

Alienation is obviously a major theme in J.D. Salinger's popular novel *The Catcher in the Rye*. Holden Caulfield, the novel's adolescent central character, seems alienated from most of his teachers and schoolmates, much of his family, and much of society at large. Although he interacts with numerous people during the three days the novel depicts, he remains fundamentally withdrawn and isolated; he is estranged and distant from others and even, to some degree, from himself. He has no real or deep friendships; most of his interactions are superficial, and many of his relationships are insincere. Holden seems fundamentally frustrated and unhappy with his life and most of the people around him. Most of those people, in turn, appear to exist—at least as they are perceived and described by Holden—in shallow, unfulfilling, and insubstantial relationships, not only with Holden but also with one another. Very few characters in Salinger's book appear to enjoy satisfying and purposeful existences; instead, they are living lives that are essentially self-centered, calculating, and insincere—lives that Holden, in perhaps the most famous word used in this book, considers fundamentally "phony."

Salinger stresses Holden's own sense of alienation. As the novel opens, Holden is expelled from the latest in a series of prep schools.

Unable to summon any enthusiasm for his studies or to build real friendships with his schoolmates, he looks on the world with premature cynicism and jaded contempt, and yet at some level he also hungers for a deeper, richer, more fulfilling existence. In the opening pages of the novel, as he prepares to leave this latest school, Holden is "hanging around" campus, "trying to feel some kind of good-by" (4). The verbs are telling: He lacks direction or purpose, and he feels suspended ("hanging around"), as if he has nothing significant to do. Not even his emotions are spontaneous; he must force himself to "try" to feel. Although he addresses the reader throughout the novel in colloquial, first-person prose, and although he shares thoughts and feelings he shares with almost no one else (with the possible exception of his younger sister, Phoebe), Holden seems remote from nearly everyone. We do get inside his head, and some readers clearly empathize with his thoughts and feelings, but Holden rarely invites us (or anyone) into genuine communion. Instead, his general attitude is cynical and judgmental, and he rarely finds—and rarely seeks—a sincere, enduring bond with another person. His relationships—except for the one with Phoebe—are fleeting, disappointing, and often disillusioning. He clearly longs for more permanent and meaningful connections, but he makes little effort to establish or sustain them.

In his restlessness, discontent, and alienation, Holden is the archetype of the disaffected teenager, the surly, rebellious youth (usually male) who rejects the values and pretensions of "adult" society without having formed any coherent or articulate set of superior values or a more successful plan for a satisfying life. The astonishing and enduring popularity of Salinger's book suggests it touches a real nerve in its depiction of the lives of American teenagers, and the book's translation into numerous other languages suggests that it also speaks to (and about) adolescent experience in other nations and cultures. Yet Carol and Richard Ohmann caution against automatically assuming that teenagers (or even simply teenage males) have been always and everywhere the same. Describing the reactions of many early reviewers of the book, the Ohmanns noted that they tended to "type Holden according to a timeless developmental standard. They [i.e., the early reviewers] do not fully agree on how to define adolescence, or on how far Holden fits the category (is he *hypersensitive?* is he *especially* bright?), but they do agree that there is a norm or model and that Holden more or less matches it" (20). Readers may find that norm attractive or unattractive, appealing or unappealing, but the Ohmanns correctly note that the existence of such a norm is often assumed in commentary on Salinger's novel. For good or for ill, Holden Caulfield is often seen as the authentic representative of many teenagers of his time and place—and perhaps of all times and all places.

In contrast, the Ohmanns try to put Caulfield in historical context by seeing him and his discontentment as a rejection of the "phoniness ... rooted in the economic and social arrangements of capitalism, and in their concealment" (29). Holden repudiates "mores and conventions that are a badge of class," they assert, and at the bottom of his alienation and "sadness are lives confined by poverty, the loss of human connectedness, the power of feelings distorted by class to overcome natural bonds of affinity and friendship" (32). "*The Catcher in the Rye*," for the Ohmanns,

> is among other things a serious critical mimesis of bourgeois life in the Eastern United States, ca. 1950—of snobbery, privilege, class injury, culture as a badge of superiority, sexual exploitation, education subordinated to status, warped social feeling, competitiveness, stunted human possibility, the list could go on.... In short, the esthetic force of the novel is quite precisely located in its rendering a contradiction of a particular [i.e., late capitalist] society, as expressed through an adolescent sensibility that feels, though it cannot comprehend, this contradiction (35).

The Catcher in the Rye, for the Ohmanns, is an implicit indictment of capitalist materialism in the immediate aftermath of the defeat of fascism in World War II and the rise of the anti-Marxist cold war. Holden is insufficiently sophisticated to offer this diagnosis himself, let alone formulate a workable remedy, but Salinger's novel clearly reveals to the Ohmanns the pervasive alienation fostered by a class-based, capitalist society. Holden, then, is not so much an archetypal, ahistorical teenager as he is a symbol of the problems of a society dominated by greed, competition, and bourgeois materialism.

If Holden (and Salinger) fail, it is not in the diagnostic intuitions they offer but rather in their apparent inability to imagine, let alone rigorously formulate, an alternative society—one the Ohmanns clearly suggest would be based on Marxist principles of economic equality, social cooperation, and ideological solidarity among people living in a society concerned with the greatest good for the greatest number. In a Marxist economy, presumably, Holden would be a happy and well-adjusted citizen.

Support for this argument can be found in Salinger's novel, which mocks the materialism of modern American life, particularly when describing a wealthy and self-satisfied alumnus who visits Holden's school (16-17). Class is explicitly emphasized when Holden describes how his efforts to befriend a less-wealthy roommate were thwarted by that student's awareness of their class differences (108-09). Moreover, the novel in general depicts humans as shallow, materialistic, competitive, and often selfish. The Ohmanns might be correct in seeing *The Catcher in the Rye* as partly an indictment of a materialistic, competitive society in which individuals put their own interests first, leaving many people alienated, estranged, and cut off from deeper attachments to others. However, a sound diagnosis of the ills of a materialistic society need not imply a Marxist cure, particularly since Marxism itself is rooted in the very materialism the novel seems to question. Nor is it certain that Salinger is suggesting that flaws in individual psychology and society are the fault of capitalism, per se.

A strong case can be made that the novel indicts any excessive investment in any materialistic philosophy, whether that philosophy is capitalist, Marxist, or another sort. The main problem with Holden and his society, one can argue, is that both have lost their traditional moorings in the spiritual and even explicitly religious values that once provided solace, satisfaction, meaning, fellowship, and hope to millions of people before the advent of modern materialism, whether capitalist or Marxist. One of the most striking aspects of the book is the secular, nonreligious, and even antireligious nature of much of the thought and behavior it presents. Holden lives in a society in which God is mostly absent, and yet references to God—mainly in the form of casual profanity—abound. Although the novel is often remembered for its frequent use of the words *phony* and *phoniness*, the word *goddam* seems to appear more often. The word seems to appear on every page and it does appear in the novel's first paragraph ("I'm not going to tell you my whole goddam autobiography or anything" [1]) and its last ("I think I even miss that goddam Maurice" [214]). In Holden's world, many people and things seem "phony," but practically everything and everybody also appears "goddamned" to Holden and others.

The effects of this pervasive profanity—the kind that takes God's name in vain—are complicated and ironic. The insistent (if irreverent) references to God keep God—and a religious perspective—constantly on our minds. Yet the casual, irreverent, and often deliberately insulting nature of these references also reminds us that Holden lives in a post-Christian and postreligious environment. His society is not stridently atheistic (for atheists, more than most people, take religion quite seriously), and many of the characters consider themselves Christians. Nevertheless, God and religion no longer occupy central places of respect, veneration, or even serious attention. Holden, his schoolmates, and many of the book's adults gratuitously toss around words such as *goddam* purely to show off and assert themselves, not because they regard either God or damnation with much conviction. The use of the word *goddam* is, like so much else in their speech and behavior, rooted in a need for self-centered display. They use it to express their frustration and exasperation with others and to demonstrate the strength and intensity of their feelings (even though the words lose their power through overuse), and it's a term with which they express and enact their alienation from others. They are living in a "goddamned" world in part because they care little for traditional ideas about God and for their fellow human beings. Their repetition of the word is both a sign of their desire to seem "mature" and "grown-up" ("Look: I can swear like a sailor") and a sign of their adolescent immaturity.

"Goddam," however, is not the only religious word or phrase Salinger incessantly repeats. Other such phrases include "for Chrissake" (20, 22, 24), "I swear to God" (21), "too damn hot" (23), "God damn it" (25), and "What the hell's" happening (25), to take just a few examples from a few pages. Similar religious phrasing includes such terms as "God" (as an exclamation [71]), "Good God" (also as an exclamation [144]), "Oh, God!" (145), and "for God's sake" (used once on page 145 and three times on page 146). And then there is Holden's particularly memorable, if skeptical, report that some actors were "absolute angels. Angels. For Chrissake. *Angels*" (127). Page 132 alone has "get the hell out," "sore as hell," and "Why the hell not?"

The Catcher in the Rye brims with religious profanity, and thus religion is never far from the reader's awareness. What is striking about the book's profanity is how little of it is profane in the more usual bodily senses of the term. Admittedly, the word *fuck* makes a thematically important appearance (202), but notable largely by their absence are the many other popular expletives of the potty-mouth, adolescent lexicon. Viewing Salinger's novel in light of the limited range of expletives, one is struck by how *little* his profanity focuses on the body and how often it has religious overtones. Surely, this is not an accident; in any case, the fact of it helps determine the flavor of the book's profanity. Salinger's characters constantly use religious language but in ways that do not take that language (and the ideas it represents) seriously. Salinger's characters are alienated from one another, but they are also alienated from God.

To say that they are "alienated from God" may be too melodramatic, as the novel's characters rarely acknowledge God's possible existence, let alone his potential importance. God and Christianity are mainly a convenient source of profanity, but there seems no denying that Salinger encourages his readers to think more seriously about religion than most of his characters do. The novel's events, for example, take place over three days during the Christmas season. Christmas is a celebration of the event that Christians view as one of the two most important events in human history, the other being the resurrection. To Christians, Christmas symbolizes the moment when God *became* man, when the fundamental alienation of man from God—an alienation inaugurated by the Fall—was suddenly and irrevocably reversed. To Christians, Christmas is a time of great joy precisely because Christ's birth proves God's love and his complete identification with his creatures. For centuries, the Christian religion and Christmas were viewed by millions of people as practical and consoling alternatives to alienation. Christ's good tidings were a message of love—God's love for man, man's love for God, and the potential love of humans for one another. Christmas also symbolized the powerful connection between the mundane and the divine, the earthly and the supernatural; it suggested that the rewards of eternal life could be hoped for even in the bleakest and most depressing of material circumstances.

Holden and most of *Catcher*'s characters live in a society that is worldly and mundane. If their lives seem shallow and joyless and their interactions aimless and pointless, that is partly because they look to nothing higher or more transcendent to give deeper meaning to their lives and relationships. They (and their culture) lack the old certitudes, the old hopes and faith that once gave structure and meaning to the lives of people living in earlier, perhaps more naïve, times. In that sense the Ohmanns are right: Holden Caulfield is less the archetype of the eternal adolescent than he is the embodiment of a postreligious age, when all the so-called "verities" no longer seem relevant.

Although the Ohmanns complain that neither Holden nor Salinger presents us with an obvious or appealing alternative to the alienated, self-centered social relations the book depicts, this is not entirely true. Both Holden and his creator give an unusual amount of attention to two characters who otherwise seem unimportant to the larger plot and who represent a real and viable alternative to the shallow materialism and egocentricity the book mocks. Those characters are the two nuns Holden meets in a sandwich bar in New York about halfway through the novel, and Holden's reflections on his interaction with them consume about six pages. The nuns are among the few adults in the book Holden genuinely respects, and they are among the few adults whose relations with him do not add to his eventual disillusionment. The nuns do not seem "phony"; they seem as genuinely interested in and concerned about Holden as he is respectful of them, and he has an ease and comfort with them that he has with few others. His first impulse upon meeting them is to "give them a hand" with their suitcases—"very inexpensive-looking suitcases—the ones that aren't genuine leather or anything" (108). When describing the nuns' cheap suitcases, Holden digresses briefly and recalls his discomfort with a one-time roommate who considered Holden and his expensive possessions too "bourgeois" (108). The Ohmanns cite this incident to support their Marxist reading of the novel, but it is also possible that Salinger inserts this episode to suggest how Christian charity, when sincerely practiced, provides an alternative to economic tensions and class conflict.

Holden's first impulse is to disdain the cheapness of the nuns' suitcases (108), but the more he gets to know the nuns, the more he respects them. One of them carries a basket to collect charitable gifts, and although the nuns are not actively seeking donations, Holden volunteers one anyway and insists that the nuns take it. He does so at a time when he needs the money, and his donation is one of his most obviously selfless and generous acts (109-10). Holden is embarrassed to be eating a full breakfast, while the nuns, apparently, can afford only "toast and coffee," and he also is impressed that the nuns think he is being too generous (110). Both nuns are teachers, yet Holden's relations with them are not as complex as his relations with most of the novel's other teachers. One nun is interested in Holden's reading habits and seems interested in literature itself—even literature (such as *Romeo and Juliet*) that appear to conflict with a nun's chastely vows. Yet Holden senses no "phoniness" in her, and he talks comfortably with her about the play. As the encounter ends, Holden tries to pay for the nuns' meager meals, but they refuse any more generosity; they take charity for others, not for themselves (111-12).

This is one of the few episodes in the book that risks becoming sentimental, although Salinger avoids this by making Holden wonder (innocently) about how the nuns react to sexual topics in literature (110) and also by making Holden fear that the nuns might proselytize for Catholicism (112). Yet, the nuns retain Holden's respect by refraining from any attempts at recruitment, and even when Holden inadvertently blows smoke in their faces, they treat him with genuine affection and forgiveness. Holden considers them "nice" and reports that he "enjoyed talking to them," and there seems no trace of irony in his words—a rarity in his descriptions of human interactions. Even after the nuns leave, he continues to think about them and contrast their genuine charity with the more ostentatious charity practiced by some of his relatives (114). The nuns, living with apparent self-sacrificing sincerity according to an ancient and possibly naïve creed that many of their contemporaries treat with indifference if not hostility, win Holden's respect and even affection. With them he enjoys a relationship free from the alienation that afflicts his relationships with so many others. Later, as his life spirals out of control, he finds himself "looking for those two nuns I'd met at breakfast the day before, but I didn't see them" (197). Later still, he famously announces that "You can't ever find a place that's nice and peaceful, because there isn't any" (204), but his encounter with the nuns in the sandwich shop proves him at least partially (if only briefly) wrong.

The nuns are hardly the only representatives of religion in Salinger's novel. The pompous, self-righteous prep-school alumnus who parades his piety but does not live according to his professed values (16-17) is another, and clearly the alumnus represents all the potential for pride and hypocrisy to which religion, like any imperfect human institution, can fall victim. Yet Holden, although an avowed atheist in a family full of avowed atheists, nevertheless is capable of feeling real respect for Jesus even when he expresses characteristic disdain for many self-important Christian preachers (99-100). Jesus, presumably, would have approved of the nuns, and so does Holden.

The Catcher in the Rye makes no effort to present Christianity or religion as an alternative or solution to the alienated condition of life in modern society. The novel is not a piece of propaganda (religious, Marxist, or otherwise). Perhaps Salinger felt that religion was no longer a viable option for most moderns, although the continued, and indeed sometimes frightening, growth of many of the world's religions suggests otherwise. Yet it seems striking that two of the few people who escape from the book with most of their dignity and character intact, and who remain free from Holden's adolescent scorn, are not a pair of recruiters for the Communist Youth League, but a couple of nuns with cheap luggage. God! Who would've predicted *that*, for Chrissakes?

BIBLIOGRAPHY

Ohmann, Carol, and Richard Ohmann. "Reviewers, Critics and *The Catcher in the Rye.*" *Critical Inquiry* 3 (1976): 15–37.

Salinger, J.D. *The Catcher in the Rye*. New York: Little, Brown, 1991.

THE CHOSEN
(CHAIM POTOK)

"The Head, the Heart and the Conflict of Generations in Chaim Potok's *The Chosen*"
by Sam Bluefarb,
in *College Language Association Journal* (1971)

INTRODUCTION

In his essay on Chaim Potok's *The Chosen*, Sam Blue-farb details how the novel depicts "two generations and the Hawthornesque split between the obsessions of the head and the impulses of the heart." This tension results in the alienation of Reuven Malter and Danny Saunders: Both boys feel out of place in their own community; they are isolated, pulled between two Jewish sects. Further-more, both are caught in a generational shift as the Jewish community, alienated from mainstream society, seeks to adapt to American culture. Thus, for Bluefarb, both boys are torn "between head and heart, tolerance and fanaticism."

Bluefarb, Sam. "The Head, the Heart and the Conflict of Generations in Chaim Potok's *The Chosen*." *College Language Association Journal* (CLA), Vol. 14, No. 4 (June 1971): 402–9.

Some Zaddikim serve the Lord in the old way: they walk on the
state road. Others at times adopt a new way: they walk on the side
road. Still others pursue a way of their own choosing: they walk on
the path. The last reach their destination first.

—Hassidic saying

Jewish tradition contains many tensions.

—Irving Malin, *Jews and Americans*

The conflict in Chaim Potok's novel *The Chosen* functions at several
levels. These are: the generational conflict; the temperamental; the
conflict between head and heart; the opposition between a petrified
fanaticism and a humane tolerance; and, finally, the split between
two visions of God and man's relationship to Him. Of all of these,
however, it is the opposition between the head and the heart which
predominates.

The locale of the story is the Crown Heights section of Williamsburg in Brooklyn from the Depression years to the founding of the
state of Israel. Although much of the story's direction is determined
by the conflict between Hassidic and Misnagdic traditions in Judaism
(as respectively represented by the Saunders and Malter families), it
is the conflict between two generations and the Hawthornesque split
between the obsessions of the head and the impulses of the heart that
carry the major thrust of *The Chosen*.

The Hassidic view originated as a revolt against the arid intellectual concerns of 18th century scholastic (i.e., Misnagdic) Judaism with
its tortuous explications in Talmudic *pilpul* and its aristocratic disdain
for the poor and illiterate Jew. This resulted in the Hassidic heresy
(according to the Vilna Gaon) toward the stress on joy and the intuitions. Yet in its turn (especially as portrayed in *The Chosen*) Hassidism
itself evolved into the very thing it had attacked. The distance between
the *Ba'al Shem Tov* (or the *Besht*, as he was affectionately called by his
followers) and his latter-day followers is relatively short, as history
goes: a mere two hundred years or so; but the distance between the
gentle piety of the founder of Hassidism and the fanaticism of his later
followers qualitatively spans a greater distance than time alone can
account for. Indeed, Reb Saunders, the Hassidic leader in *The Chosen*,
has really reverted to the earlier arid scholasticism which Hassidism
in its own beginnings had set itself up in opposition to.

However, in *The Chosen*, the quarrel between the Hassidim and the Misnagdim (these days, roughly those practicing Jews who are not Hassidim) though decreasing in intensity and bitterness after the slaughter of six million in the Nazi Holocaust, still makes up a substantial aspect of this novel. It is this group—the Misnagdim (or, to acknowledge Potok's Sephardic dialectal usage, Mitnagdim)—to which Reuven Malter, the young protagonist, belongs. We must of course remember that many Hassidim consider most Jews beyond their own circle *apikorsim* (heretics). While it is true that the Misnagdim in *The Chosen* did not actively oppose the Hassidim, the baseball game between the Misnagdic and the Hassidic schools on which the novel opens not only triggers the conflict but determines the direction the novel will take. In a sense, *The Chosen* is a kind of exercise in the "Hegelian" dialectic which the Hassidim and the Misnagdim have engaged in for the last two and a half centuries; however, in doing so, they have articulated their respective visions toward life and God, and, in a sense, have managed to exert some beneficial influence on each other.

One of the central problems in *The Chosen* is communication—or lack of it. Part of this is deliberate and "chosen." Reb Saunders, in his oddly "Talmudic" way, believes that he can best teach his son the language and wisdom of the heart by forbidding, or discouraging, what he considers "frivolous" discourse—what most of us might think of as the minimal conversational civilities. Thus Reb Saunders denies Danny what Mr. Malter the yeshiva teacher freely gives to his son Reuven: warmth, communication, and understanding. On those rare occasions when Reb Saunders permits himself to address Danny, these exchanges take place during the periodic quizzes on Talmud, which the *rebbe* subjects Danny to—or when he blows up in exasperation at his son's passivity in the face of his own religious (near violent) commitments.

On the other hand, the relationship between Reuven and *his* father is a tender one, made all the more trusting by the easy and affectionate exchange of confidences that go on between them. They, at least, can do what Danny and his father seem unable to do: communicate. In the instance of Reb Saunders it is an admixture of pride and fanatic pietism that prevents any intimacy between himself and his son (rationalized by the elder Saunders' commitment to the Talmudic *A word is worth one coin; silence is worth two*). In Danny's

case it is simply fear of his father that prevents any viable relationship between the two. Conceivably, Mr. Malter, the yeshiva teacher,
and Reb Saunders, the Hassidic Talmudist, are of a common generation, if not of a common age; yet it is Reb Saunders' rigidity, and his
stiff-necked pride, that give the illusion that he is much older than
Mr. Malter—even as Hassidism itself *appears* to be rooted in an older
tradition than its Misnagdic counterpart.

The difference between Mr. Malter and Reb Saunders expresses
itself most forcefully in their respective visions toward the Holocaust:
Reb Saunders can do little more than shed (very real) tears for the
martyred Jews of Europe. "How the world drinks our blood. . . . [But]
It is the will of God. We must accept the will of God." (Chaim Potok,
The Chosen. Fawcett Crest Edition, p. 181. All further quotations are
cited by page number within parentheses following them.) Reuven's
more Westernized father, on the other hand, attempts to counter the
existential nullity of the "world" by becoming ever more active in a
resuscitated Zionist movement. Reb Saunders, to the contrary, in
conformance with orthodox Hassidism, is bound by the Messianic
belief—that only with the coming of the Messiah will Jews achieve
the millennial dream, the ingathering of the exiles, the return to Eretz
Yisroel.

What we find in *The Chosen* is a kind of *doppelgänger* effect—
minus the *doppelgänger* itself. For Reuven and Danny are symbolically
two halves of a single (perhaps ideal? Jewish?) personality, each half
searching for its complement, which we already know can never be
found in an imperfect world (*Siz a falsher velt!*—It's a hypocritical
world! says a Yiddish Koheleth). In short, no perfection is to be
attained, except in unity. But that is precisely the problem of the
characters in *The Chosen*: Theirs is a search for that elusive (or illusory)
goal. For neither of these two boys growing into manhood can really
be said to exist at their fullest potential unless they retain some sort
of relationship with each other, which on one occasion is suspended
when Reb Saunders forbids Danny any association with Reuven for an
interval of about a year, making the two boys doubly miserable.

Reuven, whose father allows his son forays into symbolic logic,
the mathematics of Bertrand Russell, ends up a rabbi! Danny, who
throughout the novel is coerced into following Hassidic tradition, and
is expected to succeed Reb to the leadership of the sect on his father's
death, ultimately breaks away. Danny, for want of a better word—the

word has been overly used and abused, though it applies here—has been alienated—from his father, from Hassidism, and finally from the Hassidic community itself. In a sense Danny is recapitulating (suffering through) the transitions and adjustments so traumatically demanded by the exodus from the Old World to the New, adjustments required of his father and his followers, "pilgrims" who came to America from the East European *shtetle* one step ahead of Hitler's kill-squads.

The American Diaspora has also given Danny Freud and Behaviorist psychology (though initially he has mixed feelings about the latter); but after reading Graetz's *History of the Jews*, he has found that "Freud had clearly upset him in a fundamental way—had thrown him off-balance" (p. 148).

More significant than the conflict of belief in *The Chosen* is the conflict between the generations—each of which is so often collateral with the other. The novel itself could as easily, if not originally, have been called *Fathers and Sons*. For it is as much about the old split between the fathers and their offsprings as it is about the conflicts between religious views and personalities. The sons have been molded by the fathers, though in the case of Danny that influence is a negative one. For Reb Saunders is a fanatic, or at least has those propensities; he represents the archetypal, God-intoxicated Hassid. And it is he who has caused Danny to grow into a tense, coldly introverted personality. Reuven's father, on the other hand, is the tolerant (albeit religious) humanist, opposed both in mind and in heart to the cold scholasticism of the Saunderses.

In the growing estrangement between Danny and his father, the conflict of generations and of visions toward life surfaces. And it is America that is the catalyst: the old East European ambiance is gone (unless one accepts Williamsburg as a pale substitute milieu for the vanished *shtetle*); and in the second instance the old ghetto traditions have become influenced, perhaps eroded—the old acculturation-assimilation story—by the pressures of urbanism and secular intellectualism.

The relationship between Reuven Malter and his father is rooted organically, not in principle—self or externally imposed—but in tolerance and mutual respect. Mr. Malter is a yeshiva teacher, yet he can comfortably discuss the secular philosophers with Reuven as Danny's father, the Hassidic Reb Saunders, never can with him. Mr. Malter tells Reuven, "the point about mathematizing hypotheses was made by Kant. It is one of the programs of the Vienna Circle logical positivists" (p. 202). Yet with all his easy familiarity with philosophical schools and systems, his acumen in grasping them, Reuven's father allows his son to seek truth in his own way (possibly because of his own exposure to the rationalist winds of Western philosophy). Where Danny is coerced into the study of a specific mode of religious thought, Reuven is allowed by his father to roam free through the country of ideas. This seemingly minor approach to pedagogical technique—both fathers are teachers in their own ways—will determine the direction each of the boys will later take as young men.

Reuven's father hopes his son will become a rabbi—but would not coerce him into it. The elder Saunders not only expects Danny to take his place in the rabbinic dynasty when his own time comes (as Hassidic custom requires), but can hardly imagine an alternative. On the other hand fanaticism and intolerance go to form the iron bond that binds Danny to his father. What is important here, though, is that Danny becomes an object, manipulated by his father, rather than a person one relates to. This determines Danny's ultimate hostility toward Hassidism itself, so that when he rebels, he not only rebels against a religious movement but against his father, who is its representative. The worship of God gives way, in the first flush of enthusiasm, to his admiration, if not worship, of a substitute god, Sigmund Freud.

As the novel progresses, Danny the intellectual wizard, *Wunderkind*, finds himself increasingly boxed in by the restrictive ghetto mentality of the Hassidim. He sees that his father "Intellectually ... was born trapped. I don't ever want to be trapped the way he's trapped" (p. 191).

Ultimately, though, *The Chosen* is a paradigm of two visions that have not only sundered Judaism but have affected other areas of life—the split between head and heart. The Saunderses seem to have an excess of head in their (paradoxical streak of zealousness and emotional) makeup; but the Malters have heart *and* head: They are in balance. For Reuven is not only an outstanding student of Talmud but he "has a head" for mathematics and symbolic logic. Like his father, he also has a spark of tolerance that illuminates his own knowledge of human essences as opposed to ritualistic forms.

Reuven's studies are "brain" disciplines—logic, mathematics, philosophy—yet it is he who finally turns out to have more "heart" than the brilliant son of a Hassid. Danny, on the other hand, having been raised in the tradition of the *Ba'al Shem*, should have been a "heart-and-joy specialist." Yet it is he who is all brain. And this produces a keen irony, since Hassidism, a movement that was originally a revolt against arid scholasticism became (as portrayed in *The Chosen*) transformed into its opposite. Piety, joy, even learning (a latecomer to Hassidism) becomes pietism, rote learning, memorization.

In this split between head and heart, Danny Saunders shows a brilliant flare for Talmudic explication. Yet Reb Saunders, addressing Reuven Malter in Danny's presence, complains, "the Master of the Universe blessed me with a brilliant son. And He cursed me with all the problems of raising him. Ah, what it is to have a brilliant son! ... [But] There was no soul in my ... Daniel, there was only his mind. He was a mind in a body without a soul" (p. 263). Too late: Danny has already "chosen" his own path, and Reb Saunders—plausibly or not—realizes at last that it is impossible to turn back now and give his son the love (or heart) he might once have given him, an act which may well have tempered Danny's mind.

Reuven is not exactly a *graubbe yung*, a moron, himself. For in one of the terminal scenes, he proves himself a master of many Talmudic brain twisters—and this, ironically, even when he *cannot* answer one difficult proposition which the teacher himself is unable to resolve! There is enough sanity in Reuven, though—presumably the heritage his father has passed on to him—to bring him to the realization that words themselves have little meaning unless they are rooted in life. If necessary, Reuven will show that he is capable of proving a formidable rival to Danny's father in his ability to untie knotty Talmudic propositions. Yet he also knows that this hardly makes a Jew, much less a compassionate human being. For brilliance, whether in Talmud or in other mental acrobatics, may as often blind the brilliant with their own brilliance as enlighten. The major irony, then, is that Hassidism—the brand portrayed in Potok's novel—though presumably a religious movement of the heart, has become transformed into its opposite.

I should like to say a few words about the symbolic symmetry of *The Chosen*. Potok seems to have extended himself beyond plausibility here. For the conclusion of this otherwise fine and sensitive work is marred by contrivance. Perhaps this can be ascribed to a symmetry that, while possible in life, somehow doesn't ring true when placed in fictional context. In this symmetry Danny escapes the confines of the Hassidic sect while Reuven stays within the wider boundaries of a more tolerant form of Judaism. Further, in this kind of resolution, Potok unintentionally (and unfortunately) reveals his intentions long before the novel ends. It takes no great effort to guess, even early in the novel, that Danny will rebel, while Reuven, the "nice Jewish boy," will become a rabbi.

Reb Saunders' "conversion"—his resignation to Danny's break with Hassidism—doesn't convince. The novel is too mechanical in this sense—with Danny, who was to have inherited his father's leadership going off to become a clinical or behavioral psychologist, while Reuven turns to the rabbinate.[1]

The climax of the novel is illustrated by the following exchange the two young men engage in: Danny tells Reuven: "I can't get over your becoming a rabbi." Whereupon Reuven answers: "I can't get over your becoming a psychologist" (p. 247). Even the dialogue is weak here, betraying the Procrustean ending; it is virtually the antithesis to the brilliant verbal fencing—stichomythia—that the great dramatists from Shakespeare to Shaw were such virtuosos at. In this instance, the dialogue verges on the cliché.

Thus, as Reuven moves closer to Misnagdic—non-Hassidic—Judaism, so Danny moves away from its Hassidic counterpart, giving the novel this mechanical symmetry. The saving feature in spite of the contrived ending is that the choices of the two young men are as much determined by motive and character (or lack of it) as by superimposed plot strictures.

The almost explicit theme of *The Chosen*, then, is that the more repression one is forced to knuckle under to (no matter the noble intentions), the greater will be the rebellion against the source of that repression; it's the old postulate of an opposite and equal reaction for every action. In other words, the contrivance of the rebellious son against the father and the father's resignation to the son's rebellion—"You will remain an observer of the Commandments?" he pathetically asks Danny (p. 268)—are developments that make it all the more difficult to believe in Reb Saunders as a strong, if stubborn, man.

Still—and this I mean to stress—the "contrivance of symmetry" with which the novel ends is a minor flaw in a larger pattern: that of tolerance against intolerance, empty ritual against the vital deed, rote learning against eager wonder. In any effective fiction it is the process rather than the outcome that is more important. This is especially true in *The Chosen*. For in this novel Chaim Potok gives us as keen an insight into the split between head and heart, tolerance and fanaticism, the strictures of tradition against the impulses of *rachmonis* (pity) as has appeared in the Jewish-American novel in a long time.

NOTE

1. In Danny's escape from the Hassidic milieu, he is acting out the time-honored escape impulse that fills the pages of American literature generally—from Mark Twain's Huck Finn to Joseph Heller's Orr.

DUBLINERS
(JAMES JOYCE)

"Alienation in James Joyce's *Dubliners*"
by Blake Hobby,
University of North Carolina at Asheville

Initially shocking readers and printers because it criticized sacred institutions such as the Roman Catholic Church and broached sensitive subjects such as human sexuality and alcoholism, James Joyce's *Dubliners* (1904) broke from traditional ways of telling a story. As with Franz Kafka's fiction, especially such works as *The Trial* and *The Metamorphosis*, *Dubliners* is an expressionist artwork. Such works use the most penetrating means imaginable, no matter how unusual, to communicate inner thoughts and emotions—a goal that echoes Joyce's desire to describe the Dubliners "for the most part in a style of scrupulous meanness" (quoted in Ellman 210). As they depict angst-ridden lives, Joyce's stories convey a powerful sense of alienation. By quickly shifting characters and perspectives and moving through the stages of a human life—childhood, adolescence, and maturity—Joyce provides a panoramic view of turn-of-the-century Dublin as a paralyzed world.

One of the three italicized words introduced to readers on the first page of the text, *paralysis* conveys the alienation of Joyce's characters. As Joyce explains, he intended "to write a chapter of the moral history of my country and I chose Dublin for the scene because the city seemed to me the centre of paralysis" (quoted in Levin 30). Thus, like many expressionistic works of art and pieces of music, *Dubliners*

takes as its subject the modern, disillusioned person as described by
Friedrich Nietzsche and Sigmund Freud: isolated, filled with inner
conflict and anxiety, suppressed by institutions and cultural values, and
acting out in irritated rebellion against established order and accepted
forms. Stephen Dedalus, the protagonist of Joyce's novel *Portrait of
the Artist as a Young Man* (1916), yearns to be free of this same world:
"When the soul of a man is born in this country there are nets flung
at it to hold it back from flight. You talk to me of nationality, language,
religion. I shall try to fly by those nets" (*Portrait* 196). These same nets
trap the Dubliners, who inhabit a suffocating urban world.

The opening story of *Dubliners*, "The Sisters," concludes with a
silent wake, a communal ritual robbed of its efficacy. In the story's
opening paragraph, the boy remembers repeating the word *paralysis*
as a "mantra" at the priest's window (3). The word sounds strange to
him, "like the name of some maleficent and sinful being," filling the
boy with fear (3). The boy next remembers Old Cotter, who arranges
"his opinion in his mind" of the priest's demise as he smokes his
pipe before the fire (4). The story ends, however, before an empty
fireplace in a communion ritual whose painful silence causes the boy
to refuse the host-like crackers offered for fear of making noise. The
boy's aunt breaks the silence with a timid suggestion, an incomplete
thought, as she says, "I heard something . . ." (11). Although the aunt
speaks of rumors, what the reader hears in the lapse, after the silence,
is laughter. The story ends with a mysterious phrase that is repeated
like the boy's mantra at the story's opening. Eliza repeats what Father
O'Rourke has told of Flynn's condition the evening he was found in
the confessional: "Wideawake and laughing-like to himself . . ." (11).
Flynn's own laugh, co-opted by O'Rourke, reinterpreted by Eliza, and
then retold by the narrator, ends the exposition of *Dubliners*, creating
a sense of alienation in the reader that mirrors Joyce's own alienation
from Irish society.

Rituals with awkward silences and musical parodies in *Dubliners*
call attention to the alienated state of the city dwellers, highlight
their need to escape, and often set up dark "epiphanies," the expression Joyce borrows from the theological tradition to indicate sudden
moments of awareness. Music accompanies this alienated world, a
world paralyzed in its adherence to ritual, a world sick and weary from
imprisoning moral values, as Nietzsche describes in *On the Genealogy
of Morals*. Many of the collection's dark epiphanies contain awkward

silences, where word and deed have failed to make meaning. At the end of "Araby," for example, a young boy faces a dark epiphany in which his dreams of being a bold knight-errant fade as he accepts his failure (27). His epiphany, revealing that there is nothing behind the illusive shadow of the woman he fabricates and in which he believes, brings anger and anguish. The boy recognizes "a silence like that which pervades a church after a service." The music of the "fall of coins" from "two men . . . counting money on a salver" breaks his silence (26). The boy then allows "two pennies to fall against the sixpence in his pocket," an act that symbolically associates the boy with the merchants. Gazing up into the darkened bazaar, he vaults his own suffering, fictively creating himself "as a creature driven and derided by vanity," one whose own suffering and disillusionment are great (27). The music of the coins in the boy's pocket enables the reader to see the boy's self-derision as part of a larger pattern of alienation. The boy fabricates the woman as his own desire and thus falls prey to an illusion. He functions as part of a world in which the uncle and the merchants, as well as the flirtatious couple the boy overhears, are victims of their own wills, alienated creatures following thwarted desires.

Joyce describes the Dubliners as hearts that, like the strings of Orpheus, beat to the rhythm of desire. "Eveline," for example, contains many allusions to the heart and heartbeats. Literally, the story palpitates (29). As the boat separates Eveline from Frank, the narrator describes, "A bell clanged upon her heart" (32). Eveline muses on "the pitiful vision of her mother's voice" and her "life of commonplace sacrifices" (32). Similarly, "An Encounter" opens and closes with percussive palpitations: Joe Dillon "beating a tin" (12) and the "heart . . . beating quickly with fear" (20) of the little boy who yearns, like Dillon, to escape. Farrington in "Counterparts" likewise desires to escape his job and his home life. His frustrated desires culminate, after his arm-wrestling humiliation with Weathers, in a "heart [that] swelled with fury" (85). Similarly, Gabriel's heart in "The Dead" swells with another kind of fury when he desires Gretta: "The blood went bounding along his veins and then thought went rioting through his brain, proud, joyful, tender, valorous" (194). Joyce renders Gabriel's desire, along with the impotent desires and ambitions of the other Dubliners, in a musical language that captures the Dubliners' alienation: their blindness, humiliation, and powerlessness.

For example, lulled by Frank's singing, Eveline desires his song to be more than it is. The narrative voice describes: "when he sang about the lass that loves a sailor she always felt pleasantly confused" (30-31). While Frank's song distorts Eveline's intent, so does Polly's song in "The Boarding House." As the virgin Polly plays her part in the seduction of Mr. Doran, a game in which she and he become pawns, she sings a bawdy ditty:

> I'm a . . . naughty girl.
> You needn't sham:
> *You know I am.* (53)

Polly's song inflames Doran's desire and hers and makes the betrothal game of Mrs. Mooney an excessive perversion. Trapped but also playing the game, Doran meets Polly secretly at night, desiring to have her while still being virtuous in the eyes of the business community. Mrs. Mooney uses her own children in a musical exhibitionist show that lays the groundwork for Mooney's later scheming, amid the music of church bells, when she "deal[s] with moral problems as a cleaver deals with meat" (54). The story's meat-cleaving images are fantastic distortions as are the songs Polly and Jack sing with the other artistes as part of the Mooney salon floorshow. While Doran is simultaneously tricked and one who tries to turn a trick, the reader sees all the Mooney and Doran machinations as part of the show.

Although "Araby" depicts a young boy following his own elusive desires, "Clay," "The Boarding House," and "After the Race" all depict people as part of cruel games that leave individuals alone, isolated, and at odds with themselves and the world. "Clay," the midpoint in *Dubliners*, depicts Maria as the center of a cruel game. Maria sings in "a tiny quavering voice" (93) and spoils her performance as she becomes entrenched in a lyric loop, repeating lyrics like the circling horse Gabriel mimics in "The Dead" (189). Maria's first mistake (the choosing of the clay) brings snickers, but her guffaw evokes silence. Although the story's ending seems tragic and sentimental as Joe co-opts Maria's song, turning her pathetic longings for love into his own sentimental tears for the "time . . . long ago" (94), the story ends with an ambiguous image of a wine opener. The corkscrew is a sexual allusion that mocks Joe's impotence as husband, brother, father, and son and, in a strange double irony, caricatures Maria and pities her virginity.

Likewise, as the waltz and card game end in "After the Race," Jimmy counts "the beats of his own temples," knowing he has become a victim in his own game, a pawn in the world of commerce.

Bastardized rituals appear in *Dubliners* with musical descriptions and musical effects. In "Grace," "the light music of whiskey falling into glasses" accompanies the men who lure Kernan to the retreat (153). Purdon's sermon is a musical performance in which he "develop[s] the text with resonant assurance," speaking on the difficulty of "interpreting properly" and addressing an audience of "hearers" with the kind of coin-clinking music heard in "Araby" (157). Purdon's sermon rings with irony, as does all the political talk in "Ivy Day in the Committee Room," a story of political doggerel and awkward silences interrupted by the music of beer bottle *"poks!"* (118, 119, 122). The *poks* lend irony to the long-winded music of the co-opters who gather to honor Parnell and lament his demise yet participate in the same corrupt games that caused his end. The co-opters use Parnell as the race-car drivers use Jimmy and Europe uses Ireland. "A Painful Case" likewise ends with a grotesque musical scene. Duffy listens to the tram just as he listened to a musical performance the evening he met Mrs. Sinico. The tram's music reminds him of the performance Sinico gave in her own death. Although Duffy eschews the world of sound after breaking off with Sinico, the music of the tram is inescapable. The tram's music, uttering Sinico's tripartite name repeatedly as its wheels move across the tracks, comes from Duffy's perspective. The reader sees that Duffy believes he is responsible for Sinico's death and feels pride that he has power to control another's life. Duffy's narration and the newspaper account are only two perspectives, while Mrs. Sinico's perspective is conspicuously absent. Duffy's interpretation is wily, snaky, and suspicious, bringing the reader to imagine that Duffy has snaked his way into the Sinico home and perhaps even tunneled into Mrs. Sinico.

In "Araby" the boy describes himself as a harp, a thing that responds in an overstated, hyperreactive manner to the illusion he creates: "But my body was like a harp and her words and gestures were like fingers running upon the wires" (23). Lenehan and Corley of "Two Gallants" also pass a harpist in the Dublin streets who plays his instrument as they themselves play women:

> They walked along Nassau Street and then turned into Kildare Street. Not far from the porch of the club a harpist stood in

the roadway playing to a little ring of listeners. He plucked at
the wires heedlessly, glancing quickly from time to time at the
face of each newcomer and from time to time, wearily also,
at the sky. His harp too, heedless that her covering had fallen
about her knees, seemed weary alike of the eyes of stranger
and of her master's hands. One hand played the bass melody
of *Silent, O Moyle*, while the other hand careered in the treble
after each group of notes. The notes of the air throbbed deep
and full. (45-6)

The harp heard by the gallants is both woman and Ireland, a thing
played by manipulative hands, an alienated world controlled by
external forces beyond individual control. The harp also attracts the
scheming Lenehan on his return as he runs his hands along the railings of Duke's Lawn: "The air which the harpist had played began to
control his movements. His softly padded feet played the melody while
his fingers swept a scale of variations idly along the railings after each
group of notes" (47-48). Lenehan becomes the victim of his own game
and is associated with the woman, which places Lenehan in a passive
posture of waiting for Corley and alludes to his possible homosexuality.
The opening paragraph of "Two Gallants" describes the streets as an
expressionistic canvas: "The streets, shuttered for the repose of Sunday,
swarmed with a gaily coloured crowd. Like illumined pearls the lamps
shone from the summits of their poles upon the living texture below
which, changing shape and hue unceasingly, sent up into the warm
grey evening air an unchanging unceasing murmur" (41). This opening
passage associates the music of the city, its unceasing murmur, with the
shifting colors, shapes, and hues that depict inner conflict expressed
in external signs, an inner world mirrored in the cacophony of the
city. The gallants, seeking to escape the mourning music of the harp,
encounter the music of the city, "the noise of trams, the lights and the
crowd" that releases them "from their silence" (46).

Dubliners contains many frenetic spectacles that depict commerce,
social mechanisms, and the pace of modernity as a meaningless,
cacophonous game that engulfs all and leaves individuals alone and
isolated. In "After the Race," Dame Street is "busy with unusual
traffic, loud with the horns of motorists and the gongs of impatient
drivers" (37). The furious ringing of a bell opens "Counterparts" as a
voice amplified through a tube barks out Alleyne's wishes. The story

comments on the absurdity of business and the inhumanity of a world of commerce in which people are used as machines. The office's characters and machines constantly click and clack, forming the monotonous office routine that is satirized in Farrington's "Bernard Bernard" copy blunder (79). Similarly, Jack's violence, the church bells, and the bawdy singing are all part of Mrs. Mooney's economic venture in "The Boarding House." We do not feel at home in such infernal worlds; instead, we feel a sensation Freud called "the uncanny."

"The Dead" concludes *Dubliners*, opening with the music of Lily's scampering feet and the "halldoor bell" clanging (159). The reader hears "gossiping and laughing and fussing" from the dressing room upstairs, the scraping of snow from galoshes, and "the shuffling of feet" of dancers (161). As a waltz ends, hand clapping begins (165), followed by the laughter of Freddy Malins, the drunken "high-pitched bronchitic laughter" that rings throughout the story (168). The young ladies, listening to the "whiskey, . . . it's the doctor's orders" of Mr. Browne, "laugh in musical echo, swaying their bodies to and fro" (166). The music at the table is disordered and cluttered; yet it expresses the festive ritual that ends *Dubliners* and opposes the bare communion rite at the collection's opening. At the Morkans' meal, "there [is] a great deal of confusion and laughter and noise, the noise of orders and counterorders, of knives and forks, of corks and glass stoppers" (179) that simultaneously parries and mirrors the "thought-tormented music" Gabriel laments in his speech (183). The crowd gathered at the table, rapping the table until "the patting at once grew louder in encouragement and then ceased altogether," encourages Gabriel to speak (183). Applause and laughter interject Gabriel's speech, which concludes with more clapping and a sung "acclamation" to which the comic "Freddy Malins beat[s] time with his pudding fork" (187). "Peals of laughter" follow Gabriel's imitation of Johnny the circling horse (189). The evening's celebration ends as Mary Jane helps "the discussion from the doorstep with cross-directions and contradictions and abundance of laughter," a tone that changes as Gabriel watches Gretta on the stairs and asks himself, "What is a woman standing on the stairs in the shadow, listening to distant music, a symbol of ?" (190-1). Gabriel listens to the voices outside, the voices in the hall, and the music coming from upstairs as the house's voices blend. Gabriel directs his attention to "the old Irish tonality" sung with uncertainty by D'Arcy, whose "voice made plaintive by the distance and by the singer's hoarseness faintly illuminated the cadence of the air with words expressing grief" (191). D'Arcy's words, internalized by Gabriel in his own sentimental way, cause his blood to boil. Gabriel remembers "the first touch of her body, musical, strange and perfumed" (196). The silence that Gabriel and Gretta observe as they follow the innkeeper to their room feeds Gabriel's hunger as "the falling of the molten wax into the tray" echoes "the thumping of his own heart against his ribs" (196). Gretta's choking sobs leave Gabriel alone in silence as his wife drifts off to sleep (202).

Here, alone, Gabriel experiences the final moment of alienation in *Dubliners.* "The Dead" ends with "a few light taps upon the [window] pane" as Gabriel breaks the silence by describing the snow-covered countryside before him. Gabriel resists what he called in his Robert Browning review the "thought-tormented music" of modernity. Instead of the stark, scrupulous style used until now, the narrative voice shifts, rounding out the collection with lush Romantic prose. As he co-opts the story of Michael Fury and *The Lass of Aughrim,* which so occupies Gretta, and makes the song his own self-pitying, nationalistic ballad, Gabriel becomes another of the isolated voices in *Dubliners,* speaking in the night but unheard. While it's tempting to read the ending of "The Dead" as a hope-filled epiphany that converts Gabriel, such a reading discounts the continuity of Joyce's stories, the common thread of alienation that unites the Dubliners in their paralytic lives. In a collection that begins with a wake and ends with a marital crisis, Joyce creates a cohesive portrait of urbanites following vain desires, Dubliners for whom alienation is a shared condition after centuries of oppression—not just from the colonizing British but also from the social, political, and religious institutions that influence their lives. In life they seek freedom but find only emptiness echoed in "the snow falling faintly through the universe and faintly falling, like the descent of their last end, upon all the living and the dead."

BIBLIOGRAPHY

Ellman, Richard. *James Joyce: New and Revised Edition.* New York: Oxford University Press, 1982.

Joyce, James. *Dubliners.* Hans Walther Gabler and Walter Hettche, eds. New York: Vintage, 1993.

————. *Portrait of the Artist as a Young Man.* Ed. Hans Gabler. New York: Vintage, 1993.

Levin, Harry. *James Joyce: A Critical Introduction.* Norfolk, Conn.: New Directions, 1941.

FAHRENHEIT 451
(RAY BRADBURY)

"Burning Bright: *Fahrenheit 451* as Symbolic Dystopia" by Donald Watt, in *Ray Bradbury* (1980)

INTRODUCTION

In his essay on fire symbolism in *Fahrenheit 451*, Donald Watt emphasizes the real possibility that modern culture may eradicate itself in nuclear war, an ironic notion when one considers that the technological tools developed to create a greater sense of freedom ushered in an alienated age of disillusionment and paranoia. As Watt says, Montag, the book's protagonist, desires "something enduring in man's existence—history, heritage, culture. Montag seeks, in essence, a definition and a preservation of the identity of human kind." To live in a world of destruction that is quickly erasing its past is to become an exile, one who seeks to keep "the flame of man's wisdom and creativity" alive. Montag and the other exiles try to preserve humanity's accumulated wisdom by memorizing books: our tools of self-understanding and self-preservation in an alienating age. Bradbury's tale suggests

---

Watt, Donald. "Burning Bright: *Fahrenheit 451* as Symbolic Dystopia." *Ray Bradbury*. Ed. Joseph Olander and M.H. Greeberg. New York: Taplinger, 1980. 195–213.

we have lost our humanity in the search for knowledge and technological advancement. Thus, his dystopian world both represents and decries modern alienation, itself a symptom of unbridled "progress" in which, by following blind ideals, "we can hardly escape from ourselves."

❦

"It was a pleasure to burn," begins Bradbury's *Fahrenheit 451*. "It was a special pleasure to see things eaten, to see things blackened and *changed*." In the decade following Nagasaki and Hiroshima, Bradbury's eye-catching opening for his dystopian novel assumes particular significance. America's nuclear climax to World War II signalled the start of a new age in which the awesome powers of technology, with its alarming dangers, would provoke fresh inquiries into the dimensions of man's potentiality and the scope of his brutality. *Fahrenheit 451* coincides in time and, to a degree, in temperament with Jackson Pollock's tense post-Hiroshima experiments with cobalt and cadmium red, as well as the aggressive primordial grotesques of Seymour Lipton's 1948 New York exhibition—*Moloch, Dissonance, Wild Earth Mother*. Montag's Nero complex is especially striking in the context of the looming threat of global ruin in the postwar era: "With the brass nozzle in his fists, with this great python spitting its venomous kerosene upon the world, the blood pounded in his head, and his hands were the hands of some amazing conductor playing all the symphonies of blazing and burning to bring down the tatters and charcoal ruins of history."[1] Montag's intense pleasure in burning somehow involves a terrible, sadomasochistic temptation to torch the globe, to blacken and disintegrate the human heritage. As Erich Fromm observes, destructiveness "is the outcome of unlived life."[2] Modern man actively pursues destructiveness in order to compensate for a loss of responsibility for his future. Seeking escape from the new freedom he enjoys as a benefit of his new technology, man is all too likely to succumb to a Dr. Strangelove impulse to destroy himself with the very tools that gave him freedom. The opening paragraph of Bradbury's novel immediately evokes the consequences of unharnessed technology and contemporary man's contented refusal to acknowledge these consequences.

In short, *Fahrenheit 451* (1953) raises the question posed by a number of contemporary anti-utopian novels. In one way or another, Huxley's *Ape and Essence* (1948), Orwell's *Nineteen Eighty-Four* (1948), Vonnegut's *Player Piano* (1952), Miller's *A Canticle for Leibowitz* (1959), Hartley's *Facial Justice* (1960), and Burgess's *A Clockwork Orange* (1962) all address themselves to the issue of technology's impact on the destiny of man. In this sense, Mark R. Hillegas is right in labeling *Fahrenheit 451* "almost the archetypal anti-utopia of the new era in which we live."[3] Whether, what, and how to burn in Bradbury's book are the issues—as implicit to a grasp of our age as electricity—which occupy the center of the contemporary mind.

What is distinctive about *Fahrenheit 451* as a work of literature, then, is not what Bradbury says but how he says it. With Arthur C. Clarke, Bradbury is among the most poetic of science fiction writers. Bradbury's evocative, lyrical style charges *Fahrenheit 451* with a sense of mystery and connotative depth that go beyond the normal boundaries of dystopian fiction. Less charming, perhaps, than *The Martian Chronicles*, *Fahrenheit 451* is also less brittle. More to the point, in *Fahrenheit 451* Bradbury has created a pattern of symbols that richly convey the intricacy of his central theme. Involved in Bradbury's burning is the overwhelming problem of modern science: As man's shining inventive intellect sheds more and more light on the truths of the universe, the increased knowledge he thereby acquires, if abused, can ever more easily fry his planet to a cinder. Burning as constructive energy, and burning as apocalyptic catastrophe, are the symbolic poles of Bradbury's novel. Ultimately, the book probes in symbolic terms the puzzling, divisive nature of man as a creative/destructive creature. *Fahrenheit 451* thus becomes a book which injects originality into a literary subgenre that can grow worn and hackneyed. It is the only major symbolic dystopia of our time.

The plot of *Fahrenheit 451* is simple enough. In Bradbury's future, Guy Montag is a fireman whose job it is to burn books and, accordingly, discourage the citizenry from thinking about anything except four-wall television. He meets a young woman whose curiosity and love of natural life stir dissatisfaction with his role in society. He begins to read books and to rebel against the facade of diversions used to seal the masses away from the realities of personal insecurity, officially condoned violence, and periodic nuclear war. He turns against the authorities in a rash and unpremeditated act of murder, flees their lethal hunting party, and escapes to the country. At the end of the book he joins a group of self-exiled book-lovers who hope to preserve the great works of the world despite the opposition of the masses and a nuclear war against an unspecified enemy.

In such bare detail, the novel seems unexciting, even a trifle inane. But Bradbury gives his story impact and imaginative focus by means of symbolic fire. Appropriately, fire is Montag's world, his reality. Bradbury's narrative portrays events as Montag sees them, and it is natural to Montag's way of seeing to regard his experiences in terms of fire. This is a happy and fruitful arrangement by Bradbury, for he is thereby able to fuse character development, setting, and theme into a whole. Bradbury's symbolic fire gives unity, as well as stimulating depth, to *Fahrenheit 451*.

[. . .]

Bradbury continues to play variations on burning in the final sequence of Part Two, where the two different, indeed opposite, kinds of flame flicker out at each other. Montag's return to the firehouse provokes Beatty to welcome him: "I hope you'll be staying with us, now that your fever is done and your sickness over" (p. 94). For Beatty, Montag's inner burning is the result of a fever. From Beatty's point of view, this burning means that a man has been unwell. But Montag wishes to nourish the burning; he doesn't want to return to normal. Beatty, however, enervates Montag with his "alcohol-flame stare" (p. 95) and a confusing barrage of conflicting quotations. Montag feels he cannot go on burning with the firemen, yet he is as powerless to answer Beatty's onslaught as he would be to stop the Salamander, the fire engine, that "gaseous dragon roaring to life" (p. 98). Montag is chagrined by the recollection of reading a book to "the chaff women in his parlor tonight" and realizes it was as senseless as "trying to put out fires with waterpistols" (p. 99). In his typically figurative way, Bradbury is telling us that Montag's psychic temperature cannot remotely approach the 451 degrees Fahrenheit which is the minimal level of power enjoyed by the firemen. On appearance, at any rate, and for the moment, Montag's rage for individual responsibility is puny by comparison with the firepower of Beatty's crew.

The ramifications of Bradbury's two fires become clearer in Part Three, "Burning Bright," for the sequence of events portrays Montag's movement from one to the other, from the gorging arson of his own house to the comforting campfire of Granger. In this section Montag's growth develops into a belief in what Blake symbolizes in his poem, "The Tiger":

Tiger! Tiger! burning bright
In the forests of the night,
What immortal hand or eye
Could frame thy fearful symmetry?

Blake's tiger is the generative force of the human imagination, the creative/destructive force which for him is the heart of man's complex nature. Montag becomes Bradbury's tiger in the forests of the night. He becomes a hunted outcast from an overly tame society by making good his violent escape from the restraining cage of the city. In his rebellion and flight, Montag *is* burning bright. Paradoxically, the flame of his suppressed human spirit spreads through his whole being after his horrible murder of Beatty. In burning Beatty, Montag shares the ambivalence of Blake's tiger, with its symbolic combination of wrath and beauty, its "fearful symmetry."

Bradbury introduces another allusion, one connected with his major symbol, when the fire engine pulls up before Montag's house at the opening of the third section and Beatty chides him: "Old Montag wanted to fly near the sun and now that he's burnt his wings, he wonders why" (p. 100). Beatty's reference is to the mythological Icarus who soared into the sky with Dedalus, his father, on wax wings. But Icarus, carried away by the joy of flying, went too close to the sun, causing his wings to melt and making him fall. Clarisse, we recall, used to stay up nights waiting for the sunrise, and her face reminded Montag of a clock dial pointing toward a new sun. The sun, traditional symbol of truth and enlightenment, is antithetical to the dark night of ignorance that Beatty spreads across the land. The difference between Montag and Icarus—which, of course, Beatty will never live to see—is that Montag, though crippled by the Mechanical Hound, survives his own daring. Burning bright and living dangerously, Montag skirts the destruction Beatty plans for him and flees to the liberated periphery of society where pockets of truth endure undimmed.

At the beginning of Part Three, however, Beatty prevails. Montag once more enjoys the purging power of the fireman as he lays waste to his own house: "And as before, it was good to burn, he felt himself gush out in the fire, snatch, rend, rip in half with flame, and put away the senseless problem.... Fire was best for everything!" Montag destroys his house piecemeal, surprised that his twin beds go up "with more heat and passion and light than he would have supposed them to contain." Bradbury's lyrical style conveys Montag's fascination with the splendor and the transforming power of the flames. His books "leapt and danced like roasted birds, their wings ablaze with red and yellow feathers." He gives the TV parlor "a gift of one huge bright yellow flower of burning" (p. 103). Beatty affects Montag strongly with his enticing argument for burning:

> What is fire? It's a mystery. Scientists give us gobbledegook about friction and molecules. But they don't really know. Its real beauty is that it destroys responsibility and consequences. A problem gets too burdensome, then into the furnace with it. Now, Montag, you're a burden. And fire will lift you off my shoulders, clean, quick, sure; nothing to rot later. Anti-biotic, aesthetic, practical. (p. 102)

With a happy vengeance Montag levels the house where he has become a stranger to his own wife. He feels as though a fiery earthquake is razing his old life as Montag the fireman, burying his artificial societal self, while in his mind his other self is running, "leaving this dead soot-covered body to sway in front of another raving fool" (p. 104). Beatty cannot understand that at this point Montag is inwardly turning the flamethrower against its owners, that by burning his house he is deliberately destroying his niche in Beatty's system.

Only when Beatty threatens to trace Faber does Montag realize that the logical end to his action must be the torching of his chief. As Montag recognizes, the problem is, "we never burned *right* ..." (p. 105). The shrieking, melting, sizzling body of Beatty is Bradbury's horrible emblem of the end result of a civilization based on irresponsibility. Beatty has always told Montag not to face a problem, but to burn it. Montag considers: "Well, now I've done both" (p. 107). One may conclude that Montag fights fire with fire.

The remainder of the novel consists of Montag's escape from the domain of the Mechanical Hound, his immersion in the countryside, and his discovery of Granger's group of bookish outcasts. Montag is still very much in Beatty's world as he flees through the city. Stung by the Mechanical Hound, his leg is "like a chunk of burnt pinelog he was carrying along as a penance for some obscure sin" (p. 107). As he runs his lungs feel "like burning brooms in his chest" (p. 112), his throat like "burnt rust" (p. 123). In his narrow escape from a police car, the lights from the highway lamps seem "as bright and revealing as the midday sun and just as hot" (p. 112), and the car bearing down on him is "a torch hurtling upon him" (p. 113). Montag wants to get out of the distressing heat of Beatty's city and into the cool seclusion of the country. Bradbury stresses that the real insanity of the firemen's world is the pleasure people take in random violence and destruction. Accordingly, just before he sets off to elude the Mechanical Hound, Montag tells Faber that in his death scene he would like to say just one or two words "that would sear all their faces and wake them up" (p. 120). He deeply regrets what he did to Beatty, transformed now into "nothing but a frame skeleton strung with asphalt tendons," but he feels he must remember, "burn them or they'll burn you.... Right now it's as simple as that" (p. 109). It is perhaps instructive to note that one of Montag's last acts in the city is to frame the fireman named Black.

Bradbury broadens Montag's perspective on burning when Montag wades into a river and floats downstream away from the harsh glare of the pursuing searchlights. The life-saving river, a symbol of life's journey and its baptismal vitality, carries Montag into the world of nature: "For the first time in a dozen years the stars were coming out above him, in great processions of wheeling fire. He saw a great juggernaut of stars form in the sky and threaten to roll over and crush him" (p. 124). The great fires of the cosmos have been concealed from Montag by the glittering arcs of the city. Immersed in the river and free of the electric jitters of city life, Montag at last discovers leisure to think for himself. Beatty had said that one of fire's attractions for man is its semblance of perpetual motion. Montag, reflecting on the moon's light, becomes aware that the sun burns every day, burns time, burns away the years and people's lives. Before long, he knows "why he must never burn again in his life." He sees that "if *he* burnt things with the firemen and the sun burnt Time, that meant that *everything* burned!" But he feels that somehow conserving must balance consuming:

> One of them had to stop burning. The sun wouldn't, certainly.
> So it looked as if it had to be Montag and the people he had

worked with until a few short hours ago. Somewhere the saving
and putting away had to begin again and someone had to do the
saving and keeping, one way or another, in books, in records, in
people's heads, any way at all so long as it was safe, free from
moths, silver-fish, rust and dry-rot, and men with matches. The
world was full of burning of all types and sizes. Now the guild
of the asbestos-weaver must open shop very soon. (p. 125).

This key passage illuminates Montag's sensed need for some form
of permanence to counteract the instability of destruction and change.
Man should not capitulate to the tyranny of the nitrogen cycle, to the
mutability characteristic of the physical, dynamic world. Montag's
emerging desire is for something enduring in man's existence—history,
heritage, culture. Montag seeks, in essence, a definition and a preservation of the identity of human kind.

Montag's recognition of another mode of burning, therefore, is
at this stage eminently appropriate to Bradbury's theme. Enchanted
by the warmth of the country, which is implicitly contrasted with the
coldness of Mildred's bedroom, reminded of Clarisse by all the natural
smells of the vegetation surrounding him—"a dry river smelling of
hot cloves," "a smell like a cut potato from all the land," "a faint yellow
odor like parsley on the table at home," "a smell like carnations from
the yard [Clarisse's] next door" (p. 128)—Montag comes upon a
campfire which strikes him as strange "because it meant a different
thing to him" (p. 129). The difference is, he abruptly notices: "It was
not burning, it was *warming*." Men hold their hands toward this
warmth; they do not recoil in terror from it. Montag "hadn't known
fire could look this way. He had never thought in his life that it could
give as well as take. Even its smell was different." Montag feels like
some forest creature "of fur and muzzle and hoof" attracted to the
fire and "listening to the warm crackle of the flames." No longer a
fierce tiger because he has escaped the mad jungle of Beatty's city,
Montag is now like a shy, wondering animal of the woods. Free of the
ceaseless noise of "the family," Montag feels the silence as well as the
flame of the camp is different. The men around the fire have time to
"look at the world and turn it over with the eyes, as if it were held to
the center of the bonfire, a piece of steel these men were all shaping"
(p. 130). Bradbury's figure is of utmost importance, since it recalls
Faber's comment that all of civilization must be melted down and

reshaped. Involved in Montag's sighting of Granger's group is the hope that the new kind of burning may bring about some possibility of a new kind of world.

The purpose of their group, Granger explains, is to preserve man's cultural heritage through the current dark age of his history. They are keepers of the flame of man's wisdom and creativity. They live in the forests of the night, harboring their gentle light against the annihilating torches of the city's firemen. But Montag, expecting "their faces to burn and glitter with the knowledge they carried, to glow as lanterns glow, with the light in them," is disappointed. There is no inner glow to their faces, only resignation. These men are now waiting for "the end of the party and the blowing out of the lamps." They know that nuclear war is imminent, that the joyride of Beatty's society is over, that the future of man is unsure: "They weren't at all certain that the things they carried in their heads might make every future dawn glow with a purer light . . ." (p. 138). Shortly, the bombs turn the city into what Granger describes as "a heap of baking powder" (p. 145), with Mildred and the others now literally buried under the volcano in which they have burned away their existences. The contrast between fire as holocaust and fire as hearth becomes pointed as Granger's men settle around a campfire to cook bacon. Fire, like technology and knowledge, is good or bad, depending on how one uses it.

At the close, Granger compares man with the Phoenix, the mythical bird that lives for hundreds of years in the desert, consumes itself in fire, and then rises reborn from its own ashes. It appears to Granger that man periodically does the same thing, with the difference that man knows what he is doing to himself: "We know all the damn silly things we've done for a thousand years and as long as we know that and always have it around where we can see it, some day we'll stop making the goddam funeral pyres and jumping in the middle of them." Granger hopes that, with more people each generation seeing man's record of folly, some day they will "remember so much that we'll build the biggest steamshovel in history and dig the biggest grave of all time and shove war in and cover it up" (p. 146). Bradbury's mood at best is one of modified optimism, at worst, skeptical ambivalence. The question he raises but leaves unexplored is whether man can ever transcend the cycles of construction and devastation that have characterized his history. Granger's hope notwithstanding, one must remember the phoenix-disc is also one of the firemen's symbols.

Yet at the very end, Bradbury does inject the promise of at least a seasonal renewal, and perhaps more, for man. As the men put out their campfire, "the day was brightening all about them as if a pink lamp had been given more wick" (pp. 146-47). The candle figure is instructive, for it brings the reader all the way back to Clarisse and the kind, humane light she stands for. As they break camp the men, including Granger, fall in behind Montag, suggesting that he will become their leader. Montag, which means Monday in German, will conceivably light their way to a fresh beginning for man. As he wonders what he can say to make their trip upriver a little easier, Montag feels in his memory "the slow simmer" of words from the Bible. At first he remembers the initial verses from Chapter 3 of Ecclesiastes: "To everything there is a season. Yes. A time to break down, and a time to build up. Yes. A time to keep silence and a time to speak. Yes, all that." But The Preacher's words on the vanity of worldly things are not enough for Montag. He tries to remember something else. He digs into his memory for the passage from Revelations 22:2: "*And on either side of the river was there a tree of life, which bare twelve manner of fruits, and yielded her fruit every month; And the leaves of the tree were for the healing of the nations*" (p. 147). This is the thought Montag wants to reserve for noon, the high point of the day, when they reach the city. Bradbury draws on the Biblical notion of a heavenly Jerusalem, the holy city where men will dwell with God after the apocalypse. Its appeal for Montag is the final stroke of Bradbury's symbolism. In the Bible the heavenly city needs no sun or moon to shine on it, for God's glory is what keeps it lit. The nations of the Earth will walk together by this light, and there will be no night there. The light Montag bears in Granger's remnant of humanity is the Biblical hope for peace and immutability for mankind. This light is the permanent flame Montag has discovered in answer to the devouring nuclear burning invited by Beatty's society and as a counterpoint to the restless Heraclitean fire of the visible cosmos.

From its opening portrait of Montag as a singed salamander, to its concluding allusion to the Bible's promise of undying light for man, *Fahrenheit 451* uses a rich body of symbols emanating from fire to shed a variety of illuminations on future and contemporary man.[4]

To be sure, the novel has its vulnerable spots. For one thing, Montag's opposition is not very formidable. Beatty is an articulate spokesman for the authorities, but he has little of the power to invoke terror that Orwell's O'Brien has. The Mechanical Hound is a striking and sinister gadget; but for all its silent stalking, it conveys considerably less real alarm than a pack of aroused bloodhounds. What is genuinely frightening is the specter of that witless mass of humanity in the background who feed on manhunts televised live and a gamey version of highway hit-and-run. For another thing, the reader may be unsettled by the vagueness with which Bradbury defines the conditions leading to the nuclear war. Admittedly, his point is that such a lemming-like society, by its very irresponsibility, will ultimately end in destruction. But the reader is justifiably irritated by the absence of any account of the country's political situation or of the international power structure. The firemen are merely enforcers of noninvolvement, not national policy-makers. The reader would like to know something more about the actual controllers of Beatty's occupation. Who, we wonder, is guarding the guardians?

Probably a greater problem than either of these is what some readers may view as a certain evasiveness on Bradbury's part. Presumably, the controversies and conflicts brought on by reading books have led to the system of mass ignorance promulgated by Beatty. Even with this system, though, man drifts into nuclear ruin. Bradbury glosses over the grim question raised by other dystopian novelists of his age: If man's individuality and knowledge bring him repeatedly to catastrophe, should not the one be circumscribed and the other forbidden? Such novels as *A Canticle for Leibowitz, A Clockwork Orange,* and *Facial Justice* deal more realistically with this problem than does *Fahrenheit 451.* Although the religious light shining through Montag from the Bible is a fitting climax to the book's use of symbolism, Bradbury's novel does risk lapsing at the very close into a vague optimism.

Yet *Fahrenheit 451* remains a notable achievement in postwar dystopian fiction. Surely it deserves more than its recent dismissal by a noted science fiction critic as "an incoherent polemic against book-burning."[5] The book's weaknesses derive in part from that very symbolism in which its strength and originality are to be found. If *Fahrenheit 451* is vague in political detail, it is accordingly less topical and therefore more broadly applicable to the dilemmas of the twentieth century as a whole. Like the nineteenth-century

French symbolists, Bradbury's purpose is to evoke a mood, not to name particulars. His connotative language is far more subtle, his novel far more of one piece, than Huxley's rambling nightmare, *Ape and Essence*. Though the novel lacks the great impact of *Nineteen Eighty-Four*, Kingsley Amis is right when he says that *Farenheit 451* is "superior in conciseness and objectivity" to Orwell's anti-utopian novel.[6] If *Farenheit 451* poses no genuinely satisfying answers to the plight of postindustrial man, neither is the flight to the stars at the end of *A Canticle for Leibowitz* much of a solution. We can hardly escape from ourselves. By comparison with Bradbury's novel, *Facial Justice* is tepid and *A Clockwork Orange* overdone. On the whole, *Farenheit 451* comes out as a distinctive contribution to the speculative literature of our times, because in its multiple variations on its fundamental symbol, it demonstrates that dystopian fiction need not exclude the subtlety of poetry.

NOTES

1. Ray Bradbury, *Fahrenheit 451*, New York: Ballantine Books, 1967, p. 3. Subsequent page references in the text are to this edition of the novel.
2. Erich Fromm, *Escape from Freedom*, New York: Avon Books, 1966; orig. publ. 1941, p. 207.
3. Mark R. Hillegas, *The Future as Nightmare: H.G. Wells and the Anti-Utopians*, New York: Oxford UP, 1967, p.158.
4. Clearly there are many additional examples one could cite of Bradbury's uses of fire and its associated figures. An open book falls into Montag's hands at 11 North Elm and the words on the page "blazed in his mind for the next minute as if stamped there with fiery steel" (p. 34). In his initial talk with Montag, "Beatty knocked his pipe into the palm of his pink hand, studied the ashes as if they were a symbol to be diagnosed and searched for meaning" (p. 54). The Mechanical Hound comes sniffing at Montag's door, bringing "the smell of blue electricity" (p. 64). Mildred argues with Montag that the books will get them into trouble: "She was beginning to shriek now, sitting there like a wax doll melting in its own heat" (p. 68). Montag

links his stumbling into Mildred's empty pillbox in the dark with "kicking a buried mine" (p. 69). When Montag first visits his house, Faber asks: "What knocked the torch out of your hands?" (p. 73). In rebuking Montag for falling under the influence of Clarisse, Beatty tells him such do-gooders "rise like the midnight sun to sweat you in your bed" (p. 101). As Montag prepares to cross the highway during his escape, he thinks it incredible "how he felt his temperature could cause the whole immediate world to vibrate" (p. 111).

5. David N. Samuelson, "*Limbo*: The Great American Dystopia," *Extrapolation*, 19 (Dec. 1977), pp. 77–78.
6. Kingsley Amis, *New Maps of Hell*, New York: Harcourt, Brace, 1960, p. 109.

HAMLET
(WILLIAM SHAKESPEARE)

"Book IV, Chapter XIII"
by Johann Wolfgang von Goethe,
in *Wilhelm Meister's Apprenticeship
and Travels* (1865)

INTRODUCTION

This excerpt from Johann Wolfgang von Goethe's *Wilhelm Meister's Apprenticeship and Travels* includes an influential interpretation of *Hamlet* in which the young Goethe hero identifies with Hamlet's alienation and inability to avenge his father's murder. Goethe raises a key question: Why is Hamlet unable to act? Wilhelm Meister, often considered Goethe's mouthpiece, concentrates on Hamlet's psychological stress and the many causes of his alienation and inertia. According to Wilhelm, Hamlet alienates himself by retreating into a conflicted interior world. His self-imposed isolation is the result of an overactive, ever-reaching mind that circles upon itself, removing the prince of Denmark from the field of human interaction: "He winds, and turns, and torments himself; he advances and recoils; is ever put in mind, ever puts himself in mind; at last does all but lose

---

Goethe, Johann Wolfgang von. "Book IV, Chapter XIII." *Wilhelm Meister's Apprenticeship and Travels*. Trans. Thomas Carlyle. Boston: Ticknor and Fields, 1865. 229–32.

his purpose from his thoughts; yet still without recovering
his peace of mind."

⌒⋎⌒

For the first time during many months, Wilhelm felt himself in his
proper element once more. Of late in talking, he had merely found
submissive listeners, and even these not always; but now he had the
happiness to speak with critics and artists, who not only fully understood him, but repaid his observations by others equally instructive.
With wonderful vivacity they travelled through the latest pieces;
with wonderful correctness judged them. The decisions of the public
they could try and estimate: they speedily threw light on each other's
thoughts.

Loving Shakspeare as our friend did, he failed not to lead round
the conversation to the merits of that dramatist. Expressing, as he
entertained, the liveliest hopes of the new epoch which these exquisite productions must form in Germany he ere long introduced his
Hamlet, who had busied him so much of late.

Serlo declared that he would long ago have played the piece, had
this been possible, and that he himself would willingly engage to act
Polonius. He added, with a smile: "An Ophelia, too, will certainly turn
up, if we had but a Prince."

Wilhelm did not notice that Aurelia seemed a little hurt at
her brother's sarcasm. Our friend was in his proper vein, becoming
copious and didactic, expounding how he would have Hamlet played.
He circumstantially delivered to his hearers the opinions we before
saw him busied with; taking all the trouble possible to make his notion
of the matter acceptable, sceptical as Serlo showed himself regarding
it. "Well, then," said the latter, finally, "suppose we grant you all this,
what will you explain by it?"

"Much, everything," said Wilhelm. "Conceive a prince such as I
have painted him, and that his father suddenly dies. Ambition and
the love of rule are not the passions that inspire him. As a king's son
he would have been contented; but now he is first constrained to
consider the difference which separates a sovereign from a subject. The
crown was not hereditary; yet a longer possession of it by his father
would have strengthened the pretensions of an only son, and secured
his hopes of the succession. In place of this, he now beholds himself

excluded by his uncle, in spite of specious promises, most probably forever. He is now poor in goods and favour, and a stranger in the scene which from youth he had looked upon as his inheritance. His temper here assumes its first mournful tinge. He feels that now he is not more, that he is less, than a private nobleman; he offers himself as the servant of every one; he is not courteous and condescending, he is needy and degraded.

"His past condition he remembers as a vanished dream. It is in vain that his uncle strives to cheer him, to present his situation in another point of view. The feeling of his nothingness will not leave him.

"The second stroke that came upon him wounded deeper, bowed still more. It was the marriage of his mother. The faithful tender son had yet a mother, when his father passed away. He hoped, in the company of his surviving noble-minded parent, to reverence the heroic form of the departed; but his mother too he loses, and it is something worse than death that robs him of her. The trustful image, which a good child loves to form of its parents, is gone. With the dead there is no help; on the living no hold. She also is a woman, and her name is Frailty, like that of all her sex.

"Now first does he feel himself completely bent and orphaned; and no happiness of life can repay what he has lost. Not reflective or sorrowful by nature, reflection and sorrow have become for him a heavy obligation. It is thus that we see him first enter on the scene. I do not think that I have mixed aught foreign with the piece, or over-charged a single feature of it."

Serlo looked at his sister, and said, "Did I give thee a false picture of our friend? He begins well; he has still many things to tell us, many to persuade us of." Wilhelm asseverated loudly, that he meant not to persuade, but to convince; he begged for another moment's patience.

"Figure to yourselves this youth," cried he, "this son of princes: conceive him vividly, bring his state before your eyes, and then observe him when he learns that his father's spirit walks; stand by him in the terrors of the night, when the venerable ghost itself appears before him. A horrid shudder passes over him; he speaks to the mysterious form; he sees it beckon him; he follows it, and hears. The fearful accusation of his uncle rings in his ears; the summons to revenge, and the piercing oft-repeated prayer, Remember me!

"And when the ghost has vanished, who is it that stands before us? A young hero panting for vengeance? A prince by birth, rejoicing to

be called to punish the usurper of his crown? No! trouble and astonishment take hold of his solitary young man; he grows bitter against
smiling villains, swears that he will not forget the spirit, and concludes
with the significant ejaculation:

> The time is out of joint: O cursed spite,
> That ever I was born to set it right!

"In these words, I imagine, will be found the key to Hamlet's
whole procedure. To me it is clear that Shakespeare meant, in the
present case, to represent the effects of a great action laid upon a soul
unfit for the performance of it. In this view the whole piece seems
to me to be composed. There is an oak-tree planted in a costly jar,
which should have borne only pleasant flowers in its bosom; the roots
expand, the jar is shivered.

"A lovely, pure, noble and most moral nature, without the strength
of nerve which forms a hero, sinks beneath a burden which it cannot
bear and must not cast away. All duties are holy for him; the present is
too hard. Impossibilities have been required of him; not in themselves
impossibilities, but such for him. He winds, and turns, and torments
himself; he advances and recoils; at ever put in mind, ever puts himself
in mind; at last does all but lose his purpose from his thoughts; yet still
without recovering his peace of mind."

THE ILIAD
(HOMER)

"The Solitary Amphora: Alienation and Tradition in Homer's *Iliad*"
by Scott F. Crider,
University of Dallas

Late in the *Odyssey*, we learn from Agamemnon that Achilles's ashes were collected in an amphora with those of Patroklos:

> Around them then, we, the chosen host of the Argive
> spearmen, piled up a grave mound that was both great and
>   perfect,
> on a jutting promontory there by the wide Hellespont,
> so that it can be seen afar from out on the water
> by men now alive and those to be born in the future.
>   (24.80-84)

This amphora is strange for two reasons: It houses the ashes of Achilles and his friend, and it is set apart—away from Troy, now a razed city, and away from Phthia, to which Achilles will never return. Agamemnon's account provides a figure for a literary character with one friend and no city: the solitary amphora.

In *Politics*, Aristotle recognizes that human beings are essentially social: The life of a person is lived in common with other people, and the institution of that common life is the city or *polis*. A person who is unable to share in common life or is so self-sufficient that he or she chooses not to is either an animal or a god (1.1). Unlike the animal and the divine, however, the *human* life is by nature political. This association is guided toward some end or good that contributes to the flourishing life. Consequently, the defining characteristic of human association is an agreement upon the end or good to be sought together, an agreement achieved through language.

Even though we are political beings, we can choose not to be: A person may be apolitical, "alienated" from human association and its shared goods. For Aristotle, this is not a good thing, and his simile for the apolitical person is "an isolated piece at draughts" (1.1.9), a piece whose purpose is defined by the game and the other pieces from which he or she is isolated. Imagine a knight alienated from other chess pieces and the board: That is Aristotle's apolitical being—now either an animal or a god but not a human being.

Homer agrees, but not entirely—first, because the classical *polis* of Aristotle's era does not exist in Homer's, and second, because, while Homer believes that human alienation from the city and its good is tragic, he does not believe it is inhuman. Indeed, although it can lead—and does lead in the *Iliad*—to inhumanity, it can and will in the poem also lead to a renewed humanity.

Through parentage and martial excellence, Achilles is a kind of god because his mother, Thetis, is immortal. Although he does act like an animal in the savagery of his violence, he is also the most supremely human of all the human characters in the *Iliad*. By alienating himself from the shared good of his own polity, specifically its cultural tradition of honor, and from the natural and divine orders of the world itself, Achilles alone enacts a new good—or rather an old good too long neglected and not fully understood: a pity that becomes love for an enemy.

The *Iliad* stands at the beginning of the Western, Hellenic tradition's understanding of itself, and it contributes a radical and tragic conception of tradition: It is not enough for us to master and reproduce cultural traditions; we must alter them to renew them and master them to become alienated from them. For Homer, mere cultural reproduction is the tragedy of the Trojan prince Hektor, who is guided by the cultural good of honor—although, to be fair, he may also be guided by another good: the freedom of his wife, Andromache (6.447-464). Cultural alienation and innovation are forms of Homeric tragedy, like that of Achilles, the alienated master. Without such tragedy, though without the radical devastation that accompanies it—including the death of that which we love most—there might be no Hellenism, for Hellenism may essentially be a dynamic, violent response to its own mastery of, alienation from, and innovation within its traditional conception of the good life. At each moment of Achilles's alienation, he is a poet of culture.

Achilles's anger, or *mênis*, is Homer's subject (and the first word of the epic poem); it is the great warrior's mania in response to Agamemnon's injustice. The mania alienates him from the war effort and persuades him to be apolitical. Homer represents the cause of the mania in the quarrel of Book 1. The good of the Achaean polity is, of course, honor or *timê*. Achilles threatens Agamemnon's authority by calling an assembly or *agorê* (1.53-56) to deliberate a response to the plague that Apollo brought upon the Greeks after Agamemnon enslaved the daughter of Apollo's priest (9-52); thus the strife between Achilles and Agamemnon is inevitable. Agamemnon returns the priest's daughter but declares he will take Briseis, a woman given to Achilles as a prize of war, a sign of *timê*. Achilles's reaction is a rage so overwhelming that Athena has to restrain him from murdering Agamemnon (188-222).

Aristotle explains in *Rhetoric* that anger is a response to an unjust slight: "Let us then define anger as a longing, accompanied by pain, for a real or apparent revenge for a real or apparent slight, affecting a man himself or one of his friends, when such a slight is undeserved" (2.2.1). Agamemnon's treatment of Achilles is undeserved, because Achilles is responding to a real need in the community to address the plague. So when Agamemnon steals the woman who signifies Achilles's *timê*, hence duplicating the crime Paris committed against Menelaos (157-160), the alienating effect upon Achilles is immediate: "Now I am returning to Phthia, since it is much better / to go home again with my carved ships, and I am minded no longer / to stay here dishonored [*atimos*] and pile up your wealth and your luxury" (169-171). That alienation leads him to reflect poetically upon the shared good of just honor within the Achaean polity as he holds the scepter:

> But I will tell you this and swear a great oath upon it:
> in the name of this scepter, which never again will bear leaf nor
> branch, now that it has left behind the cut stump in the
> mountains,

nor shall it ever blossom again, since the bronze blade stripped
bark and leafage, and now the sons of the Achaeans
carry it in their hands in state when they administer
the justice of Zeus. And this shall be a great oath before you:
some day longing for Achilles will come to the sons of the
　　Achaeans,
all of them. Then stricken at heart though *you* be, *you* will be able
to do nothing, when in numbers before man-slaughtering
　　Hektor
they drop and die. And then *you* will eat out the heart with-
　　in you
in sorrow, that *you* did no honor to the best of the Achaeans.
(233-244, emphases mine)

"[Y]ou did no honor [*ouden etisas*] to the best of the Achaeans
[*ariston Akhaiôn*]": Achilles's anger is not surprising, as Agamemnon is
dishonoring the aristocratic martial excellence that is the foundational
good of the culture that Agamemnon, Achilles, and all present share.
Yet Achilles's response is remarkable for a number of reasons.

First, Achilles will revenge himself not only upon Agamemnon
for the injustice but also upon *all* of the Achaeans: His anger is
excessive. (Achilles will learn just how imprudent that "all" is when
Patroklos dies.) Though it is clear that Achilles's "you" is second-
person singular—he is speaking directly to Agamemnon alone—he
will harm many more than the king, as the poem's opening makes
clear: This is an anger "which put pains thousandfold upon the
Achaeans, / hurled in their multitudes to the house of Hades strong
souls / of heroes" (1.2-4). Achilles is the first revenger in Western
literature, and revenge has a tendency to exceed the original harm.
That excess is no doubt due to the second remarkable characteristic
of Achilles's response: his agonized grasp of the culturally destructive
nature of Agamemnon's injustice against him. He swears an oath by
the scepter that is a sign of justice—a cultural object fashioned from
nature by people inspired by the god of justice, Zeus—right before
he throws it to the ground (245-246). Achilles's lyric description of
the scepter's fashioning indicates his awareness that Agamemnon
is denying him just honor, the only good of their association, and
thereby undermining the principle of that association. His oath here
indicates alienation from the Achaean enterprise. Once he hands

Briseis over, he moves away from even his own Myrmidons, the warriors under his command: "Achilles / weeping went and sat in sorrow apart from his companions / beside the beach of the grey sea looking out on the infinite water" (348-350). When he persuades Thetis to supplicate Zeus on his behalf to punish the Achaeans, it is the extreme act of a man alienated from his polity because it has unjustly abandoned its own foundational principle. He will now remain apart near the sea, neither speaking in the assembly nor fighting in battle but only consuming his own heart (490-492).

Phoenix reminds Achilles that Peleus, Achilles's father, directed him to teach Achilles to be a speaker of words and a doer of deeds (9.443), and speech in the assembly and action in war are the two forms of human excellence or *areté* the Homeric world values, with the latter more important than the former in the *Iliad*. (Even Nestor, "the lucid speaker of Pylos" [1.248], has a history of martial valor, as he continually reminds his younger fellow soldiers.) Achilles's oath inaugurates a departure from his military excellences and a transformation of his intellectual and verbal ones.

When we next encounter Achilles in Book 9 after a long absence, his alienation has led him to reflect upon the associative good of honor and to determine that it is only one good unequal to the good of life itself. The war has turned against the Achaeans (Books 6-8), and Agamemnon has decided with Nestor's counsel to rehonor Achilles (9.89-181). Odysseus, Ajax, and Phoenix visit Achilles to offer him the honor he was earlier denied, including the return of Briseis. Yet Achilles has changed between the first and ninth books: His alienation from the polity encouraged a philosophical critique of the tradition that constituted his self-understanding until the cultural strife of the poem's opening. His critique began with a deconstruction of that tradition without offering much in the way of a reconstruction.

Achilles ignores all but one of Odysseus's appeals (9.260-299), because he no longer believes in honor or its signs, and he no longer believes in the war that has been the occasion for acquiring both. The rejection of the good of honor indicates an alienation from the cultural values that it once enraged him to see undermined by Agamemnon:

> Fate is the same for the man who holds back, the same if he
> fights hard.
> We are all held in a single honor, the brave with the weaklings.

> A man dies still if he has done nothing, as one who has done
>   much.
> Nothing is won for me, now that my heart has gone through its
>   afflictions
> in forever setting my life on the hazard of battle. (318-22)

The fate, portion, or *moira* of all human beings is the same—death or *thanatos*—and all humans, therefore, have the same *timê*. Finitude is the human condition. By implication, the excellences that encourage us to imagine that death can be challenged or conquered are meaningless because no human excellence, nor the honoring or recognizing of it, can alter the fact of human mortality.

Paradoxically, Achilles's alienated reflection upon death gives him more appreciation of life, and his description of his two fates indicates his recognition that the city of war is not the only city:

> For my mother Thetis the goddess of the silver feet tells me
> I carry two sorts of destiny toward the day of my death. Either
> if I stay here and fight beside the city of Trojans,
> my return is gone, but my glory shall be everlasting;
> but if I return home to the beloved land of my fathers,
> · the excellence of my glory is gone, but there will be long life
> left for me, and my end in death will not come quickly to me.
> (410-416)

This conflicts with what Thetis says earlier (1.416-417), yet Achilles believes he has two fates from which to choose: glory or *kleos* that will honor his actions in war, or *nostos*, long life or *aiôn*. Life is now of greater value to Achilles than honor. Achilles will be unable to act upon that reevaluation of the relative goods of honor and of life because he does not return home; even so, his rejection of the embassy's offer of renewed honor elevates life above the cultural forms that give it expression and from which Achilles is alienated. The ambassadors respond to Achilles's rejection with silent wonder (430-431). Phoenix appears not to hear the reason for the rejection as his account of Meleagros (526-599) presumes the very honor that Achilles is rejecting. Both Odysseus and Phoenix appeal also to pity or *eleos* (300-302 and 496-497, respectively). Neither knows that Achilles persuaded his mother to enlist Zeus in the destruction of the Achaeans (1.407-412), but, in his alienation from his own culture, Achilles is not ready for *eleos*; he is ready only to recognize that his life is a good greater than their honor of him.

This philosophical recognition is tragic, of course. Achilles's refusal leads to the (almost total) destruction of the Greeks at the hands of Hektor, a destruction that Homer narrates in Books 11-15. Witnessing this, Achilles sends Patroklos out, and Patroklos returns in Book 16, bearing Nestor's request that Achilles allow Patroklos and the Myrmidons to reenter the war (11.761-805). It is Zeus's plan now for the Achaeans to be harmed "until the thing asked by the son of Peleus has been accomplished" (15.74). In Book 1, Achilles sets in motion the circumstances he responds to in Book 11. That leads indirectly to Patroklos's request in Book 16, in response to which Achilles makes his tragic error, his *hamartia*, of sending Patroklos to war as his martial double. According to Aristotle, an *hamartia* is not a tragic "flaw"; it is a tragic "error" in deliberation and choice that leads to the tragic actor's reversal of fortune, or *peripeteia*, which leads to a recognition of the error, an *anagnôrisis*, suffering and death. Achilles's tragic error is that he can neither completely extricate himself from the culture whose first principle he no longer believes in by sailing for Phthia and the long life that is one of his fortunes, nor can he completely renew his participation in that culture by fighting for the honor the Greeks will give him when he rescues them from Hektor. He imagines he can maintain philosophical uncertainty in response to a choice; indeed, he is so confused that he begins to be reanimated by the desire for honor (16.83-90) and by a romance of martial friendship in which he and his friend are the only two people living after Troy's ruin:

> Father Zeus, Athena and Apollo, if only
> not one of the Trojans could escape destruction, not one
> of the Argives, but you and I could emerge from the slaughter
> so that we two alone could break Troy's hallowed coronal.
>   (97-100)

This is a kind of premonition of the golden amphora. Achilles imagines he can control the battle, as we see in his advice to Patroklos (80-100) and his prayer to Zeus (233-248) to let his friend return—a prayer Zeus sees (232) and hears (249) but denies (249). Achilles commits a tragic error, which he will recognize as he suffers over the death of Patroklos: "I stayed too long out of the fighting" (18.125). A man who sees the value of his own life recognizes that another life has value—but only after he has lost the one most valued.

Achilles's response is an inhuman savagery unlike anything seen earlier, during which, in a "sorrow beyond endurance" (19.367), he challenges natural, human, and divine laws, becoming a god of death, "like something more than a mortal" (20.493): The alienated becomes the nihilist. (In the last book, Achilles is figured as a Hades and Priam's visit to his encampment a kind of descent into the underworld, with Hermes the escort leading the way.) His nihilism is surreal: His horse Xanthos speaks with him (19.392-424); he battles the river Skamandros (21.211-382); and the gods themselves descend to fight him (20.32 ff.).

His violence against other people is horrific. Homer describes his killing of Hektor and desecration of Hektor's corpse in apocalyptic terms: "It was most like what would have happened, if all lowering / Ilion had been burning top to bottom in fire" (22.410-11). The poet's understated report of the sacrifice of Trojan soldiers during Patroklos's funeral startles the reader. Before he murdered the soldiers "with the stroke of iron," Achilles sacrificed Patroklos's nine dogs (23.172-178).

Earlier, in response to Hektor's desire for proper burial, Achilles fantasized about cannibalism: "I wish only that my spirit and fury would drive me / to hack your meat away and eat it raw for the things that / you have done to me" (22.346-348). Achilles deconstructs the order of his cosmos, and the compulsive repetition of his failure to dismember Hektor's corpse (the gods protect the corpse from dissolution) figure a man on fire whose flame is waning: He has burned everything out, including himself, and the fusion of savagery and indifference in the penultimate book indicates that his reunion with Agamemnon is meaningless; it simply restores the associative good of *timê* that Achilles has demolished through reflection.

It is only with Achilles's *eleos* in response to Priam's supplication and his return of the body of the old man's son that our tragic hero reconstructs his own culture upon a new good that acknowledges the value of human life. Achilles knows he cannot return to that good. Only in losing his friend does he realize the value of a *shared* good. Achilles cannot wish this good for his friend's sake—part of

Aristotle's definition of friendship or *philia* in the *Nichomachean Ethics* (8.2.3)—because Achilles's friend is dead. Throughout the poem, wishing a friend a good for his or her sake seems at odds with wishing for honor for oneself: Hektor sacrifices Andromache's day of liberty out of shame (22.99-130), and Achilles sacrifices Patroklos's life out of concern for recognition (16.1-100). When Priam visits Achilles, however, the latter has no honor left to gain, even if it did mean anything to him. (We know, and Achilles may see, that he will suffer the dishonor of dying at the hands of Paris [22.355-366].) Achilles's response to Priam is guided neither by desire for honor nor fear of the gods (even though Zeus, Apollo, and Hermes orchestrate the exchange [24.1 ff.]); instead, it is guided by the old man's appeal to his *eleos*: "[T]ake pity upon me / remembering your father" (24.503-504). Priam's appeal to *eleos* is rhetorically successful:

> So he spoke, and stirred in the other a passion of grieving
> for his own father. He took the old man's hand and pushed him
> gently away, and the two remembered, as Priam sat huddled
> at the feet of Achilles and wept close for manslaughtering
>   Hektor
> and Achilles wept now for his own father, now again
> for Patroklos. The sound of their mourning moved in the house.
>   (507-512)

Through mutual mourning for shared loss—Priam for his son, and Achilles for his father and friend—the two enemies share a moment of love: In Achilles, Priam sees Hektor; in Priam, Achilles sees Peleus. Aristotle defines *eleos* in *Rhetoric* thus: "Let *eleos* then be a kind of pain excited by the sight of evil, deadly or painful, which befalls one who does not deserve it; an evil which one might expect to come upon himself or one of his friends, and when it seems near" (2.8.2). (Aristotle explains that the evils humans pity are those that arrive by fortune or *tukhê*, and it is difficult to imagine he does not have in mind Homer's lines for Achilles's speech on the "two urns" of fortune [24.517-551].) Yet *eleos* is not *philia*: That Achilles pities Priam does not necessarily mean that he loves him. Achilles may only restore an economy of pity for the suppliant that preceded the action of the *Iliad*. Before Priam left on his mission, though, the old man prayed for both—"[G]rant that I come to Achilles for love [*philon*] and pity [*eleeinon*]" (309)—and the episode reveals that he received both. In giving Priam the body, in lifting it onto the litter and treating the body with a respect absent in his earlier treatment of it (587-591), and in promising Priam to retard the destruction of Troy so Hektor can be properly buried (656-670), Achilles acts out of *eleos* and *philia* because Achilles is doing a good for the Trojan and his city that he will not share. It is a limited good, but nowhere else have we seen this *philia* for an enemy. This interpretation may seem excessive. After all, Priam operates within the conventional mode of supplication, Achilles himself is aware that his *mênis* may overwhelm his *eleos* (581-586), and Troy will fall. But this only makes Achilles's accomplishment more subtle and its qualified degree of cultural reconstruction more credible.

Achilles's achievement is actually that of Homer, the shaping intelligence of the poem, whether there was one such poet or not. Homer is alienating himself from the cultural good of honor to discern another good, one apparently discerned for the first time in the ancient pagan world during the eighth century B.C., long before another mortal god in gospels written in the same language discovered the good of love in response to shared suffering. Yet, as attractive as it might be to see the Lord's Prayer—"Give us this day our daily bread. And forgive us our debts as we forgive our debtors" (KJV, Matthew 6: 11-12)—in enemies mourning and eating together, we must remember that Jesus claims to be suffering on behalf of a loving cosmos. Achilles's invention of the love of one's enemy takes place, as Achilles says, in an indifferent universe:

> Such is the way the gods spun life for unfortunate mortals,
> That we live in unhappiness, but the gods themselves have no
>   sorrows.
> There are two urns that stand on the door-sill of Zeus. They are
>   unlike
> for the gifts they bestow: an urn of evils, an urn of blessings.
> If Zeus who delights in thunder mingles these and bestows
>   them
> on man, he shifts, and moves now in evil, again in good
>   fortune. (24.525-530)

Unknown to Achilles, the gods have arranged his interview with Priam. Of course, Zeus will complain in the *Odyssey* that Achilles's accusation is untrue because human beings bring greater suffering upon themselves than fate has in store because of their own errors (1.26-43). With his invention of Achilles's love of his enemy, Homer suggests that, although the gods provide occasion for goodness and human beings suffer more than fated, love is nonetheless the distinct accomplishment of those who are neither gods nor animals but human beings, who must, as this beautifully terrible poem suggests, question and destroy everything assumed in their associations in order to learn how to love. The *Odyssey* will supplement this tragic wisdom with another wisdom related, yet distinct—one in which one can achieve both *kleos* and *nostos* but only with the help of an intelligent spouse—but, by itself, the *Iliad* is a solitary amphora marking the place where the most difficult *philia* is born.

INVISIBLE MAN
(RALPH ELLISON)

"Alienation as Narrative Strategy in Ralph Ellison's *Invisible Man*"
by Aimable Twagilimana,
Buffalo State College, SUNY

As he sits isolated in the belly of the Earth, far away from the society that has manipulated him for so long, the Invisible Man recounts the chaotic events of his life. In this fictional autobiography, he attempts to make sense of his alienation from America's historical, cultural, economic, ideological, and literary landscape. To a degree, his alienation is self-imposed due to his repeated blind allegiance to authority. Though it would appear these authorities eventually force this alienation upon him, the Invisible Man's movement underground is a demonstration of his freedom. He consciously acknowledges his invisibility and proclaims, "I am nobody by myself" (15), telling us his "hibernation"—his alienation from society—"is over" (580).

In explaining his own life, the abolitionist and former slave Frederick Douglass proclaimed, "you have seen how a man was made a slave; you shall see how a slave was made a man" (75). Like Douglass, the Invisible Man frees himself by telling his story. In the epilogue, he proclaims his faith in the "principle on which the country was built and not the men, or at least not the men who did the violence," even though such men have violated him (574). The Invisible Man is alienated, and yet he is also part of a tradition dating back to July 4, 1776.

When Thomas Jefferson and many others put pen to page that day, they proved that liberation is primarily an act of language and rhetoric. Despite his embitterment with his country, the Invisible Man believes in the same ideas Jefferson espoused many years before. He adopts Jefferson's language and ideology, as well as those of other authors and thinkers, to examine America's need for change. Though he cites other works, the tale the Invisible Man relates is his story alone; after telling it, he emerges to make the change he seeks. His epilogue is his personal declaration of independence.

Ralph Ellison drafted his novel in the 1940s, the gestational years of the modern civil rights movement. *Invisible Man* appears prophetic considering the movement's development in the two decades after the novel's publication. Its title character preaches the rhetoric of inclusion that some civil rights leaders, particularly Martin Luther King Jr., later embraced. Rooted in reality, the Invisible Man's alienation allowed him to experience and critique American society. His experiences were tragic and yet enabling, for they allowed him to see all the misfortunes the world had to offer, both on a personal and political front. As such, Ellison's protagonist is suited to comment on America's inequalities. Ironically, it is because America never truly sees him that the Invisible Man truly sees America. His embittering experience can be seen as an accumulation of American history and ideology in his day that can be found in the Invisible Man's autobiography, his speeches, and his writing. To empower his character with such cultural knowledge and wisdom, Ralph Ellison refers his protagonist to a vast number of literary works that bespeak his condition almost as much as his own narrative does.

Julia Kristeva's term *intertextuality* refers to the references a text makes to other literary works. In alluding to another writer's work, authors can retell, question, parody, revise, and enrich their own works, as well as the works they comment on. By invoking authoritative texts that precede their own, writers place themselves in the company of literary forefathers, at times employing this authority to become what Percy Bysshe Shelley called "unacknowledged legislators of the world" (765). Intertextual links also manifest the author's trust in the reader's ability to use background knowledge to make sense of what is new, to establish connections, have expectations, and make predictions while reading. They guide readers to meaning. Ellison's literary craft resonates with what Roland Barthes called the "impossibility of living outside the infinite text" (36). By referencing and adopting the language used by previous authors, the Invisible Man claims his own authority. He gains access to America's multiple discourses and is thus able to make bold and informed statements in the novel's prologue and epilogue. Like Umberto Eco's character Adso in *The Name of the Rose*, the Invisible Man "realized that not infrequently books speak of books; it is as if they spoke among themselves" (286).

Writers, like the books they write, also speak among themselves. In an interview with Robert B. Stepto and Michael S. Harper, Ralph Ellison said writers "are sons of many fathers, or at least the sons of many writers' styles" (3). Considering the kaleidoscopic nature of *Invisible Man*, Ellison's proposition is probably an understatement. The 1952 novel is virtually an encyclopedia of world literature. The texts the novel references—directly or indirectly—run the gamut: the Declaration of Independence, the Constitution, the Bill of Rights, Melville's *Benito Cereno*, T.S. Eliot's play *Family Reunion*, Fyodor Dostoevsky's *Notes from Underground*, Louis Armstrong's "What Did I Do to Be So Black and Blue," Mark Twain's *The Adventures of Huckleberry Finn*, Ralph Waldo Emerson's "Self-Reliance," Booker T. Washington's *Up from Slavery*, and Richard Wright's "The Man Who Lived Underground." By citing such works, the *Invisible Man*, both the novel and character, is able to comment effectively on America's founding documents, history, politics, literary models, and culture.

Perhaps more importantly, this high level of intertextuality highlights the Invisible Man's alienation: Despite abundant references to other works from other times, he is unable to make the right connections at the right moments. Failing to read correctly, Ellison seems to suggest, has serious consequences, including the repetition of past mistakes. Continuous allegiance to authority condemns the Invisible Man to a Sisyphean life that ends when he plummets through an open manhole and into the underground. This move saves his life, however, and from this place he will tell his story. The possibility of death at the hands of both the Brotherhood and Ras the Destroyer's men forces him to examine his life and his world. He does so much in the manner of Cervantes, who mocked the Spanish society of the sixteenth century in *Don Quixote*, or like Mark Twain, who derided slavery and racism in pre–Civil War America in *The Adventures of Huckleberry Finn*. Like the protagonists of these works, the Invisible Man must move to have access to different constituencies. Paradoxically, it is his naïveté that keeps him moving to another model, another experience, and another place. The Invisible Man, like Don Quixote and Huck Finn, is a figure of mobility who dissects society's varying layers in order to satirize its hypocrisy.

The Invisible Man moves from ideology to ideology but also from place to place. The first six chapters take place in the South, the remaining nineteen in the North. This movement from South to North mimics that of the slave narratives, in which former slaves recount their lives in slavery and their journeys north to freedom. Like the typical slave narrative, *Invisible Man* is an example of what Robert Stepto called a "narrative of ascent" in his *From Behind the Veil: A Study of Afro-American Narrative*. As opposed to the narrative of immersion, which shows the protagonist journeying to a real or symbolic South and being accepted into a group, the narrative of ascent tells of alienation. The protagonist escapes from the group and journeys to a real or symbolic North, appropriates dominant discourses, and suffers loneliness and isolation. Self-creation is central to the hero's quest, as he is without family or community. Invisible Man's main problem, however, is that his literary proficiency is not sufficient to help him navigate the politics of the people he meets. Unlike Frederick Douglass, William Wells Brown, and Harriet Jacobs in their times, the Invisible Man is unable to achieve complete freedom before the epilogue because his literacy is not developed enough to allow him to reclaim himself. This is a calculated weakness, on Ellison's part, that allows his character to step naïvely into tragedy again and again. Eventually these experiences enable the Invisible Man to better tell his tale and give him the strength to emerge from the manhole a fully grown man. His alienation is necessary.

After surveying the prejudice, racism, and segregation of the South as well as the accommodationist and hypocritical college he attended there, Invisible Man heads to the North to do more surveying. In the South, the Invisible Man first witnesses African-American alienation: in the hotel housing the "Battle Royal" (where he delivers an impassioned speech to an amused white gathering); in the Negro College, where the master-slave structure of slavery is in full effect; and in the Golden Day Tavern, where many African Americans go to drink and combat their feelings of isolation. He heads North to escape these things and to improve himself and his literary proficiency.

Misinterpretation or misuse of the texts he seeks leads to intoxication of the mind, as it did with Don Quixote, who reinvented himself as a knight after reading many books of chivalry. Likewise, the radiance of authority continuously blinds the Invisible Man. He fails to perceive the racism and hypocrisy first manifested by the white supremacists in the first chapter of the book. He does not notice the accommodationist hypocrisy of what Leon Forrest calls the "Barbee-Founder-Bledsoe trinity" (271). Nor does he acknowledge the colonizing mind of Mr. Norton, who has been for "forty years a bearer of the white man's burden" (37). He only truly recognizes the deadly ideologies espoused by the Brotherhood and Ras the Destroyer's men when he is nearly killed by them. In each of these situations, the Invisible Man fails to interpret correctly until he is deceived and has to move on, apparently without learning from the experience. Unexamined models, Ellison seems to suggest, can easily lead to perdition. Yet, as battered as he is by each episode, the Invisible Man always gets a chance to start anew and learn again. What is more, he has the last word: He uses his writing to manipulate those who manhandled him.

Black leaders, such as the subservient Bledsoe, are tolerated because of their blind and hypocritical obedience to rich whites. The protagonist moves to New York City after being expelled from college for driving one of the college's white benefactors through an unsightly black neighborhood. In New York City, the protagonist successively falls under the spells of white and black deceivers without becoming more discerning. His experiences at the Liberty Paints factory and with the Brotherhood and Ras the Destroyer allow him to study the ideologies supposedly intended to help end African-American disenfranchisement. Ultimately, he finds that the Communist Party (the Brotherhood) and Black Nationalism (represented by Ras the Destroyer's group) offer inadequate solutions to black alienation. Many black intellectuals joined the white-dominated Communist Party in the 1930s only to conclude later that it did not understand or care about the African-American experience. The Invisible Man also rejects the Black Nationalist ideology of racial separation preached by Ras the Destroyer, whose spear he narrowly ducks and returns to pierce his attacker's chest.

Invisible Man's fall through the open manhole to the underground saves his life, though he initially experiences "a kind of death

... death alive" (566-567). From this total darkness will beam 1,369 lights, and what is potentially a place of terror becomes a place of redemption through writing. Instead of being haunted by terrifying creatures, he is haunted by the memory of his own life, reflected in his favorite Louis Armstrong recording "What Did I Do to Be So Black and Blue." The underground conjures up many things for the Invisible Man—displacement, flight, hiding, isolation, escape, secrecy, exploration, investigation, darkness, and even death—but in his fictional autobiography it is a space free from danger and the manipulations of the society overhead. The sewer houses no master in the form of Bledsoe, Mr. Norton, or Brother Jack. In this new place, as Valerie Smith argues, the Invisible Man reenacts the writing of eighteenth- and nineteenth-century slave narratives, wherein former slaves reclaimed their very being by "naming themselves before a culture that denied them full humanity" (192). In this hole, he develops sufficient literacy to complete the symbolic journey north to freedom.

Like the protagonists in Fyodor Dostoevsky's novella *Notes from Underground* (1864) and Richard Wright's short story "The Man Who Lived Underground" (1942), Ellison's Invisible Man is an outsider, a stranger to the dominant civilization. But, unlike Dostoevsky and Wright, Ellison's underground man synthesizes his experiences and suggests alternatives. For different reasons, the main characters in the three stories live isolated from society and muse over the meanings of their lives. Wright's Fred Daniels escapes through a manhole after he is wrongfully accused of killing a white woman. After considering different groups from his underground dwelling, he comes to the existentialist conclusion that life is absurd and decides to turn himself in as a way of assuming responsibility for the evil nature of the human condition. The underground man in Dostoevsky's story explains his alienation from society by claiming to be a "sick," "spiteful," and "unattractive man" who has exercised his free will by choosing to shun societal institutions and living his individualistic life. Unlike the other two underground men, however, the Invisible Man uses his setting to ascend to a Platonic contemplation of light, symbolically expressed by the excessive lighting in his new home. Even though he dwells in a place of darkness (the cave in Plato's allegory), he has defeated it by attaining enlightenment, which allows him to see the "principle." Unlike the other two characters, Ellison's Invisible Man plots a new course. Having diagnosed the racial and ideological ills of American society, he uses his writing to "give pattern to the chaos" (580), to recast the idea of America imagined by its founders. He finally understands his grandfather's advice: "I want you to overcome 'em with yeses, undermine 'em with grins, agree 'em to death and destruction, let 'em swoller you till they vomit or bust wide open" (16). The grandfather affirmed the principle (574), and his grandson takes ownership of it through his deep examination of it. It is an epiphany for him.

To contemplate the principle as it is, the Invisible Man first proclaims his self-awareness. In the manner of Dostoevsky's underground man, Ellison's Invisible Man resolutely affirms: "I am an Invisible Man." From his harsh experiences, he knows that to be black in America between the end of the Civil War and the 1940s (and beyond) means to live in a liminal place, an "alien nation" plagued, according to W.E.B. Du Bois, by "double-consciousness":

> a peculiar sensation . . . this sense of always looking at one's self through the eyes of others, of measuring one's soul by the tape of a world that looks on in amused contempt and pity. One ever feels this two-ness—an American, a Negro; two souls, two thoughts, two unreconciled strivings; two warring ideals in one dark body, whose dogged strength alone keeps it from being torn asunder. (38)

Du Bois describes the African American as covered with a veil, a metaphor that suggests invisibility to American society, the viewer. From this threshold, he would like "to merge his double self into a better and truer self" (39). The Invisible Man's inability to achieve a true self reflects his embrace of models whose ideological consequences he does not understand, as shown in his regurgitation of Booker T. Washington's Atlanta Exposition Address before the inattentive white men in the "Battle Royal." Washington was willing to accept racial alienation, as he articulated in his 1895 Atlanta address: "In all things that are purely social we can be as separate as the fingers, yet one as the hand in all things essential to mutual progress" (143). Thus Washington, one of the Invisible Man's intellectual mentors, subscribed to the segregationist law of "separate but equal." Washington also wrote that "the wisest among my race understand that the agitation of questions of social equality is the extremest folly, and that progress in the enjoyment of all the privileges that will come to us

must be the result of severe and constant struggle rather than of artificial forcing" (144). In his speech to white patrons in the first chapter
and during all his time at college before his expulsion, the Invisible
Man seeks to emulate Booker T. Washington and his ideological
incarnations, Dr. Bledsoe and the blind Barbee. Initially exposed to
accommodationist principles, the Invisible Man is shaped by models
that accept exclusion and alienation; he seems willing to postpone his
rights to a later date and exile himself from the American body politic,
which he reclaims in the epilogue with the invocation of "E pluribus
unum" and the appeal to the "principle."

Many critics have ignored what Du Bois wrote in *The Souls
of Black Folk* after discussing the veil, the color line, and double
consciousness as metaphors of the African-American identity in
post-Reconstruction America. In Chapter 3, "Of Mr. Washington,"
he critiques Washington's educational and political ideology. Du
Bois accounts for the blues, songs of sorrow that convey the historically vicious and corrupt treatment of the black person in America,
but he does not wallow in them; instead he reaffirms "the higher
aims of life" that come with manhood and American citizenship in
his criticism of Washington (Du Bois 67). He reaffirms his strong
belief in the inalienable rights promised to every American citizen
in the Declaration of Independence, Constitution, Bill of Rights,
and the Thirteenth, Fourteenth, and Fifteenth Amendments. This
is the same principle that Ellison's Invisible Man appeals to in his
epilogue. Having used the main story to sing his blues ("What Did I
Do to Be So Black and Blue"), the Invisible Man determines that an
aesthetic of loss, survival, and temporary catharsis, no matter what its
imaginative possibilities, cannot help him overcome his plight. He
embraces the "principle."

Like Martin Luther King Jr. after him, Ellison engages both
white and black America by exposing the country's broken promises.
Significant individuals, periods, and ideologies directly and indirectly
invoked by *Invisible Man* include Thomas Jefferson (and through him
the founding ideas of the U.S. Constitution), the American renaissance in literature (Emerson), slavery and the struggle for freedom
(Frederick Douglass), the Civil War, Reconstruction and post-Reconstruction (Booker T. Washington and W.E.B. Du Bois), Jim Crow
laws and the myth of white supremacy, the great migration north and
the "New Negro Renaissance," and the emergence of the Communist

Party (the Brotherhood) and Black Nationalism (Ras the Destroyer). At the novel's end, the Invisible Man concludes that many of these historical ideologies and counterideologies have contributed to the alienation of African Americans only because the principle of constitutional democracy and the promise of inalienable rights have been betrayed since America's founding. He believes, however, that the principle remains sound, because it is "greater than the men, greater than the numbers and the vicious power and all the methods used to corrupt its name" (574). Martin Luther King's speech "I Have a Dream" first lists the African-American nightmares since the Emancipation Proclamation in 1863 (first invoking its author, President Abraham Lincoln, and then repeating "one hundred years later" to underscore the American betrayal of its black population) and then projects a better future, when the rights guaranteed by the founding documents (the Constitution and the Declaration of Independence) will become a reality for all Americans. The protagonist of *Invisible Man* sees a redemption in those same principles.

The Invisible Man's story laments the corruption and betrayal of the American covenant, the "promissory note to which every American was to fall heir" (King 80). The novel reenacts Ralph Waldo Emerson's optimism and Du Bois's democratic idealism; it foreshadows King's admonition and dream of social equality. Like Du Bois and King, Ellison also goes beyond the litany of suffering and imagines an America saved from the chaos and darkness of the past and basking in freedom for all its citizens. From this perspective, Ralph Ellison's seminal novel is an exercise in the definition of America. In attempting to define the country, the Invisible Man sought the words of those who had defined it in the past: Jefferson, Emerson, Melville, Douglass, and Du Bois, among many others. In reading these writers' works and then writing his own, the Invisible Man finally sheds his self-imposed alienation.

BIBLIOGRAPHY

Barthes, Roland. *The Pleasure of the Text*. Trans. Richard Miller. New York: Hill & Wang, 1975.

Douglass, Frederick. *Narrative of the Life of Frederick Douglass, an American Slave, Written by Himself*. Ed. David W. Blight. Boston: Bedford Books, 1993. [1845]

Du Bois, W.E.B. *The Souls of Black Folk*. ed. Robert Gooding-Williams. Boston: Bedford Books, 1997. [1903]

Eco, Umberto. *The Name of the Rose*. Trans. William Weaver. London: Vintage, 1998.

Ellison, Ralph W. *Invisible Man*. New York: Vintage Books, 1995. [1952]

King Jr., Martin Luther. "I Have a Dream." *Norton Anthology of African American Literature*. Ed. Henry Louis Gates, Jr. & Nellie Y. McKay. New York: W.W. Norton & Company, 1997. 80-83.

Shelley, Percy Bysshe. "A Defence of Poetry." *Norton Anthology of English Literature*. Sixth Edition, Vol. 2. ed. M.H. Abrams. New York: W.W. Norton & Company, 1993. 752–65.

Smith, Valerie. "The Meaning of Narration in *Invisible Man*." *Ralph Ellison's Invisible Man: A Casebook*. Ed. John F. Callahan. New York: Oxford University Press, 2004. 189–220.

Stepto, Robert B. *From Behind the Veil: A Study of Afro-American Narrative*. Urbana: University of Illinois Press, 1979.

Stepto, Robert B. & Michael S. Harper. "Study and Experience: An Interview with Ralph Ellison." *The Critical Response to Ralph Ellison*, ed. Robert J. Butler. Westport, Conn., Greenwood Press, 2000. 3–16.

Washington, Booker T. *Up from Slavery*. ed. W. Fitzhugh Brundage. Boston: Bedford/St. Martin's, 2003. [1901]

MRS. DALLOWAY
(VIRGINIA WOOLF)

"Divided Selves"
by Jeremy Hawthorn, in *Virginia Woolf's Mrs. Dalloway: A Study in Alienation* (1975)

INTRODUCTION

In his study of alienation in *Mrs. Dalloway*, Jeremy Hawthorn argues that madness in Virginia Woolf's novel "is seen both as a symbol and a result of alienation." Such alienation, according to Hawthorn, cuts the individual off from society, denies the individual "full human contact," and exacerbates "any predisposition towards mental disorder in an individual who had difficult in making contact with other people." Focusing primarily on Septimus Smith's mental instability, Hawthorn concludes that the alienation of the individual at odds with society animates the work, ultimately making "Septimus a sort of hero *manqué*," who willingly accepts death "in order to preserve his own existential unity."

There seems little doubt that Virginia Woolf's experience of what she called 'madness' contributed to her sense of the dissolution of

---

Hawthorn, Jeremy. "Divided Selves." *Virginia Woolf's Mrs. Dalloway: A Study in Alienation*. London: Sussex University Press, 1975. 28–44.

human identity. Yet it would be a mistake to see the whole question of self-dissolution or division in *Mrs. Dalloway* as a clinical matter. Certain social forces which had been developing in British society for some time were making a sharp division between the public and the private necessary for more and more people. It is worth remarking on the fact that in one sense Septimus Smith, the 'mad' character in *Mrs. Dalloway*, is *not* 'divided' in the way that other characters are, and it is arguable that it is his attempt to synthesise the public and the private that results in his inability to conform to the requirements of his society. Joan Bennett has suggested that after 1919 Virginia Woolf was not capable of including the clearly defined human character among those aspects of life in which she could believe with conviction.[1] Her experience of madness was probably a contributory factor in this change of attitude, but more important social developments—both on a wider scale and also relating to her particular social circle—are certainly involved. Her own artistic development has parallels in the development of other major contemporary writers and other artists. In 1923, in the early stages of writing *Mrs. Dalloway*, she stated in her diary that character '. . . is dissipated into shreds now . . .', and this theme recurs constantly in her writing at this time. In 'Mr. Bennett and Mrs. Brown', written in 1924, she 'hazarded the assertion' that '. . . in or about December, 1910, human character changed'. The date mentioned seems almost certainly to refer to the first post-Impressionist exhibition in London, which was organised by Roger Fry. It is worth linking her views on 'time', 'life' and 'reality' not only with Einstein's *Theory of Relativity*, but also the work of Joyce, Proust, Kafka and Musil.[2] Another name that might be added to this list is that of Joseph Conrad, of whom Virginia Woolf remarked that he was composed of two people who had nothing in common. In *Mr. Conrad: A Conversation*, she suggested that Conrad was not one and simple, but complex and many—words almost identical to those that Bernard, in *The Waves*, uses at one point to describe himself.

When we turn to *Mrs. Dalloway*, therefore, and consider the relationship between the divided selves of a single character, we need to bear in mind that we are dealing not with an eccentric offshoot of Virginia Woolf's madness, but with a specific example of a phenomenon which appears so insistently in the literature of this period that it suggests some common, fundamental reality underlying it. In her 1928 *Introduction* to the novel, Virginia Woolf claimed that a first version of the novel was written in which Septimus Smith did not appear, and that he was introduced later as Clarissa Dalloway's 'double'. It is as if the novelist has taken the divided selves of one character, and has turned them into two people. In this same *Introduction*, Virginia Woolf also informed the reader that in this first version of the novel, Clarissa was, '. . . originally to kill herself, or perhaps merely to die at the end of the party'. Kitty Maxse, who, according to Quentin Bell's biography of Virginia Woolf, was to some extent the model for the character of Clarissa Dalloway, died suddenly in 1922 after a fall from the top of a flight of stairs. Virginia Woolf believed that she had committed suicide and this may be one possible explanation of the rather opaque suggestions in Virginia Woolf's notes to the novel that Clarissa's progress from one level to another up her stairs has some sort of symbolic significance—a significance which the completed novel does not manage to convey in any clear form.

We do not need the evidence of her *Introduction* to see that there are close affinities and relationships between Septimus and Clarissa, even though they never meet. Virginia Woolf's fear that the reviewers would say that the mad scenes did not connect with the Dalloway scenes seems to have been unwarranted. Poetic techniques are used to relate Septimus and Clarissa with each other in the novel; both are beak-nosed, bird-like, associated with similar patterns of imagery and literary echoes such as the refrain from *Cymbeline* (which is sung in the play to Imogen, in the mistaken belief that she is dead). Septimus thinks that 'something tremendous [is] about to happen', Clarissa that 'something awful was about to happen'. Such parallels and contrasts can be added to. Clarissa 'feels' the death of Septimus whereas he had been unable to feel the death of Evans (it is not correct to say, as does Leon Edel, that it is a common 'failure to feel' that makes Septimus and Clarissa doubles).[3]

What do these parallels and contrasts add up to? Winifred Holtby sees the relationship between the two characters as metaphysical and psychological,[4] which may be the case but which certainly needs further elucidation. Perhaps more germane to our enquiry at this point is the insistence upon the *social* significance of the relationship of the two characters that Bernard Blackstone makes:

> Without the Dalloways there would be no Warren Smiths. Behind the Dalloways there rises the massive edifice of

civilisation, the Houses of Parliament, St. Paul's Cathedral, the
War Office, the Law Courts, the professional classes, Harley
Street.[5]

'Civilisation' is a trigger-word in *Mrs. Dalloway*, used ironically rather
than in a laudatory sense, and whatever one may think about the restric-
tiveness of Virginia Woolf's social and political vision there are some
significant flashes of insight into the relationships between personal
and social phenomena in the novel. Is Sally Seton's suggestion that the
well-bred but secretly lustful Hugh Whitbread is 'responsible' for the
fate of 'those poor girls in Piccadilly' so far-fetched? Certainly Richard
Dalloway—who has an unusually well-developed sense of social relationships for a Conservative Member of Parliament—sees prostitution
to be the fault of our social system, and Peter Walsh even feels that:

> ... God knows, the rascals who get hanged for battering the
> brains of a girl out in a train do less harm on the whole than
> Hugh Whitbread and his kindness! (*MD* p. 190)

Now *Mrs. Dalloway* is not *Waiting for Lefty*, and it would be absurd
to interpret it as a developed Marxist analysis of Virginia Woolf's
society. But on the other hand it would, I feel, be equally misleading
to ignore the fact that it consistently tries to uncover hidden relationships both between different characters, and also between characters
and social institutions. In many cases a character—Sir William Bradshaw for example—represents an aspect of her society rather than
a particular example of human individuality for Virginia Woolf. I
think that the few fleeting references to prostitution in *Mrs. Dalloway*
show how Virginia Woolf was concerned to relate individual and
social phenomena. Put simply, I think that it is *true* that there is a
connection between the hypocritical attitudes of Hugh Whitbread
with his external correctness and concealed lust and the 'poor girls in
Piccadilly'. It is probable that very little that Marx wrote would have
interested Virginia Woolf directly, but the following comment might
perhaps have caught her attention:

> Prostitution is only a *specific* expression of the *general* prostitution
> of the *labourer*, and since it is a relationship in which falls not
> the prostitute alone, but also the one who prostitutes—and the

latter's abomination is still greater—the capitalist, etc., also comes under this head. (*EPM* p. 133(n))

It is certainly important to be constantly aware that Septimus is a victim of the war, whilst the Dalloways are representative of politics and government. Years before the writing of *Three Guineas* Virginia Woolf had a very clear idea of the connection between the brutality of war and the 'screen-making habits' of English males of the governing classes. I want it to be clear that I am not arguing for an interpretation of *Mrs. Dalloway* in terms of an overt, consistent political message. What I am saying is that Virginia Woolf saw important connections between social institutions and individual characteristics, and that the relationship between Clarissa and Septimus in the novel is not just metaphysical and psychological, but has an important *social* dimension too.

I would suggest, therefore, that Septimus's madness plays a complex and multiple role in the novel. On one level it is an extreme *symbol* of that alienation from human contact that all of the characters suffer from to a greater or a lesser extent. On another level, as a result of the specifically social links which are drawn between Septimus (who lost the ability to feel through the war), and characters such as Sir William Bradshaw (who is a servant and eager supporter of that 'civilisation' which is associated with the war), Septimus's madness is seen as the *result* of particular pressures engendered by an alienating society.

Certainly, the introduction of a mad character into the novel allows the presentation of an extreme form of alienation. Madness is the supreme isolator, and the more a man needs other men, the more madness is feared. Samuel Johnson, that most fervent believer in man's social nature and the most suspicious critic of enthusiasm and private experiences of truth, in the midst of experiencing a stroke which was partially to paralyse him, prayed to God that however He might afflict his body, He should spare his mind. Madness cuts off Septimus from nearly all real human contact:

But Rezia could not understand him. Dr. Holmes was such a kind man. He was so interested in Septimus. He only wanted to help them, he said. He had four little children and he had asked her to tea, she told Septimus.

So he was deserted. (*MD* p. 102)

Dr Holmes's invitation to his wife makes Septimus feel deserted in just the same way that Lady Bruton's invitation to her husband makes Clarissa feel that she is alone. Both need people and are terrified of solitude, but Clarissa, although often apparently teetering on the edge of the horror that encompasses Septimus, has certain lifelines which preserve her. Both Septimus and Clarissa make gifts. But Septimus's gift of his life only completes his isolation in death, symbolised by the enclosing ambulance representative, as Peter Walsh feels, of 'civilisation'. Clarissa's gift of her party, on the other hand, really does succeed in bringing people together for a short time.

> Communication is health; communication is happiness. Communication, he muttered.
> 'What are you saying, Septimus?' Rezia asked, wild with terror, for he was talking to himself. (*MD* pp. 103, 104)

The bitter irony of this 'exchange' contrasts with the fact that even though Richard cannot bring himself to tell Clarissa that he loves her, there is still enough contact between the two to preserve Clarissa's sanity. Thus when she hears of Septimus's death, Clarissa understands that

> Death was defiance. Death was an attempt to communicate, people feeling the impossibility of reaching the centre which, mystically, evaded them; closeness drew apart; rapture faded; one was alone. There was an embrace in death. (*MD* p. 202)

This passage echoes many of the phrases in an earlier passage describing Clarissa's vicarious indulgence in the described sexual passion of another woman:

> Then, for that moment, she had seen an illumination; a match burning in a crocus; an inner meaning almost expressed. But the close withdrew; the hard softened. (*MD* p. 36)

The embrace that Septimus finds in death is sought because he cannot find it in that human contact achieved momentarily at her party that recharges Clarissa's spiritual reserves. The traditional association of sex and death surely stems from a recognition that sex involves some extinction of privacy, some breaking down of the walls of the self, that prefigures the complete extinction of the self in death.

Septimus's dying words—'I'll give it you!'—are thus extremely significant, as they point to the thing that both he and Clarissa most want to do—to *give*. The final extinction of self that Septimus throws himself to in his suicide jump is described in terms that have been used to describe heterosexual passion earlier on, because Virginia Woolf sees close and significant parallels between the act of giving a life and giving in sex. It is Clarissa's fear of 'losing herself' as Septimus loses himself that accounts for her lack of 'something central that permeated', for her inability to give herself—as we say, 'body and soul'—to a sexual relationship. It is thus revealing that there is a distinctly sexual element in Clarissa's imagination of Septimus's death-scene:

> He had thrown himself from a window. Up had flashed the ground; through him, blundering, bruising, went the rusty spikes. There he lay with a thud, thud, thud in his brain, and then a suffocation of blackness. (*MD* p. 202)

Clarissa concludes that there is an embrace in death, but in the descriptions of her inability to give herself to either Peter Walsh or, sexually, to Richard, we can see her fear that there is death in an embrace, that abandonment to passion is beyond her because she fears the loss of self—seen symbolically magnified in Septimus's death—that it threatens.

I have said that in *Mrs. Dalloway* madness is seen both as a symbol and a result of alienation. Because madness does cut the individual off from other people, it is to be expected that many of the characteristics resulting from mental disorder may resemble those which result from a society which denies its members full human contact. Furthermore, such a society would be likely to exacerbate any predisposition towards mental disorder in an individual who had difficulty in making contact with other people. Even if Septimus were a real person and not a character in a novel, it would be difficult to say whether or not the need to shut out the horrors of war caused, or encouraged, his inability to feel. What one can say is that once such an inability has become apparent, a society in which it is necessary not to feel for other people in certain circumstances will not encourage recovery.

Septimus is possessed of many of the paradoxical impulses that recent research has revealed to be common in cases of schizophrenia, and in which we can sometimes see, albeit in a distorted or magnified form, impulses that are experienced by those not suffering from any mental disorder. Septimus wishes to communicate but is scared of self-exposure, and his 'madness' clearly has a defensive function for him, which the following passage, with its vague echoes of *King Lear*, points to:

> But he would not go mad. He would shut his eyes; he would see
> no more. (*MD* p. 26)

In this instance, Septimus's eye-lids are screens which preserve his sense of identity, which prevent him from 'dissolving utterly'. But screens, we remember, can threaten to destroy that which they protect, just as it is possible that in shutting herself off from Peter Walsh, Clarissa may have caused the death of her soul. When Septimus shuts his eyes in sleep, much later in the novel, the destructive side of this attempt to preserve his self becomes apparent:

> He was very tired. He was very happy. He would sleep. He
> shut his eyes. But directly he saw nothing the sounds of the
> game became fainter and stranger and sounded like the cries of
> people seeking and not finding, and passing farther and farther
> away. They had lost him!
>
> He started up in terror. What did he see? The plate of
> bananas on the sideboard. Nobody was there (Rezia had taken
> the child to its mother; it was bedtime). That was it: to be alone
> for ever. That was the doom pronounced in Milan ... (*MD*
> pp. 159, 160)

It was in Milan that he realised the implications of his inability to feel the death of Evans. An inability to feel may have temporary advantages, but it impoverishes and isolates, it eventually destroys what it is intended to protect. As Marx expresses it, man's relation to himself only becomes objective and actual through his relation to the other man, and Septimus's inability to feel the death of the 'other man' leads to a loss of what R.D. Laing calls ontological security.

In an unpublished comment written at the time she was working on *Mrs. Dalloway*, Virginia Woolf suggested that Septimus was to be:

> ... only real in so far as [Rezia] sees him. Otherwise to exist in his view of things: which is always to be contrasting with Mrs. Dalloways. (*sic*) [6]

Septimus, in other words, has a very low level of ontological security. We all exist and are real only in so far as other people see us, but we do not normally need to be seen by other people all the time. Septimus lacks the reserves of strength given by a secure sense of self, and needs constant, immediate self-confirmation through contact with Rezia. Once again we can note that this is an exaggerated version of a normal human need, rather than something totally removed from any familiar human experience. Septimus lacks a secure sense of self and therefore needs another person more than is usual; Miss Kilman, who describes herself, interestingly, as a wheel without a tyre at one point in the novel, lacks a close personal relationship, and thus needs to develop a more than normally secure sense of self—much is made in the novel of her 'armour'.

Virginia Woolf talks of screens; we can perhaps raid the vocabulary of the astronaut to suggest that the 'normal' person has various forms of emotional air-lock which allow in only that which does not threaten the individual's ontological security, and which enable him to communicate with other people. Septimus has no such air-lock apart from Rezia, and so the attempt to separate him from her is a threat to his very existence as an independent human being. Another comment of Virginia Woolf's on Septimus is interesting in this context:

> [Septimus] might be left vague—as a mad person is—not so much character as an idea—This is what is painful to her [Rezia]—becomes generalised—universalised. So can be partly R; partly me. [7]

If we wish to know what this generalisation and universalisation consist of, we need to have some way of relating Septimus's isolation to the situation of other characters in the novel—particularly Clarissa—who are not 'mad' in the same sense.

Leonard Woolf has claimed that there was a real distinction between Virginia Woolf's mad and sane states, which could be expressed as the distinction between an 'awareness and acceptance of the outside world and a rational reaction to it' and 'a refusal to admit or accept facts in the outside world'. The distinction is one that can fruitfully be applied to the distinction between Septimus and Clarissa, and yet in spite of this there are important parallels as well as contrasts between their respective situations. Septimus's internal alienation is compounded by the fact that his only contact with a human reality is through one who is herself an alien;[8] Rezia feels that, 'I am alone; I am alone!'. Clarissa too feels isolated from other people although she desperately needs them, and it is worth asking whether her rejection of Peter Walsh is to be seen as in some way parallel to Septimus's inability to feel the death of Evans. R.D. Laing has written that we all share the psychotic's paradoxical need to reveal and conceal himself, and that in most cases we have reached the more or less satisfactory solution of having our secrets and our needs to confess. He suggests that it is when we tell our first lie that we realise that in certain respects we are irredeemably alone, and that 'within the territory of ourselves there can be only our footprints'. This phrase is strikingly similar to one to be found in Virginia Woolf's essay 'On Being Ill' (a situation in which the individual feels more than normally cut off from other people): 'There is a virgin forest in each; a snowfield where even the print of birds' feet is unknown.' Laing claims that genuine privacy is the basis of genuine relationship, and it is perhaps to preserve the last few square feet of untrodden snow in his soul that Septimus kills himself.

My insistence on the importance of human privacy may seem to run counter to the general drift of my argument that the disjunction between the public and the private is a product of human alienation, and is to be regretted. I think that it is important to make a distinction between a situation where the private and public selves of an individual are not only completely separate but are contradictory, which I associate with alienation, and a situation where the individual enjoys some 'untrodden snow in his soul' which confirms his own human individuality without implicitly or explicitly denying the human individuality of others. Having said this, it is necessary to add that in a society not founded upon the sort of contradictions to which I have drawn attention, the individual would (and does) feel far less need for a secure area of personal privacy either within him or herself, or within an exclusive personal relationship. Whether such a need could ever disappear completely in a different social situation, I am not sure.

Septimus is irredeemably alone because, unlike Clarissa, he has completely shut himself off from feeling rather than taking risks and exposing his vulnerability—although to this it must be added that his experience of the war placed a greater pressure on him than did Clarissa's more restricted social experience. Clarissa's parties, as I want to argue more fully in a later chapter, involve vulnerability and risk as well as being an offering; they enable her to regenerate her sense of identity through the development of relationships based on openness and honesty. Earlier I drew a parallel between Virginia Woolf's description of the creative process of writing a novel, and Clarissa's behaviour at her party. In both cases some alternation between retreat and exposure, privacy and communion is necessary. Septimus has lost this ability, and is fixed in a privacy inescapable until he makes that tragic contact with Rezia immediately before his death. Septimus's form of madness is simply loneliness intensified beyond the point of human endurance.[9] Clarissa may shut herself off from a concern with the persecuted Armenians (or Albanians), but her ability to feel Septimus's death, while it makes her vulnerable, keeps her sane.

Some screens are necessary. Whereas Septimus thinks about large questions of life and death but feels nothing on a more immediately personal level, Clarissa:

> ... cared much more for her roses than for the Armenians. Hunted out of existence, maimed, frozen, the victims of cruelty and injustice (she had heard Richard say so over and over again)—no, she could feel nothing for the Albanians, or was it the Armenians? but she loved her roses (didn't that help the Armenians?)—the only flowers she could bear to see cut. (*MD* p. 133)

The implication is, as T.S. Eliot puts it in 'Burnt Norton', that human kind cannot bear very much reality. The impossibility of reconciling a knowledge of the movements of large social and political forces with the values of one's personal life stems, surely, from the fact that public and private lives are based on different and mutually exclusive value systems. Clarissa's choice of her roses rather than the Armenians can be contrasted with the choice made by Doris Kilman, who:

> ... would do anything for the Russians, starved herself for the Austrians, but in private inflicted positive torture, so insensitive was she, dressed in a green mackintosh coat. (*MD* p. 14)

It is difficult to avoid the feeling that a false pair of alternatives is being presented to the reader here, although there is the example of Richard Dalloway's concern for Armenians *and* roses that needs to be considered.

Why should Virginia Woolf apparently load the dice at this point? I would like to suggest that in a deeper sense it is true that, given her belief in the unchangeable nature of her world, Clarissa cannot reconcile a love for humanity at large with a love for those symbolic roses. Boris Kuznetsov, writing about Dostoyevsky, has shown how eagerly writers in the nineteenth century seized on the example of an Euclidean harmony which ignored microscopic processes as a parallel to the harmony of their social order which also ignored microscopic processes—that is, the fates of individual men and women. He argues that just as the physicist is still trying to find an order which encompasses both the macro- and microscopic process, so too:

> Modern notions of moral harmony require that an individual existence be determined by its importance to the collective destiny.[10]

This is the sort of reconciliation that neither Septimus, nor Miss Kilman, nor Clarissa—any more than Wemmick or Brecht's heroine— can achieve, for all of them accept a social order which contains a fundamental disjunction between public and private, individual and collective destiny.

Miss Kilman, as much as Charles Tansley in *To the Lighthouse* and *The Man who loved his Kind* in Virginia Woolf's short story of that name, would like to have personal relationships based on love rather than aggression and competition, and we are told at the beginning of *Mrs. Dalloway* that Clarissa would like to have been 'interested in politics like a man', but this sort of reconciliation is open to neither of them. The one character who succeeds in reconciling public and private is Septimus—and the success drives him mad.

I am perhaps giving Virginia Woolf the benefit of a little too much special pleading at this point, however. There is no doubt that Clarissa Dalloway's attitudes reflect a partly culpable blindness on the part of Virginia Woolf to the fate of those not immediately before her. Quentin Bell tells a revealing anecdote about how the realities of unemployment were brought home to her only when a fainting unemployed girl knocked at her door and asked for a drink of water. Whatever the contradictions in our society, they do not force this sort of blindness upon its members.

Virginia Woolf was deeply suspicious of those with causes, in which she detected egotism and the desire to force other people's souls. In her diary in 1923 she wrote that she was 'a great deal interested suddenly in my book. I want to bring in the despicableness of people like Ott.' 'Ott' was Lady Ottoline Morrell. In *Beginning Again*, Leonard Woolf commented that:

> [The Morrells] were leading members of that stage army of British progressives who can be relied upon to sign a letter to *The Times* supporting an unpopular cause or protesting against a pogrom or judicial murder. (*BA* p. 198)

The suggestion is that anyone who pretends to feel deeply about 'a pogrom or judicial murder' must be being hypocritical. Now it may well be true that there was more than a residual element of posturing in the causes adopted as their own by the Morrells, but many readers will surely feel that if so, such posturing is to be preferred to an inability to feel anything for the Albanians or the Armenians.

Lady Bruton, who writes a letter to *The Times* with the aid of Hugh Whitbread and Richard Dalloway, is not given the benefit of supporting such unimpeachable causes however, and is seen to be obsessed by what appears to be near forcible emigration (doubtless the more comfortable contemporary term, 'repatriation', would have appealed to her). She wants to push people around against their wills just as Sir William Bradshaw wants to move Septimus against his will, and both have the symbolic backing of the state. Whilst rejecting the view that roses are more important than Armenians (and there is no definite authorial support for this attitude of Clarissa's—or criticism of it), we need to remember that causes, political and religious, can sometimes make their adherents forget the humanity of those for whom they are ostensibly striving. We also need to remember that a separation of private from public morality is fundamental to capitalist society.

I think that there are interesting parallels that can be drawn between *Mrs. Dalloway* and Joseph Conrad's *The Secret Agent* in this context. Obviously, on one level, the latter novel suggests that people who espouse causes end by treating other people as tokens to be manipulated rather than as people, but there is a more significant parallel than that. In *The Secret Agent* we again have a mentally-disturbed or retarded character—Stevie—who is unable to reach a satisfactory relationship with the world which includes sympathy but excludes horror. Horrified by the condition of a cab-horse, Stevie is even more horrified to learn from the cabman that the security of the latter's family *depends* on the horse's ill-treatment:

> 'Poor! Poor!' stammered out Stevie, pushing his hands deeper into his pockets with convulsive sympathy. He could say nothing; for his tenderness to all pain and all misery, the desire to make the horse happy and the cabman happy, had reached the point of a bizarre longing to take them to bed with him. And that, he knew, was impossible. For Stevie was not mad. It was, as it were, a symbolic longing . . .

In a society where not only does the happiness of cabmen seem to depend on the unhappiness of cab-horses, but where the happiness of one man can depend upon the unhappiness of another man, then such symbolic longings will, in default of a desire to change society itself, tend to emerge.

Other interesting parallels between the two novels are worthy of note. There is a strong suggestion in *Mrs. Dalloway* that Septimus's insanity is in some ways a logical—even sane—response to the insanity of war, a paradox explored with remorseless logic by Joseph Heller in *Catch 22*. Certainly it is only by inhumanity—that is, obliviousness to the pains of the Armenians—that Clarissa retains her humanity and avoids madness, just as Mr Verloc in *The Secret Agent*, who thinks of himself as just doing a job of work and remains oblivious to the fact that it results in people's deaths, stays sane. Significantly *The Secret Agent*, like *Mrs. Dalloway*, is set in London, and it is worthy of note that Mr Verloc's 'front' (revealing word) for his nefarious activities is the sale of pornography—the ultimate symbol of the reduction of human beings to objects alienated from one another. Most of all, Conrad, like Virginia Woolf in her portrayal of Septimus, brings out the *self-destructiveness* of the isolation which these conditions produce: the ghastly figure of the professor, living in his own fantasy world and prepared to blow himself up with the explosive he carries continually if the police attempt to arrest him, is a symbol of something that goes far beyond *The Secret Agent* in its significance.

Returning to England after the war, Septimus feels, as his train leaves Newhaven, that it might be possible that the world itself is without meaning. The contrast between his experiences during the war and the 'civilisation' which was responsible for the war but which appears to be unaware of it is too much for Septimus, too great to have any meaning imposed upon it. Whatever impression of social rarification the reader of *Mrs. Dalloway* may initially receive, the novel constantly uncovers connections between many seemingly diverse phenomena. The first reference in the novel to a suppression of the emotions in order to preserve 'public' decorum comes on the second page, when Lady Bexborough opens a bazaar with the telegram announcing the death of her favourite son in her hand. The war is thus related to that 'manliness' that conceals natural emotions and drives a wedge between the public and the private. Clarissa thanks Heaven that the war is over, but it is not over for the shell-shocked Septimus who relives it in his memory, and shows in a heightened way what Virginia Woolf shows in many other characters, that we 'are', in part, what we have been. *Mrs. Dalloway* is saturated with references to the war, which remains a lingering symbolic presence throughout the novel, and is specifically associated, through Holmes and Bradshaw, with the state and with the habit of separating public and private experience. Septimus cannot reconcile post-war Newhaven with his war-time experiences; he lacks that 'sense of proportion' that allows Bradshaw to ignore awkward connections, relationships. Rezia cannot understand Septimus's obsessions, for '. . . such things happen to every one. Every one has friends who were killed in the war. Every one gives up something when they marry.'

In view of the symbolic significance that the war comes to have in the novel, we are not surprised to learn that Lady Bruton 'could have led troops to attack', and that although Doris Kilman lost her post for attacking jingoism in the war, she has become possessed of 'the power and taciturnity of some prehistoric monster armoured for primeval warfare'. Septimus claims to have stopped feeling in the war, but we have Rezia's recollection that he was 'only suffering sometimes through this terrible war', and at his death he is saluted in the manner of men killed in battle by the apron of Mrs Filmer, which resembles a flag:

> 'The War?' the patient asked. The European War—that little shindy of schoolboys with gunpowder? Had he served with distinction? He really forgot. In the War itself he had failed.
>   'Yes, he served with the greatest distinction,' Rezia assured the doctor; 'he was promoted.' (*MD* p. 106)

The paradox is presented forcibly here; Septimus feels that his outward distinction in the war is really a failure. The word 'failure' gathers around itself a number of pregnant echoes in *Mrs. Dalloway*, and becomes suggestive of its opposite. To fail in a system that is inhuman may be testimony to one's humanity, and it is to the credit of characters such as Septimus and Peter Walsh (who is referred to as a failure on a number of occasions) that they do fail to measure up to the public standards of their society. Septimus's 'failure-in-success' is not confined to his war record:

> 'And they have the very highest opinion of you at your office?'
> Sir William murmured ... (*MD* p. 106)

—just as they have of Wemmick.

It is Sir William's achievement of a sense of proportion which, in one of the most powerful passages in the novel, is revealed as life-denying and the real failure. The connection between Sir William's personal obnoxiousness and the state he defends and represents is made quite unambiguous.

> In short, this living or not living is an affair of our own? But there they were mistaken. Sir William had a friend in Surrey where they taught, what Sir William frankly admitted was a difficult art—a sense of proportion. There were, moreover, family affection; honour; courage; and a brilliant career. All of

these had in Sir William a resolute champion. If they failed, he had to support him police and the good of society, which, he remarked very quietly, would take care, down in Surrey, that these unsocial impulses, bred more than anything by the lack of good blood, were held in control. (*MD* pp. 112, 113)

Sir William's 'sense of proportion' involves a refusal to see that the human values he appeals to are not to be reconciled with the values of the state whose servant he is and whose authority he upholds. His sense of proportion is an acceptance of hypocrisy, of the necessary disjunction of private and public values, coupled with a brutal attack on those who seek to reveal this disjunction and to overcome it. Whereas Sir William's sense of proportion is an acceptance of the inevitability of the self being divided, what makes Septimus a sort of hero *manqué* is his refusal to accept this division, and his willingness to accept death in order to preserve his own existential unity.

NOTES

1. Joan Bennett. *Virginia Woolf: Her Art as a Novelist.* Cambridge, 1964.
2. A point made by Arnold Kettle, *Mrs. Dalloway.* Milton Keynes, 1973. (This is unit 30 of the Open University course "The Nineteenth-Century Novel and its Legacy.")
3. Leon Edel. "The Novel as Poem." *The Modern Psychological Novel.* New York, 1964.
4. Winifred Holtby. *Virginia Woolf.* London, 1932.
5. Bernard Blackstone. *Virginia Woolf as Commentary.* London, 1932.
6. Quoted by Charles G. Hoffmann. "From Short Story to Novel: the Manuscript Revisions of Virginia Woolf's *Mrs. Dalloway.*" *Modern Fiction Studies*, 14.2.
7. *ibid.*
8. A point made by Hoffmann, *op. cit.*
9. A point made by Frank Baldanza in "Clarissa Dalloway's 'Party Consciousness.'" *Modern Fiction Studies*, 2.1.
10. Boris Kuznetsov. *Einstein and Dostoevsky.* Translated by Vladimir Talmy. London, 1972.

NOTES FROM UNDERGROUND
(FYODOR MIKHAILOVICH DOSTOEVSKY)

"The Journal Epoch,
Notes from Underground"
by Konstantin Mochulsky,
in *Dostoevsky: His Life and Work* (1967)

INTRODUCTION

Konstantin Mochulsky's essay on *Notes from Underground* focuses on the underground man's alienation, which Mochulsky attributes to the underground man's over-analytical mind and awareness of his inability to affect the world—the way that his "Consciousness is a sickness, leading to inertia." As with Hamlet, "Consciousness kills feeling, corrupts the will, paralyzes action." For Mochulsky, the underground man is a "human tragedy." Quoting Dostoevsky's *Diary of a Writer*, Mochulsky finds what might be called the alienated condition of modernity, in which we know we cannot end suffering: "The consciousness of our own utter inability to help or to bring, if only some, benefit or relief to suffering mankind, . . . can even *transform the love of mankind in your heart into hatred for it."*

Mochulsky, Konstantin. "The Journal Epoch, *Notes From Underground*." *Dostoevsky: His Life and Work*. Trans. Michael A. Minihan. Princeton, N.J.: Princeton UP, 1967. 242–69.

Notes from Underground is a "strange" work. Everything in it is striking: the structure, style, the subject. The first part consists of the underground man's confession in which the most profound problems of philosophy are examined. As for strength and daring of thought, Dostoevsky yields neither to Nietzsche nor Kierkegaard. He is near to them in spirit, he is "of their kin." The second part is the tale *Apropos of the Wet Snow*. The underground man, having explained his *credo*, relates his memoirs. The tie between the philosophical considerations and the shameful "anecdotes" from the hero's life seems utterly artificial. Only in the end is their organic unity disclosed.

In the works of the period prior to his exile, "idealistic dreaming" was the writer's central theme; he devoted many inspired pages to the dreamer's psychology, the aesthetic value of fantasy, and a moral condemnation of that illusory life which is "horror and tragedy." The underground is the natural culmination of "dreaming." The dreamer-romantic of the forties has in the sixties been transformed into a cynic-"paradoxalist." For forty years he has remained seated in his corner, like a mouse in the underground, and now he gets the desire to recount what he has experienced and thought in his angry solitude. The underground man's social and historical condition is defined by the same marks which earlier characterized the dreamer's state. This is "one of the representatives of a generation still living," i.e., an intellectual of the "Petersburg period of Russian history," poisoned by European culture, divorced from the soil and the people; an historical type who "not only can, but also must exist in our society." He is the product of a milieu, a bookish education, and an "abstract" civilization; not a living man, but a *"stillborn universal man."* The author imputes to him the crime which earlier he had imputed to the dreamer: a betrayal of *living life*. "... We all have lost the habit of *life*.... We have lost the habit even to such an extent that at times we feel a certain loathing toward actual *living life*.... Why, we have come nearly to looking upon actual living life as a toil, almost as an obligation.... Why, we do not even know where *that which has life, is living* now, and what such a thing is, what name it bears." To the stillborn, who "for a long time have been born not of living fathers," to the homunculi out of test tubes, there is always opposed that same foggy-mystical ideal of "living life." Its content is not revealed: why, "we do not even know where that which has life is living." The significance of this mystery is lost. And so, the underground man is defined as an historical type and ascribed to the past: "one of the characters of recent times." But the historical mask is easily removed; the hero is not only in the past, but also in the present, not only "I" but also "we." The author steadily emerges beyond the confines of the personality of the Russian intellectual and limitlessly broadens his framework. The underground man proves to be a "man of the 19th century"—"a decent man who can talk only about himself," "a conscious individual" in general. He ventures to expound his own thoughts in the name of "every intelligent man," and, finally, *simply of man.*

Consequently, the underground man's paradoxes are not the whims of some half-mad eccentric, but a new revelation *of man about man.* The consciousness of the angry mouse, crushed in the underground, proves to be *human consciousness in general.*

We are hitting upon the enigma of consciousness. A man becomes a man if he possesses consciousness. Without consciousness man is an animal. But consciousness arises only out of conflict with reality, from a breach with the world. Consciousness must pass through isolation and solitude; it is *pain.* On the other hand—solitary consciousness does not exist; it is always joined with all mankind, it is *organically collective.* In this tormenting contradiction is the tragedy of personality. The "acutely developed personality" thrusts itself back from the world, desperately upholds its self-legitimacy and at the same time is attracted to people, understands its dependence upon them. All the relations between personality and the world, in Dostoevsky, are permeated by a fatal dichotomy. His heroes always love while hating, and hate while loving; his romantics are cynical, while his cynics are full of exultation. The author suggests the idea of duality to the reader in the stylistic devices of the first part of the *Notes.* This is not logical argumentation, addressed toward reason, but a direct hypnotic suggestion by voice and intonations. We perceive almost physiologically the underground man's division through the unsightliness of his style, the disharmony of syntax, the irritating brokenness of his speech. All Dostoevsky's heroes are characterized by their language, but the verbal portrait of the man from underground is the most expressive.[1]

Most of all, one is astounded by the contrast between the confession's exterior and inner form. This is a monologue in which each sentence constitutes a dialogue. The hero asserts that he is writing exclusively for himself, that he does not need any readers, yet meanwhile his every word is directed toward another, is calculated upon an impression. He despises this other, ridicules him, abuses him, but at the same time curries his favor, exculpates himself, argues and persuades. Cries of complete independence of another's opinion alternate with the most piteous efforts to win the enemy's regard.

The "underground" begins with the words: "I am a sick man. . . . I am a spiteful man. I'm an unattractive man. I think my liver is diseased." After the very first sentence: "I am a sick man," there are a series of dots and a glancing round at the reader. As it were, the narrator has already observed a compassionate smile and taken offense. The reader will still think that he requires his pity. Wherefore, there is the impudent: "I am a spiteful man. I'm an unattractive man." Then he continues willfully: "I'm not being treated and have never been treated, although I respect medicine and doctors." And again there is a look around: does he not now appear naive to the reader? In order to correct the impression, there follows the elegant pleasantry: "Besides, I'm still extremely superstitious, well, if only so far as to respect medicine." And again the apprehension: what if he seems reactionary to the enlightened reader? This leads to a new unsuccessful pleasantry in parentheses: "(I'm well educated enough not to be superstitious, but I am superstitious.)" But the reader can ask, then why is he not being treated? His answer must be shocking: "No, sir, I don't want to be cured out of malice." The reader shrugs his shoulders in confusion. This assumed reaction already provokes the narrator and he responds insolently: "Here you, to be sure, do not deign to understand this. Well, sir, but I understand it." And, running ahead, he anticipates the objection: "I, *of course*, won't be able to explain to you whom precisely I will irk in this case by my malice; I know *perfectly well* that I won't in any way 'sully' the doctors by the fact that I'm not consulting them; *I know better than everyone* that by all this I'll injure only myself and no one else." You were thinking to catch me, and here I caught you. I, it turns out, knew all your arguments better than you. But all the same, I am not being treated, so it is "from malice." You are surprised. Well, be surprised. That's just what I wanted. What's to be done; I'm already such a paradoxalist.

And so it is in each sentence. The polemics with an imaginary enemy, one cunning and venomous, are conducted in a strained, passionate tone. There are constant reservations, self-justifications, and refutations of another, presumed opinion. "Doesn't it seem to you, gentlemen, that now I am repenting before you?" Or: "Doubtlessly, you are thinking, gentlemen, that I want to make you laugh?" All these glances about ought to attest to a thorough indifference toward the reader, but they prove, to the contrary, a servile dependence upon him. Here is the source of all the narrator's growing irritability and rage. . . . In order to free himself from the power of another's consciousness, he attempts to besmut and distort his own reflection in this mirror; he tells dreadful things about himself, exaggerates his "unseemliness," cynically ridicules everything "noble and beautiful" in him. This is the self-defense of despair. The image, which will be impressed on another's consciousness, will be a mask unlike him. He is hidden beneath it, he is free, he has escaped from witnesses and again disappeared underground. Lastly, even after the most resolute affirmations there always remains a loophole: to deny one's words or completely to alter their meaning. "I swear to you, gentlemen, that I do not believe a single, not one single little word of what I have now scribbled down! *That is, I also believe it*, if you like, but at the same time, for some unknown reason, I feel and suspect that I'm lying like a shoemaker."

Such is the unending circle through which the sick consciousness is revolved. Indifference toward the hostile world and a shameful dependence upon it—this is a mouse's scurrying about, a *perpetuum mobile*.

The underground man is not only split in two, but is also without character; he has not been able to become anything; "not evil, nor good, nor an infamous scoundrel, nor honorable, nor a hero, nor an insect!" And this is because "the man of the 19th century must and is morally obliged to be a creature preferably without character; and the man with character, the doer, a creature preferably narrow minded." Consciousness is a sickness, leading to inertia, i.e., to a "conscious sitting-with-arms-folded." Thus Dostoevsky poses the problem of contemporary *Hamletism*. Consciousness kills feeling, corrupts the will, paralyzes action. "I exercise myself in thinking, and consequently with me every primary cause immediately draws after it another still more primary, and so on, into infinity." The causal chain extends to an ugly infinity, and in this perspective, every truth is not absolute, every good is relative. For the new Hamlet there remains one occupation: "intentional pouring water through a sieve." From consciousness comes inertia, from inertia there is boredom. Not acting, not living, man out of boredom begins to "compose life": insults, events, romances. The underground existence becomes fantasy; this is a game in front of a mirror. The man suffers, rejoices, is angry and, as it were, with complete sincerity. But each sensation is reflected in the mirror of consciousness; in the actor there sits a spectator who appraises his art. The underground man turns a prostitute's soul with noble speeches; he talks ardently, sincerely, goes as far as a "throat-spasm," and at the same time not for a minute does he forget that all this is a game. He gives Liza his address, but is terribly afraid that she will come. The voice of the on-looker says in him: "And again, again to put on this dishonorable, lying mask." The voice of the actor objects: "Why dishonorable? What dishonorable? I was speaking sincerely yesterday. I remember, there was then genuine feeling in me. . . ." But such is the nature of self-consciousness: to break everything down into "yes" and "no"; what "directness and sincerity" can there be in a game before a mirror?

Consciousness opposes itself to the world. It is alone, against it is everything. As a result it feels itself brought to bay, persecuted; hence the morbid sensitivity of the underground man, his self-love, vanity, suspicions. Like a harassed mouse, he hides in his hole and from distasteful reality escapes into fancy. The breach in his personality yet increases. On the one hand, there is vicious, petty debauchery; on the other, lofty dreams. "It is amazing that these influxes of 'everything beautiful and noble' used to come in me during periods of dissipation, and just when I found myself at the very bottom, used to come so, in separate little spurts, as it were, reminding me of themselves, but not putting an end, however, to the debauchery by their appearance. They rather, as it were, seemed to enliven it by contrast." Duality is experienced as a contradiction and suffering, becomes the matter of "tormenting inner analysis," but out of suffering there suddenly grows a "decisive pleasure."

Here is this remarkable passage: "I came to the point of feeling a sort of secret, abnormal, mean enjoyment in returning home to my corner on some most foul Petersburg night and being acutely aware that now even today I had again committed a repulsive deed, that that which has been done, can never again be reversed, and inwardly, secretly, gnawing, gnawing myself for this with my teeth, plaguing and consuming myself to the point that the bitterness would be turned, at last, into a kind of shameful, accursed sweetness, and, finally, into a decisive, serious pleasure! Yes, into pleasure, into pleasure! I insist on that." This paradoxical assertion is one of Dostoevsky's real psychological disclosures. In consciousness there occurs *a substitution of the aesthetic plane for the ethical plane.* Degradation is a torture, but a "too clear awareness" of degradation can afford pleasure. Looking into a mirror, it is possible to forget about *what* is reflected and to lose oneself in *how* it is reflected. The aesthetic experiencing of a sensation makes its embodiment in life superfluous. To dream about a feat is easier than accomplishing it. The underground man's need for love is completely satisfied by "ready established forms, stolen from poets and novelists." "There was so much of it, of this love, that afterward the need to apply it in reality was not even felt; that would have been a superfluous luxury."

His investigation of consciousness brings the author to a conclusion regarding its perversity. "I swear to you, gentlemen, that to be overly conscious—this is a sickness, a real, out-and-out sickness." And nevertheless it is better to be "an acutely conscious mouse" than a "so-called direct man and agent." It is better to be an abnormal man than a normal animal. The source of consciousness is suffering, but man will not renounce suffering just as he will not renounce his *humanity.* Thus in the *Notes the sick consciousness is revealed to us as a human tragedy.*

After the analysis of consciousness there follows a "critique of pure reason." The ill-disposed readers, with whom the underground man is polemizing, begin to acquire concrete features. They are the positivists from *The Contemporary* and the *Russian Word.* These are the utilitarians and the rationalists like Chernyshevsky. Dostoevsky is defending man from the inhuman philosophy of necessity. With a boldness not inferior to that of Nietzsche and Kierkegaard, he rises up against the "stone wall" of impossibility. Reason sees the greatest wisdom in bowing down to necessity; can one really argue with the laws of nature, the conclusions of the natural sciences and the axioms of mathematics? Hegel's "world reason" very placidly crushes individual persons under the wheels of its triumphal chariot; the poisoning of Socrates and Galileo's burning do not affect it in the least. To reason's declaration: "it is impossible," the underground man answers defyingly: "I don't want to" and "I don't like it." "Lord God," he cries, "and what do I care for the laws of nature and arithmetic, when for some reason these laws and twice two is four displease me? Of course, I will not break through such a wall with my forehead if I really have not the strength to knock it down, but I am also not going to be reconciled to it simply because it is a stone wall, and I don't have enough strength."

This recalls the lamentations of Job contesting with God. The thrusts against the laws of reason are clothed in a blindingly paradoxical form. The underground man does not deliberate, but mocks and "sticks out his tongue." "Twice two is four, after all, is a truly insufferable thing," he declares. "Twice two is four, why this, in my opinion, is simply an effrontery, sir. Twice two is four looks like a fop, stands across your road, arms akimbo, and spits. I am agreed that twice two is four is an excellent thing; but if we are to give everything its due, then twice two is five is also sometimes a very charming little thing."

The formula twice two is four is the victory of necessity and death. To believe in the ultimate future triumph of reason means to bury man in advance. When a list of all "reasonable" courses of action will be composed and all "reasonable" desires are calculated beforehand, then man will no longer have free will. The will will merge with intellect, and man will be converted into an organ stop or a piano key. Fortunately, this dream of the rationalists is not destined to be fulfilled, for intellect is not everything in a man, but only a part, whereas the will is the "manifestation of his entire life." The narrator most emphatically asserts that man is an *irrational* being whose chief aim is to preserve his humanity, i.e., free will.

[...]

The whole meaning of human existence, the whole meaning of human history lies in the self-assertion of the *irrational will* ("wild caprice, mad fancy"). The world process does not have any goal; progress does not exist; mankind is by no means striving after prosperity and order. It loves to construct and be happy, but perhaps it enjoys destruction and suffering not a bit less. Man is eternally condemned to go somewhere, but he has no desire at all to arrive there; he suspects that the end, once attained, is something in the nature of a mathematical formula, i.e., death. Consequently, he upholds his independence, *"to whatever it may lead,"* opens a road *"to wherever it may be."* The underground man ends his investigations of the will with the taunt: "In a word, man is structured comically; there is obviously a joke contained in all this." The paradoxalist scoffs at the *tragedy of the will* which has been opened before him.

[...]

The underground man's confession is the philosophical preface to the cycle of the great novels. Before Dostoevsky's work is disclosed to us as a vast five-act tragedy (*Crime and Punishment, The Idiot, The Devils,*

A Raw Youth, and *The Brothers Karamazov*), *Notes from Underground* introduces us to the *philosophy of tragedy*. In the bilious and "unsightly" chatter of the paradoxalist the Russian philosopher's greatest insights are expressed. Through the sharpened edge of analysis the sickness of consciousness is uncovered, its inertia and dichotomy, its inner tragedy. The struggle against reason and necessity leads to impotent "weeping and gnashing"—*to the tragedy of Nietzsche and Kierkegaard*. Investigation of the irrational blind will, being cast about in void *self-formation*, reveals the *tragedy* of personality and freedom. Finally, the critique of socialism concludes with an assertion of the *tragedy of historical process*, purposeless and bloody, and the *tragedy of world evil*, which cannot be cured by any socialistic "earthly paradise." In this sense *Notes from Underground* is the greatest *attempt at a philosophy of tragedy* in world literature. The malicious despair and intrepid cynicism of the underground man unmasks all the idols, all the "sublimating frauds," all the "noble and beautiful," all the comforting illusions and salutary fictions, everything by which man has enclosed himself from the "dark abyss." Man is on the brink of a precipice—here is the *paysage* of tragedy. The author leads us through terror and destruction, but does he bring us to mystical purification, to a catharsis? Is it possible that "sitting with arms folded" and "intentional pouring water through a sieve" are the final word in his skeptic philosophy? To consider the *Notes* as an expression of "metaphysical despair" would mean not to observe what is *most important* in their design. The force of the underground man's revolt stems not from indifference and doubt, but from a passionate, exalted faith. He contends so vehemently with falsehood because a new truth has been opened for him. He still cannot find a *word* for it and is forced to speak in hints and circumlocutions.

[...]

And so, the dream of a genuine earthly paradise is central to *Notes*. The mockery and blasphemy are only "for form's sake," for the heightened contrast, to lend as much reinforcement as possible to the negative argumentation. In answer to it there had to appear a religious affirmation: "the need of faith and Christ." One can conjecture that at the base of the structuring of an "earthly paradise" the author would have placed that profound idea of brotherhood which he had contemplated in the *Winter Notes on Summer Impressions*. The union of personality with the communal would be justified religiously: by faith in Christ.

[...]

In the perspective of such a design the *Notes'* metaphysical significance becomes apparent to us. Dostoevsky is not investigating that
abstract "universal man" contrived by Jean-Jacques Rousseau, whom he
derisively calls the *homme de la nature et de la verité*, but the concrete
man of the 19th century in all his moral "unsightliness." He is talking
not about the "normal" consciousness which exists only in the bookish
theories of humanists, but about the real consciousness of the civilized
European. This consciousness is split in two, distorted, sick. Translating this definition into religious terms, we will say: Dostoevsky is
analyzing the *sinful consciousness of fallen man.*

[...]

By means of "negative argumentation," so characteristic of the
writer, the fundamental lie of humanism is refuted: that it is possible
to reeducate man through reason and advantage. Dostoevsky objects:
"No, evil is not overcome by education, but by a miracle. What is
impossible to man, is possible to God. Not reeducation, but *resurrection.*" Here is the reason for the "need of faith and Christ."

The second part of the *Notes*, the tale *Apropos of the Wet Snow*, is
joined to the first stylistically. The underground man's confession is an
inner dialogue, a polemic, a struggle against an imaginary enemy. In
the tale the inner dialogue becomes external, the fight is transferred
from the sphere of ideas into the plane of life, the imaginary enemies
are embodied in real ones: colleagues in the service, his obnoxious
servant Apollon, his former school companions, at the head of whom
stands the officer Zverkov, a dull, self-centered "normal man." The
paradoxalist creeps out of his underground into the light of day,
encounters the hostile world and, in conflict with it, suffers a shameful
defeat: This practical experience completes the "tragedy of the solitary
consciousness."

[...]

The underground man wants to find out: "whether it is possible
to be completely open if only with one's own self and not fear the
whole truth?" His confession has a religious significance; this is the
repentance of a sinner. He is writing it down since it will appear more
solemn on paper.... "*There will be a greater judgment upon one's self.*"

And he judges himself mercilessly. He is "a coward and a slave";
he has a monstrous intolerance and aversion toward people; in the

chancery he despises and hates all his fellow clerks. He leads a dissipated life "in seclusion, at night, secretly, timorously, sordidly, with shame," and in his corner escapes into everything "beautiful and noble," imagining himself a hero and benefactor of mankind. [...]

The tragedy of human communality—here is the theme of the tale *Apropos of the Wet Snow*. It is developed in two aspects: upon the tragedy of friendship follows the still more profound tragedy of love.

After the night spent with the prostitute Liza, the underground man "turns her soul upside down" with his noble pathos. He represents to her the horror of her life, draws an idyllic picture of the family, of love for a husband and child. Liza is overwhelmed and torn by confusion; for a long time she weeps bitterly, hiding her face in the pillow. The hero speaks with ardor and sincerely, but all this is a "game." He knows that the underground has already killed his every capacity for living life, that all his feelings are a "mirage" and self-deception, that he is doomed to the most shameful impotence. And from the awareness his tenderness toward Liza reverts to hatred. He runs about the room and curses: "It's like that, the damned romanticism of all these *pure hearts!* Oh, the obscenity, oh, the stupidity, oh, the poverty of these wretched sentimental souls!"

Love, goodness, purity arouse a demonic enmity in the doomed sinner; for his own sin he takes vengeance upon the just. Liza comes; she has left the "bawdy house" for good; love has transformed her. She surrenders her heart trustingly and modestly to her "savior." But instead of a "savior" she meets a malicious and dirty avenger who profanes her by his diabolic lust. "She guessed that the outburst of my passion had been simply revenge, a fresh humiliation for her, and that to my recent, most causeless hatred was now added a *personal* hatred, *born of envy.* ..." The underground man completes his hideous revenge with a final "villainous act"; he shoves money into the hand of his deathly pale victim. ...

So ends the dreamer-romantic who for forty years has sat in the underground. The "noble and beautiful" does not elevate, but corrupts; "natural good" turns into demonic evil. It is useless to preach the justification of the humiliated and restoration of the fallen, and the disillusioned philanthrope's love reverts to frenzied hate. The story of Liza is a parody on the romantic theme of the corrupted woman's salvation through love. Nekrasov's humane verses serve as an epigraph to it:

> When out of the darkness of error,
> By an ardent word of persuasion
> I rescued your fallen soul,
> And filled with profound torment,
> Wringing your hands, you cursed
> The vice which had enveloped you. . . .

The author interrupts the quotation with a mocking "Etc., etc., etc."

The tragedy of the underground man's love is the shattering of all romantic ethics. "Natural love" is as impotent as "natural good." This is one of the fundamental ideas of Dostoevsky's world outlook. It is most pointedly expressed in the *Diary of a Writer* for 1876: "Moreover, I assert," writes the author, "that the consciousness of our own utter inability to help or to bring, if only some, benefit or relief to suffering mankind, while at the same time remaining completely convinced of this suffering, can even *transform the love of mankind in your heart into hatred for it.*"

Notes from Underground is a turning point in Dostoevsky's creative work. Fallen Adam is cursed and condemned, and it is impossible to save him through human powers. But out of the "shadow of death" there is revealed a way to God, the "need of faith and Christ." The tragic philosophy is a religious philosophy.

NOTE

1. M.M. Bakhtin, *Problemy tvorchestva Dostoevskogo* (Problems of Dostoevsky's Creative Work), Leningrad 1929.

ONE FLEW OVER THE CUCKOO'S NEST (KEN KESEY)

"The Grail Knight Arrives"
by Raymond M. Olderman,
in *Beyond the Waste Land* (1972)

INTRODUCTION

In his study of *One Flew Over the Cuckoo's Nest*, Raymond M. Olderman compares the book's asylum with the world described in T.S. Eliot's poem *The Waste Land*, often interjecting lines from the Eliot poem to describe the site of imprisonment in Kesey's novel: "The waste land of the asylum is characterized not only by mechanization and efficiency but by sterility, hopelessness, fear, and guilt. The inmates are aimless, alienated and bored; they long for escape; they 'can connect / Nothing with Nothing,' not even picture puzzles; they are enervated and emasculated; their dignity is reduced to something less than human." Noting the alienating effects of the institution and the way such institutions "symbolize that immense power that reduces us," Olderman comments on the way we internalize systems of power with all their dictates while failing to make sense of an irrational world, "a world gone mad." Thus, for Olderman, to live in modern society means being caught in an alienated space in which

Olderman, Raymond M. "The Grail Knight Arrives." *Beyond the Waste Land.* New Haven: Yale UP, 1972. 35–51.

stems from both the institutions that overshadow us and the irrational drives that make us believe the waking world is a fantasy that excludes us.

∽⋎∽

Randle Patrick McMurphy sweeps into the asylum wasteland of Ken Kesey's *One Flew Over the Cuckoo's Nest* like April coming to T.S. Eliot's wasteland: "mixing / Memory and desire, stirring / Dull roots with spring rain." He literally drags the unwilling asylum wastelanders out of the tranquilized fog that protects them—a fog that is forever "snowing down cold and white all over" (p. 7),[1] where they try to hide "in forgetful snow, feeding / A little life with dried tubers." And, by dragging them from their retreat, he cures the Fisher King, Chief Bromden—a six-foot-eight-inch giant from a tribe of "fish Injuns," who is wounded, like all other wastelanders, in his manhood. The cure takes hold most dramatically on a fishing trip when McMurphy supplies the Chief and eleven other disciples with drink for their thirst, a woman for their desires, stimulation for their memories, and some badly needed self-respect for their shriveled souls—and all this despite the fact that the Chief "fears death by water." ("Afraid I'd step in over my head and drown, be sucked off down the drain and clean out to sea. I used to be real brave around water when I was a kid." [p. 160]) The silent Chief's voice is restored and he becomes the prophet who narrates the tale, while the false prophet—the enemy, the Big Nurse, Madam Sosostris, who has the "movement of a tarot-card reader in a glass arcade case" (p. 188)—is deprived of her voice in the last moments of the book.

The tale takes place in the ward of an insane asylum where an iron-minded, frost-hearted nurse rules by means of one twentieth-century version of brutality—mental and spiritual debilitation. Her patients are hopeless "Chronics" and "Vegetables," or they are "Acutes" who do not, according to McMurphy, seem "any crazier than the average asshole on the street" (p. 63). McMurphy comes to the asylum from a prison work farm. He has been a logger, a war hero, a gambler, and generally a happy, heavily muscled, self-made drifter and tough guy. A contest develops between McMurphy (whose initials, R.P.M., urge us to note his power) and the Big Nurse (whose name, Ratched, tips us off about her mechanical nature as well as her offensive function as a "ball-cutter"). The implications of the contest deepen; it becomes a battle pitting the individual against all those things that make up the modern wasteland, for the Nurse represents singly what the institution and its rules really are. The drama of the battle is intense, and the action seesaws as McMurphy gradually discovers he must give his strength to others in order to pry loose the Big Nurse's hold on their manhood. As they gain in health, McMurphy weakens, and his ultimate victory over the Big Nurse is a mixed one. He is lobotomized, a "castration of the frontal lobes," but he gives his lifeblood to Chief Bromden who breaks free and leaves behind in the Nurse and the Institution not a destroyed power, but a shrunken, silent, and temporarily short-circuited one. Beautifully structured, the novel provides us with both a brilliant version of our contemporary wasteland and a successful Grail Knight, who frees the Fisher King and the human spirit for a single symbolic and transcendent moment of affirmation.

The world of this wasteland is mechanically controlled from a central panel, as the narrator sees it, so that everything in it is run by tiny electrical wires or installed machinery. People are often robots or are made of electric tubing and wiring and springs, as the "adjusted" ones seem to be. The Big Nurse is only one agent of a "Combine" which rules all things, including time and the heart and mind of man. *Combine*, as the word implies, is not just an organization; it is a mechanism, a machine that threshes and levels; its ends are Efficiency and Adjustment. According to Chief Bromden, the Combine had gone a long way in doing things to gain total control,

> things like, for example—a *train* stopping at a station and laying a string of full-grown men in mirrored suits and machine hats, laying them like a hatch of identical insects, half-life things coming pht-pht-pht out of the last car, then hooting its electric whistle and moving on down the spoiled land to deposit another hatch. (pp. 227–28)

Those are the adjusted ones. The ones who cannot adjust are sent to the asylum to have things installed so that the Combine can keep them in line.

> The ward is a factory for the Combine. It's for fixing up mistakes made in the neighborhoods and in the schools and the churches, the hospital is. When a completed product goes back out into society, all fixed up good as new, *better* than new sometimes, it brings joy to the Big Nurse's heart; something that came in all twisted different is now a functioning, adjusted component, a credit to the whole outfit and a marvel to behold. Watch him sliding across the land with a welded grin, fitting into some nice little neighborhood. (p. 38)

He is a "Dismissal," spiritually and morally empty, but "happy" and adjusted. If you do not fit, you are a malfunctioning machine— "machines with flaws inside that can't be repaired, flaws born in, or flaws beat in over so many years of the guy running head-on into solid things that by the time the hospital found him he was bleeding rust in some vacant lot" (p. 4). That is what is called a "Chronic." Some people do escape in a way. People like McMurphy who keep moving, and people like Pete Bancini who are just too simple, are missed by the Combine, and if they are lucky, they can get hidden and stay missed.

All this is only the view of the narrator, a paranoid Indian. But there is enough evidence in the way the world around Chief Bromden runs to make his terms more and more acceptable as the novel progresses. Among the few characters on the "Outside" that Kesey takes the time to describe is one of the insulting loafers who taunt the patients while they wait to board their boat for the fishing trip. The man is described as having "purple under his eyes," the same kind of purple that appears under the eyes of all the ward's finished, lobotomized products. There is, at least for a moment, a frightening suggestion that the Combine's inmates may truly be everywhere. For Chief Bromden, it is no madman's logic—after seeing the actual persecution of his father, family, and tribe by the U.S. Department of the Interior—to posit a large central organization that seeks the doom of all things different.

The wasteland of the asylum is characterized not only by mechanization and efficiency but by sterility, hopelessness, fear, and guilt. The inmates are aimless, alienated, and bored; they long for escape; they "can connect / Nothing with Nothing," not even picture puzzles; they are enervated and emasculated; their dignity is reduced to something less than human. Most of all, they are run as the asylum is run—by women; it is a "matriarchy," and behind almost every ruined man is a grasping, castrating female whose big bosom belies her sterility but reveals a smothering momism. So, McMurphy perceives almost immediately that Big Nurse Ratched is pecking at their "everlovin' balls." But the same has been true of Harding's wife, and Chief Bromden's mother, and Billy Bibbit's mother—and these are just about the only women we see in the novel, except a couple of sweet whores named Candy and Sandy. However, what is more startling about this terrible world is its leveling sense of order and its rules. In one incident McMurphy wants to brush his teeth before the proper teeth-brushing time. He is told that the toothpaste is locked up. After questioning the aide about what possible harm anyone could do with a tube of toothpaste, he is advised that the toothpaste is locked up because it is the rule, and rules are rules. After all, what would happen if everyone just started brushing his teeth whenever he had a mind to. Kesey's point by this time is clear; the true madness, the real dry rot of the wasteland is not the patient's irrationality, but the deadly order, system, and rationality of the institution. What is normal is perverted, and reason becomes madness, while some small hope for salvation lies in the nonrational if not the downright irrational.

All of what the institution means and its effect on humanity come together in the single person of the Big Nurse, who causes the patients' hopelessness, their inadequacy, fear, anxiety, and alienation. She is the institution itself, the wasteland personified. White and starched stiff, she suggests Melville's plunge into the dreadful ambiguity and possible evil that could live in the heart of what is white. (McMurphy wears fancy shorts with jumping white whales on them, given to him by an Oregon State coed who called him a "symbol.") But with the Big Nurse the ambiguity is only superficial and thrives only on the name of respectability—her real villainy is clear. She is the enemy, the "Belladonna," obstacle to the Grail Knight. She enervates her patients by playing upon their fears, guilts, and inadequacies. She and all other castrators are "people who try to make you weak so they can get you to toe the line, to follow their rules, to live like they want you to. And the best way to do this, to get you to knuckle under, is to weaken you by gettin' you where it hurts the worst" (p. 58). She is relentless in her crippling pity and capable of using any weapon in order to preserve her control. She has handpicked her aides, three shadowy and sadistic

black men who are hooked to her by electrical impulses of hate. They
have been twisted by white brutality, and their response is savage. As
weapons in the Big Nurse's arsenal, they serve as symbols of the force
of guilt, which she uses to torment her patients. Guilt and the black
man twine identities in the white mind to cut deeper into its already
vitiated self-respect.

[. . .]

   One Flew Over the Cuckoo's Nest is a modern fable pitting a
fabulous kind of good against a fabulous kind of evil and making
use of many of the traditional devices of American romance. . . . For
example, [the novel] emphasizes plot and action (not character), and
it employs myth, allegory, and symbol. There are equally obvious
points of contact between the themes of Kesey's book and traditional
American themes, [such as] the rebellion against old orders and old
hierarchies, and the need for communal effort in the face of an alien
and overwhelmingly negative force. [*Cuckoo's Nest*] is closely tied to
American tradition, yet there is much in it that offers a paradigm
for what is different about the characteristic vision in the American
novel of the 1960s. It does not return to the past, gaze toward the
future, or travel to the unknown to get its "romance" setting. The
setting is the static institution which sums up both the preoccupation of our age with the mystery of power, and the substitution of
an image of the wasteland for the image of a journey between Eden
and Utopia. It is shot through with the vitality of its use of the here
and now. We are constantly shocked into discovering how the book
is really tied to the recognizable, not to the distant or strange, but to
our very own world—to the technology we know, the clichés we use,
the atmosphere possible only in the atomic tension of our times. Just
as no one can confidently say who is mad and who is not in Kesey's
novel, no one can say in what sense his story is real and in what sense
it is fiction. The narrator sounds a note that echoes everywhere in
the sixties: "You think this is too horrible to have really happened,
this is too awful to be the truth! But please. It's still hard for me to
have a clear mind thinking on it. But it's the truth even if it didn't
happen" (p. 8). The romance elements in the book are not based on
devices that whisk us away to some "theatre, a little removed from the
highway of ordinary travel,"[2] and then whisk us back fueled up with
truth. We suspect with horror that what we are seeing very possibly *is*
our highway of ordinary travel, fantastic as it may seem.

[. . .]

The Big Nurse, The Combine, The Asylum—all three seem to symbolize that immense power that reduces us, and that seems to be mysteriously unlocatable. Kesey is one of those writers of the sixties who explore some mystery about Fact itself that portends mostly defeat for man. This sense of mystery adds complexity to the paradoxes of what is mad and sane, real and unreal, for it drives us to seek its heart in some huge force conspiring against us. Although it arises in connection with the image of the wasteland, this mystery is the antipathy of Eliot's hoped-for God. It is only a further cause of divisive fear.

The mystery is best represented, to Kesey, by the asylum itself, but he leaves us with two possible locations of the mystery's source. It could be located somewhere external to us as Chief Bromden sees it, or as McMurphy tries to explain, maybe blaming it on a Combine is "just passing the buck." It may be our own "deep-down hang-up that's causing the gripes." Perhaps there is some big bad wolf—and then perhaps there is only us. In the past the essential shock in American fictional experience has been a character's discovery that deep down he too is capable of evil; the shock in the sixties is the character's discovery that deep down he may be the source of unrelenting insanity. Down there, perhaps, that unknowable and seemingly immense power against us comes into being and then mounts to become a world gone mad. Against that or within that, the writer, the prophet, sees new paradoxes of reason and irrationality, fact and mystery, and writes his novels no longer sure of what is fact or fiction and where malevolence lies—within or without. His only rationale can be the one stated by one of Kesey's characters: "These things don't happen. . . . These things are fantasies you lie awake at night dreaming up and then are afraid to tell your analyst. You're not *really* here. That wine isn't real; *none* of this exists. Now, let's go on from there" (p. 285).

NOTES

1. Page numbers for citations will be included parenthetically in the text.
2. Nathaniel Hawthorne, "Preface" to *Blithedale Romance* (New York: Norton, 1958), p. 27.

THE STRANGE CASE
OF DR. JEKYLL AND MR. HYDE
(ROBERT LOUIS STEVENSON)

"Masks in the Mirror: The Eighteen-Nineties"
by Masao Miyoshi,
in *The Divided Self: A Perspective
on the Literature of the Victorians* (1969)

INTRODUCTION

Part of a larger work on the "double" in Victorian fiction, Masao Miyoshi's essay on *The Strange Case of Dr. Jekyll and Mr. Hyde* depicts late Victorian England as a "wasteland, truly a de-Hyde-rated land unfit to sustain a human being simultaneously in an honorable public life and a joyful private one." This tension between private and public sustains Miyoshi's argument about the duplicity and hypocrisy of the self. As Miyoshi explains, "To Stevenson, the real world was not so boring really as it was simply unmanageable. More precisely, it was the self that was unmanageable, problematic in relation to the rest of life, for the biggest problem was what to do about the hypocrisy of one's own life and the lives around one." Caught in this dance of doubles, the Victorian person, according to Miyoshi, is alienated, pulled between the public

---

Miyoshi, Masao. "Masks in the Mirror: The Eighteen-Nineties." *The Divided Self: A Perspective on the Literature of the Victorians.* New York: New York University Press, 1969. 289-340.

and private, revealed and unrevealed—the world of Dr. Jekyll
and Mr. Hyde.

෴

Life imitates Art far more than Art imitates Life.
"The Decay of Lying"

We make out of the quarrel with others, rhetoric, but of the
quarrel with ourselves, poetry.
"Per Amica Silentia Lunae"

André Gide met Oscar Wilde several times during the early nineties,
and on one occasion that he recalls, Wilde inquired of him what he
had been up to since their last meeting. Gide, a serious young man
already taking sincerity seriously, recounted a few trifling incidents,
which prompted Wilde to ask, Did he really do that? Was he *really*
telling the truth? "Absolutely," said Gide, apparently gulled. "Then why
repeat it?" countered Wilde. "You must see that it is not of the slightest
importance." And he continued lecturing, "You must understand that
there are two worlds—the one exists and is never talked about; it is
called the real world because there is no need to talk about it in order
to see it. The other is the world of Art; one must talk about that,
because otherwise it would not exist."[1]

This Wildean anecdote, like the Wildean epigram, comprises the
time, Wilde himself being, of course, its most perfect exemplar. If life
seemed on the whole dull and inconsequential, art at least was something to talk about, and perhaps of occasional consequence. The argument is inescapable: One must live one's life as though it were art. But
to consciously imitate art is finally to switch roles with it. Dorian Gray
trades lives with his art-double, the idealized portrait, and makes for
a time a beautiful life for himself—one is tempted to say, a life pretty
as a picture. Of all the writers of the nineties it is surely in Wilde that
the art of the self is at its most deliberate, its most artificial. Ultimately
Wilde's art is the art of the lie, staged spectacularly as in a Cecil
Beaton production. Next to the glories of that negotiated life, ordinary
existence—even Dorian's monstrous reality as disclosed at last in the
portrait—diminishes and dies.

To Stevenson, the real world was not so boring really as it was simply unmanageable. More precisely, it was the self that was unmanageable, problematic in relation to the rest of life, for the biggest problem was what to do about the hypocrisy of one's own life and the lives around one. In a sense, his essay into the double life, *Dr. Jekyll and Mr. Hyde*, is a more conventional statement than *Dorian Gray*, for all their thematic similarity. In Stevenson, hypocrisy, the lie at the very core of life, is still moralistically conceived. While Jekyll and his ilk continue to live the lie of respectability, the "idealized" double who is Jekyll's joyboy must carry the burden of disguise. Jekyll fears disclosure of the Hyde who is his "true" identity in the same way that the Puritan fears disclosure of his secret sexuality, not for reason primarily of shame but for fear of losing forever the exquisite pleasure of that second life. The paradox of Stevenson is that his joy can never free itself, whether in art or in the art of life, from the brand of gutter guilt that was his heritage.

[. . .]

The double, whether as epipsyche, self-portrait, or monster, is for these writers the vehicle of self-creation. Indeed, consciousness of self implies doubleness, the consciousness aware of itself. Whether it is the "metaphysical" double of Hardy's novels or the "aesthetic" double of Wilde, the writers of the nineties take the insufficiency of the mere *ur*-self, the born identity, as axiomatic. Life experience, the development of self-consciousness, is for them mere matter for the life of art. At the point where art is found to be illusion, a lie at last, the life which is its source, and which in turn models its further life on art, is unavoidably a lie—and this, whether the lie is looked upon as salvation (Wilde) or damnation (Hardy). Either way the autonomy of art relative to life is beyond compromise. Wilde is clear on this in "The Decay of Lying": "As long as a thing is useful or necessary to us, or affects us in any way . . . it is outside the proper sphere of art."[2]

This distinction was present, too, in the theory of the novel at that time. It was abruptly in the eighties, fully a hundred years after Walpole's Preface, that the novel-romance controversy flared again among English writers. This time the romance genre was contrasted with the naturalistic novel of Zola. One of Stevenson's early theoretical statements, "A Gossip on Romance" (1882), argues that a romance should "embody character, thought, or emotion in some act or attitude that shall be remarkably striking to the mind's eye."[3] Although an author will certainly draw his material from ordinary life, mere representation is not his purpose. "Fiction," Stevenson believes, "is to the grown man what play is to the child" (201). The following year, he attacked the overuse of detail in modern literature, arguing that the contemporary interest in realism has little to do with the "fundamental truth" of a work of art, being simply concerned with its "technical method" ("A Note on Realism"). The romance, just as the novel, must of its nature tell the truth. The distinction between the two forms rests rather on their differing degrees of inclusiveness: The realist tends in his "insane pursuit of completion," to "immolate his readers under facts"; the romancer, in contrast, is likely to become "merely null and lose all grip of fact, particularity, or passion."[4]

In "A Humble Remonstrance" (1884), Stevenson agrees with Henry James's "Art of Fiction" but goes further (James had denied any difference either between the novel and the romance or between the novel of character and the novel of incidence), asserting that there is no distinction between fiction in prose and fiction in verse, or even between fiction and "nonfiction" such as history or biography. Common to all genres is the art of narrative, which is not representative of real life. Stevenson, borrowing a phrase from James, insists that no art can be expected to "compete with life." Where life is "monstrous, infinite, illogical, abrupt, and poignant," art is "neat, finite, self-contained, rational, flowing, and emasculate."[5] Like a proposition in geometry, an art object expresses existence, but it cannot reproduce it. It is not a "transcript of life" but a "simplification of some side or point of life, to stand or fall by its significant simplicity" (p. 100). To Stevenson art cannot *be* life, though it can *have* a life of its own.

After more than a century of theory, which strictly segregated the two streams of English fiction—the novel and the romance—the men of the nineties, already redefining their lives, redefined their books. However "realistic" a literary work may be, it cannot be a point-by-point reproduction of "reality," because "reality" is unascertained. Rather, the artist makes reality by shaping the inchoate material often called "reality." Understanding this, these artists were led to another notion, which Wilde would so nicely formulate, that art is to a far greater degree independent of mere life than the realist or the naturalist would accept. Art leads a life of its own, with the consequence that the artist can employ in his art whatever he finds suitable, however irrational or inexplicable it may be. In fact, the artist begins about this time to surrender the common sense and commonplace entirely to the life-styles of the "ordinary" middle classes, while appropriating the extraordinary and the improbable as his proper domain. And, just as the poet forges his language of symbolism—unintelligible to all but the initiate—to express his vision of reality, so the novelist discovers new forms and techniques—point of view, altered time sequence, and stream of consciousness[6] —that alone express his.

Intricately involved in this asserted alienation of the artist is the marked resurgence of Gothicism. That this mode had been all along highly attractive to many writers is clear from the strong current of the Gothic imagination throughout Victorian literature. However, the earlier restraints on it (Charlotte Brontë's dominion over the "nether world," for instance) are no longer very effective. The sudden plethora of dual-personality stories in the nineties,[7] partly the result, no doubt, of the huge circulation figures run up by both *Dr. Jekyll and Mr. Hyde* and *Dorian Gray*, is surely better explained in terms of the great impetus the form provided writers to explore the dark side of human nature.

Dr. Jekyll and Mr. Hyde (1886) was by no means the first product of Stevenson's fascination with the dual personality. From childhood he had been familiar with the legend of Deacon Brodie, daylight cabinetmaker and moonlight burglar, and a full twenty years before *Dr. Jekyll and Mr. Hyde* he was already working on a play based on Brodie's life.[8] In 1883 he wrote a wretched and revolting story ("The Travelling Companion"), which was turned down by his publisher and which he himself soon decided to destroy. He called it a "carrion tale," and later explained why he had written it: "I had long been trying to write a story on this subject, to find a body, a vehicle, for that strong sense of man's double being which must at times come in upon and overwhelm the mind of every thinking creature."[9]

[. . .]

It is best to envision the world of the story—the men and the landscape—before turning to the Jekyll-Hyde relationship itself. To begin with Mr. Utterson, a highly respected citizen and counselor: In his professional life, he is always correct and trustworthy, yet there is something furtive and suppressed about him. He is "austere with himself." He never smiles. He is "cold, scanty, and embarrassed in discourse" (Chapter 1).[10] He claims to like the theater, though he has not been to a play in twenty years. He makes no new friends and socializes only with men he has known well for a very long time. As for his renowned tolerance of other people's misconduct, this looks suspiciously to be the result not of sophistication or even good will but of indifference, though there is the subtlest suggestion of vicarious pleasure. Utterson, too, it turns out, has a past not quite innocent. When it occurs to him that blackmail may be at the root of Hyde's connection with Jekyll, he considers the possibility of a similar threat to himself: "And the lawyer, scared by the thought, brooded a while on his own past, groping in all the corners of memory, lest by chance some Jack-in-the-Box of an old iniquity should leap to light there" (Chapter 2). When his friend and client Sir Danvers Carew is murdered, the event stirs no deeper feeling in him than worry "lest the good name of another should be sucked down in the eddy of the scandal" (Chapter 5). And when his relative Mr. Enfield correctly observes the unspoken rule of never asking questions—"the more it looks like Queer Street, the less I ask" (Chapter 1)—Utterson concurs. Only the sight of Mr. Hyde's unpleasant face cracks the smooth varnish of his existence, making him feel "(what was rare with him) a nausea and distaste of life" (Chapter 2).

Dr. Hastie Lanyon is, by contrast, an outwardly healthy and genial man, yet he too is shielded from life by an imposing respectability. Estranged from Dr. Jekyll for ten years, Dr. Lanyon is a scientist of "practical usefulness" (Chapter 9), who sees Jekyll as a man gone wrong with his "scientific heresies" (Chapter 3). As it happens, when the great Dr. Lanyon confronts a phenomenon which his matter-of-fact science cannot explain, his life is "shaken to its roots" (Chapter 9). He says to Utterson, "I sometimes think if we knew all, we should be more glad to get away" (Chapter 6). Too late he has learned something of the ghastly aspect of life, and, with undiminishing horror at it all, he shrivels and dies.[11]

The important men of the book, then, are all unmarried, intellectually barren, emotionally stifled, joyless. Nor are things much different in the city as a whole. The more prosperous business people fix up their homes and shops, but in a fashion without chic. Houses give an appearance of "coquetry," and store fronts invite one like "rows of smiling saleswomen" (Chapter 1). The rather handsome town houses in the back streets of Dr. Jekyll's neighborhood are rented out to all sorts—"map-engravers, architects, shady lawyers, and the agents of obscure enterprises" (Chapter 2). Everywhere the fog of the dismal city is inescapable, even creeping under the doors and through the window jambs (Chapter 5). The setting hides a wasteland behind that secure and relatively comfortable respectability of its inhabitants.

In such a milieu Dr. Jekyll stands out as "the very pink of the proprieties" (Chapter 1). Although his studies tend toward "the mystic and the transcendental" (Chapter 10), like those of Faust and Frankenstein before him, he still manages to maintain a considerable scientific reputation. Despite Jekyll's social and professional caste—in fact, because of it—it is he, rather than Utterson or Lanyon, who brings forth Mr. Hyde.

It will be remembered that, for a period long before the emergence of Mr. Hyde, Dr. Jekyll had experienced a "profound duplicity of life"; alongside his "imperious desire" for dignity and reputation, there was that "impatient gaiety of disposition" (Chapter 10). But for those in the Victorian wasteland, gaiety and respectability are not easily reconciled. Dr. Jekyll, in particular, sees the two as mutually exclusive: A respectable pleasure would be a contradiction in terms. The exacting nature of his moral ambition was such that the most innocent delight resulted in shame. Meanwhile, his Faustian studies, which had already made him conscious of the "perennial war among [his] members" (Chapter 10), suggested a practical means of settling the whole question. However, where Faust was Promethean, irrepressible, by definition, Jekyll, the latter-day Faust, must at all costs button himself down, hold his place as a reputable man and even rise in the establishment if he can. And so, though pleasure had been suppressed for a long time by the dreary decency that was his life, Dr. Jekyll will enjoy it, after all, in the person of a totally new identity, Edward Hyde.

Hyde, once unleashed, arouses disgust in everyone. Dr. Jekyll's servant, for one, feels "kind of cold and thin" in his marrow after meeting Hyde for the first time (Chapter 8), and even the "Sawbones" has the urge to do away with him. To catch sight of Hyde is to be reminded of the hidden "*je*" in each of us, the "troglodytic" (Chapter 2) animal that lies in wait for the moment of release.

In most societies men are not required to suppress the "*je*" totally, and they agree to curb it. But in Jekyll's world, the "*je*" must be ruthlessly suppressed—most unequivocally so by the man known as "the very pink of the proprieties," Dr. Henry Jekyll, the most thoroughgoing "*je*-killer" of them all.

Hyde, at once Jekyll's Mephistopheles and his (Frankenstein) monster, looks like the very incarnation of evil, but at the beginning he is in fact merely Jekyll's unrepressed spontaneous existence. Going about in the guise of Mr. Hyde, Dr. Jekyll discovers a new freshness and joy in his life. He feels "younger, lighter, happier in body" and is conscious of a "heady recklessness," of a "current of disordered sensual images running like a mill-race in my fancy, a solution of the bonds of obligation, an unknown but not an innocent freedom of the soul" (Chapter 10). Not respectable certainly, and therefore utterly despicable by the standards of the Utterson-Enfield-Lanyon world.

However, Hyde gradually shows himself dissatisfied with his role as mere "impatient gaiety" and becomes scornful of the rights of others. His "every act and thought [are] centred on self" (Chapter 10). In fact, his pleasure comes to depend on his torturing others. At this point, the self and society are enemies to the death.

Soon after the episode in which Hyde tramples the child, the Jekyll-Hyde metamorphosis becomes involuntary. The doctor goes to bed Henry Jekyll and awakes as Edward Hyde. The hidden "*je*" released by the social "I" threatens now to overpower it. Yet he believes it is still within his strength to control Hyde. Resolving to forego the "leaping impulses and secret pleasures," he determines to live once again the life of an "elderly and discontented doctor" (Chapter 10). Of course, having once allowed his "*je*" the taste of freedom, he finds he cannot long suppress it. Soon Edward Hyde leaps out "roaring" (Chapter 10) from the cave of Henry Jekyll. When the brutal murder of Sir Danvers Carew is disclosed, Jekyll's remorse is intense, if short-lived, recalling the amnesiac reaction of countless Gothic villains after indulging their sadism. Hyde is now a known criminal, hunted down not only by Utterson (who calls himself "Mr. Seek" [Chapter 2]) but also by the police, and the doctor can no longer risk taking advantage of the Hyde persona for his sojourns in the netherworld. The next time he goes out it is in the guise of Dr. Henry Jekyll. No wonder, then, that the metamorphosis should have become completely involuntary and the magic drug virtually ineffectual. There are no longer any marks to distinguish the two. The hideous face is forever joined to the social mask. The joining, however, is in no sense a reconcilement of the Jekyll-Hyde duality. Rather, it signals a return to the starting point of Jekyll's whole experience. Only the annihilation of one of the two selves "reconciles" them: at the end of the story the doctor finally suppresses the "*je*" by murdering Hyde, thereby, of course, becoming a "self-destroyer" (Chapter 8), a suicide.

Chesterton is the first to have pointed out the autobiographical elements in *Dr. Jekyll and Mr. Hyde*. He argues that Edinburgh, not London, is the scene of the story, on the basis that the black and white distinction of good and evil, the horror of tainting respectability with the disclosure of human failings, is Puritan, especially Caledonian. Chesterton sees Jekyll's fastidiousness as the trait of one who "knew the worst too young; not necessarily in his own act or by his own fault, but by the nature of a system which saw no difference between the worst and the moderately bad." [12] Stevenson himself, being the only child of a very pious couple, suffered from their Puritanical suppressions from his earliest days. Although he did rebel in adolescence, leaving home for a bohemian love-life in the Edinburgh slums, he was soon being suppressed again, this time by his wife, the respectable Fanny Osborne Stevenson. Since he did require her secretarial services, it gradually developed that both his work and his personal correspondence were regimented and censored by her. [13] No one has yet, of course, disclosed a Hyde lurking in the shadows of Stevenson's life, and the biographical interest must remain ancillary to the book itself. On its own, quite apart from its author's problems, *Dr. Jekyll and Mr. Hyde* is fascinating for its depiction of the two levels of man's being. It also provides a very convenient epithet ("Jekyll-and-Hyde") for the psychopath. For these reasons we can say that Stevenson was perhaps too successful in both story idea and execution. For the mastery of the book is the vision it conjures of the late Victorian wasteland, truly a de-Hyde-rated land unfit to sustain a human being simultaneously in an honorable public life and a joyful private one.

NOTES

1. André Gide, *Oscar Wilde: A Study*, trans. Stuart Mason (Oxford, 1905), pp. 27-28.

2. "The Decay of Lying," *The Complete Works of Oscar Wilde* (Garden City, 1923), V, p. 24.

3. *The Works of Robert Louis Stevenson*, Vailima Edition (London, 1922), XII, p. 193. Unless otherwise stated, references are to this edition throughout the discussion of Stevenson.

4. *Works*, IV, pp. 417 and 422.

5. *Henry James and Robert Louis Stevenson*, ed. Janet Adam Smith (London, 1948), pp. 90 and 92.

6. The phrase was of course used by William James in *The Principles of Psychology* (1890). There is a chapter in the book, incidentally, "The Consciousness of Self," which discusses the problem of the divided self, and he again pursues the question in *The Varieties of Religious Experience* (given as lectures in 1901 and 1902) in a chapter called "The Divided Self, and the Process of its Unification."

7. Gothicism responded quickly to the temper and taste of the mass reader with such books as Arthur Machen's *The Three Impostors*, George Manville Fenn's *The Man with a Shadow*, Sir Walter Besant's *The Ivory Gate*, Ella D'Arcy's *The Death Mask*, Robert Smyth Hichens' *Flames: A London Fantasy*, and Lyman Frank Baum's *Tod and Tot*—all but forgotten nowadays.

8. "Deacon Brodie; or, the Double Life" was coauthored by W.E. Henley, published in 1880, and produced in 1883. Later Stevenson revised it and published the new version in 1892.

9. *The Letters of Robert Louis Stevenson*, ed. Sidney Colvin (New York, 1911), II, p. 282, and "A Chapter on Dreams," *Works*, XII, p. 247.

10. *Works*, VII, Chapter 1. The chapters are not numbered in this edition, but I have done so here for ease of reference.

11. Dr. Lanyon's fate bears a strong resemblance to Captain Brierley's in *Lord Jim*.

12. *Robert Louis Stevenson* (New York, 1928), p. 53.

13. This is the view of Malcolm Elwin in his *The Strange Case of Robert Louis Stevenson* (London, 1950). Unfortunately, Elwin's

scanty documentation makes it hard to judge the correctness of his view of the author's personal life. Mr. Bradford Booth has informed me that his forthcoming edition of Stevenson's letters will correct Mr. Elwin's interpretation on many matters.

THE STRANGER AND THE MYTH OF SISYPHUS
(ALBERT CAMUS)

"Camus' *The Outsider*"
by Jean-Paul Sartre,
in *Literary and Philosophical Essays* (1955)

INTRODUCTION

As Jean-Paul Sartre argues, *The Myth of Sisyphus* is a philosophical companion to *The Stranger* (sometimes translated as "The Outsider"). In it, according to Sartre, "we find the theory of the novel of absurdity." Presenting Camus' philosophical ideas and applying them to the novel, Sartre focuses on alienation—the way the novel's protagonist, Meursault, exists outside of social norms: "The outsider he wants to portray is precisely one of those terrible innocents who shock society by not accepting the rules of its game. He lives among outsiders, but to them, too, he is an outsider. . . . And we ourselves, who, on opening the book are not yet familiar with the feeling of the absurd, vainly try to judge him according to our usual standards. For us, too, he is an outsider." Sartre defines the absurd as "both a state of fact and the lucid awareness which certain people acquire of this state of fact. . . . Chance, death, the irreducible pluralism of

Sartre, Jean-Paul. "Camus' *The Outsider*." *Literary and Philosophical Essays*. Trans. Annette Michelson. New York: Criterion, 1955. 26–44.

life and of truth, the unintelligibility of the real—all these are
extremes of the absurd." Sartre's essay stresses displacement, alienation—the absurdity Meursault and reader know.
For Camus and Sartre, life is alienating, absurd; we inhabit
an irrational world as exiles, separated from meaning, denied
truth, and abandoned by God.

☙❧

M. Camus' *The Outsider* was barely off the press when it began to
arouse the widest interest. People told each other that it was "the best
book since the end of the war." Amidst the literary productions of its
time, this novel was, itself, an outsider. It came to us from the other
side of the Equator, from across the sea. In that bitter spring of the
coal shortage, it spoke to us of the sun, not as of an exotic marvel, but
with the weary familiarity of those who have had too much of it. It was
not concerned with re-burying the old regime with its own hands, nor
with filling us with a sense of our own unworthiness.

We remembered, while reading this novel, that there had once
been works which had not tried to prove anything, but had been
content to stand on their own merits. But hand in hand with its
gratuitousness went a certain ambiguity. How were we to interpret
this character who, the day after his mother's death, "went swimming,
started a liaison with a girl and went to see a comic film," who killed
an Arab "because of the sun," who claimed, on the eve of his execution,
that he "had been happy and still was," and hoped there would be a lot
of spectators at the scaffold "to welcome him with cries of hate." "He's
a poor fool, an idiot," some people said; others, with greater insight,
said, "He's innocent." The meaning of this innocence still remained to
be understood.

In *The Myth of Sisyphus*, which appeared a few months later, M.
Camus provided us with a precise commentary upon his work. His
hero was neither good nor bad, neither moral nor immoral. These cate-
gories do not apply to him. He belongs to a very particular species for
which the author reserves the word "absurd." But in M. Camus' work
this word takes on two very different meanings. The absurd is both a
state of fact and the lucid awareness which certain people acquire of
this state of fact. The "absurd" man is the man who does not hesitate to
draw the inevitable conclusions from a fundamental absurdity.

There is the same displacement of meaning as when we give the name "swing" to the youthful generation that dances to "swing" music. What is meant by the absurd as a state of fact, as primary situation? It means nothing less than man's relation to the world. Primary absurdity manifests a cleavage, the cleavage between man's aspirations to unity and the insurmountable dualism of mind and nature, between man's drive toward the eternal and the *finite* character of his existence, between the "concern" which constitutes his very essence and the vanity of his efforts. Chance, death, the irreducible pluralism of life and of truth, the unintelligibility of the real—all these are extremes of the absurd.

These are not really very new themes, and M. Camus does not present them as such. They had been sounded as early as the seventeenth century by a certain kind of dry, plain, contemplative rationalism, which is typically French and they served as the commonplaces of classical pessimism.

Was it not Pascal who emphasized "the natural misfortune of our mortal and feeble condition, so wretched that when we consider it closely, nothing can console us"? Was it not he who put reason in its place? Would he not have wholeheartedly approved the following remark of M. Camus: "The world is neither (completely) rational, nor quite irrational either"? Does he not show us that "custom" and "diversion" conceal man's "nothingness, his forlornness, his inadequacy, his impotence and his emptiness" from himself? By virtue of the cool style of *The Myth of Sisyphus* and the subject of his essays, M. Camus takes his place in the great tradition of those French moralists whom Andler has rightly termed the precursors of Nietzsche.
[...]

The Myth of Sisyphus teaches us how to accept our author's novel. In it, we find the theory of the novel of absurdity. Although the absurdity of the human condition is its sole theme, it is not a novel with a message; it does not come out of a "satisfied" kind of thinking, intent on furnishing formal proofs. It is rather the product of a thinking which is "limited, rebellious and mortal." It is a proof in itself of the futility of abstract reasoning. "The fact that certain great novelists have chosen to write in terms of images rather than of arguments reveals a great deal about a certain kind of thinking common to them all, a conviction of the futility of all explanatory principles, and of the instructive message of sensory impressions." [1]

Thus, the very fact that M. Camus delivers his message in the form of a novel reveals a proud humility. This is not resignation, but the rebellious recognition of the limitations of human thought. It is true that he felt obliged to make a philosophical translation of his fictional message. *The Myth of Sisyphus* is just that, and we shall see later on how we are to interpret this parallel commentary. But the existence of the translation does not, in any case, alter the gratuitousness of the novel. [. . .]

The Outsider is not, however, to be regarded as a completely gratuitous work. M. Camus distinguishes, as we have mentioned, between the *notion* and the *feeling* of the absurd. He says, in this connection, "Deep feelings, like great works, are always more meaningful than they are aware of being. . . . An intense feeling carries with it its own universe, magnificent or wretched, as the case may be." [2] And he adds, a bit further on, "The feeling of the absurd is not the same as the *idea* of the absurd. The idea is grounded in the feeling, that is all. It does not exhaust it." *The Myth of Sisyphus* might be said to aim at giving us this *idea*, and *The Outsider* at giving us the feeling.

The order in which the two works appeared seems to confirm this hypothesis. *The Outsider*, the first to appear, plunges us without comment into the "climate" of the absurd; the essay then comes and illumines the landscape. Now, absurdity means divorce, discrepancy. *The Outsider* is to be a novel of discrepancy, divorce and disorientation; hence its skilful construction.

We have, on the one hand, the amorphous, everyday flow of reality as it is experienced, and, on the other, the edifying reconstruction of this reality by speech and human reason. The reader, brought face to face with simple reality, must find it again, without being able to recognize it in its rational transposition. This is the source of the feeling of the absurd, that is, of our inability to *think*, with our words and concepts, what happens in the world. Meursault buries his mother, takes a mistress and commits a crime.

These various facts will be related by witnesses at his trial, and they will be put in order and explained by the public prosecutor. Meursault will have the impression that they are talking of someone else. Everything is so arranged as to bring on the sudden outburst of Marie, who, after giving, in the witness-box, an account composed according to human rules, bursts into sobs and says "that that wasn't it, that there was something else, that they were forcing her to say the opposite of what she really thought." These mirror-tricks have been used frequently since *The Coiners*, and they do not constitute M. Camus' originality. But the problem to be solved imposes an original form upon him.

In order to feel the divergence between the prosecutor's conclusions and the actual circumstances of the murder, in order, when we have finished the book, to retain the impression of an absurd justice, incapable of ever understanding or even of making contact with the deeds it intends to punish, we must first have been placed in contact with reality, or with one of these circumstances. But in order to establish this contact, M. Camus, like the prosecutor, has only words and concepts at his disposal. In assembling thoughts, he is forced to use words to describe a world that precedes words. The first part of *The Outsider* could have been given the same title as a recent book, *Translated from Silence*. Here we touch upon a disease common to many contemporary writers and whose first traces I find in Jules Renard. I shall call it "the obsession with silence." M. Paulhan would certainly regard it as an effect of literary terrorism.

It has assumed a thousand forms, ranging from the surrealists' automatic writing to Jean-Jacques Bernard's "theatre of silence." The reason is that silence, as Heidegger says, is the authentic mode of speech. Only the man who knows how to talk can be silent. M. Camus talks a great deal; in *The Myth of Sisyphus* he is even garrulous. And yet, he reveals his love of silence. He quotes Kierkegaard: "The surest way of being mute is not to hold your tongue, but to talk."[3] And he himself adds that "a man is more of a man because of what he does not say than what he does say." Thus, in *The Outsider*, he has attempted *to be silent*. But how is one to be silent with words? How is one to convey through concepts the unthinkable and disorderly succession of present instants? This problem involves resorting to a new technique.

What is this new technique? "It's Kafka written by Hemingway," I was told. I confess that I have found no trace of Kafka in it. M. Camus' views are entirely of this earth, and Kafka is the novelist of impossible transcendence; for him, the universe is full of signs that we cannot understand; there is a reverse side to the décor. For M. Camus, on the contrary, the tragedy of human existence lies in the absence of any transcendence. "I do not know whether this world has a meaning that is beyond me. But I do know that I am unaware of this meaning and that, for the time being, it is impossible for me to know it. What can a meaning beyond my condition mean to me? I can understand only in human terms. I understand the things I touch, things that offer me resistance."

He is not concerned, then, with so ordering words as to suggest an inhuman, undecipherable order; the inhuman is merely the disorderly, the mechanical. There is nothing ambiguous in his work, nothing disquieting, nothing hinted at. *The Outsider* gives us a succession of luminously clear views. If they bewilder us, it is only because of their number and the absence of any link between them. M. Camus likes bright mornings, clear evenings and relentless afternoons. His favorite season is Algiers' eternal summer. Night has hardly any place in his universe.

When he does talk of it, it is in the following terms: "I awakened with stars about my face. Country noises reached my ears. My temples were soothed by odours of night, earth and salt. The wonderful peace of that sleepy summer invaded me like a tide."[4] The man who wrote these lines is as far removed as possible from the anguish of a Kafka. He is very much at peace within disorder. Nature's obstinate blindness probably irritates him, but it comforts him as well. Its irrationality is only a negative thing. The absurd man is a humanist; he knows only the good things of this world.

The comparison with Hemingway seems more fruitful. The relationship between the two styles is obvious. Both men write in the same short sentences. Each sentence refuses to exploit the momentum accumulated by preceding ones. Each is a new beginning. Each is like a snapshot of a gesture or object. For each new gesture and word there is a new and corresponding sentence. Nevertheless, I am not quite satisfied. The existence of an "American" narrative technique has certainly been of help to M. Camus. I doubt whether it has, strictly speaking, influenced him.

Even in *Death in the Afternoon*, which is not a novel, Hemingway retains that abrupt style of narration that shoots each separate sentence out of the void with a sort of respiratory spasm. His style is himself. We know that M. Camus has another style, a ceremonious one. But even in *The Outsider* he occasionally heightens the tone. His sentences then take on a larger, more continuous, movement. "The cry of the news-vendors in the relaxed air, the last birds in the square, the calls of the sandwich-vendors, the wail of the trams on the high curves of the city and the distant murmur in the sky before night began to teeter over the port, all set before me a blind man's route with which I was familiar long before entering prison."[5]

Through the transparency of Meursault's breathless account I catch a glimpse of a poetic prose underneath, which is probably M. Camus' personal mode of expression. If *The Outsider* exhibits such visible traces of the American technique, it was deliberate on M. Camus' part. He has chosen from among all the instruments at his disposal the one which seemed to serve his purpose best. I doubt whether he will use it again in future works.

Let us examine the plot a little more closely; we shall get a clearer notion of the author's methods. "Men also secrete the inhuman," writes M. Camus. "Sometimes, in moments of lucidity, the mechanical aspect of their gestures and their senseless pantomime make everything about them seem stupid."[6] This quality must be rendered at once. *The Outsider* must put us right from the start "into a state of uneasiness when confronted with man's inhumanity."

But what are the particular occasions that create this uneasiness in us? *The Myth of Sisyphus* gives us an example. "A man is talking on the telephone. We cannot hear him behind the glass partition, but we can see his senseless mimicry. We wonder why he is alive?"[7] This answers the question almost too well, for the example reveals a certain bias in the author. The gesturing of a man who is telephoning and whom we cannot hear is really only *relatively* absurd, because it is part of an incomplete circuit. Listen in on an extension, however, and the circuit is completed; human activity recovers its meaning. Therefore, one would have, in all honesty, to admit that there are only relative absurdities and only in relation to "absolute rationalities."

However, we are not concerned with honesty, but with art. M. Camus has a method ready to hand. He is going to insert a glass partition between the reader and his characters. Is there really anything sillier than a man behind a glass window? Glass seems to let everything through. It stops only one thing: the meaning of his gestures. The glass remains to be chosen. It will be the Outsider's mind, which is really transparent, since we see everything it sees. However, it is so constructed as to be transparent to things and opaque to meanings.

"From then on, everything went very quickly. The men went up to the coffin with a sheet. The priest, his followers, the director and I, all went outside. In front of the door was a lady I didn't know. 'Monsieur Meursault,' said the director. I didn't hear the lady's name, and I gathered only that she was a nurse who'd been ordered to be present. Without smiling, she nodded her long, bony face. Then we stood aside to make room for the body to pass." [8]

Some men are dancing behind a glass partition. Between them and the reader has been interposed a consciousness, something very slight, a translucent curtain, a pure passivity that merely records all the facts. But it has done the trick. Just because it is passive, this consciousness records only facts. The reader has not noticed this presence. But what is the assumption implied by this kind of narrative technique? To put it briefly, what had once been melodic structure has been transformed into a sum of invariant elements. This succession of *movements* is supposed to be rigorously identical with the *act* considered as a complete entity. Are we not dealing here with the analytic assumption that any reality is reducible to a sum total of elements? Now, though analysis may be the instrument of science, it is also the instrument of humour. If in describing a rugby match, I write, "I saw adults in shorts fighting and throwing themselves on the ground in order to send a leather ball between a pair of wooden posts," I have summed up what I have *seen*, but I have intentionally missed its meaning. I am merely trying to be humorous. M. Camus' story is analytic and humorous. Like all artists, he *invents*, because he pretends to be reconstituting raw experience and because he slyly eliminates all the significant links which are also part of the experience.

That is what Hume did when he stated that he could find nothing in experience but isolated impressions. That is what the American neo-realists still do when they deny the existence of any but external relations between phenomena. Contemporary philosophy has, however, established the fact that meanings are also part of the immediate data. But this would carry us too far afield. We shall simply indicate that the universe of the absurd man is the analytic world of the neo-realists. In literature, this method has proved its worth. It was Voltaire's method in *L'Ingénu* and *Micromégas*, and Swift's in *Gulliver's Travels*. For the eighteenth century also had its own outsiders, "noble savages," usually, who, transported to a strange civilization, perceived facts before being able to grasp their meaning. The effect of this discrepancy was to arouse in the reader the feeling of the absurd. M. Camus seems to have this in mind on several occasions, particularly when he shows his hero reflecting on the reasons for his imprisonment.

It is this analytic process that explains the use of the American technique in *The Outsider*. The presence of death at the end of our path has made our future go up in smoke; our life has "no future," it is a series of present moments. What does this mean, if not that the absurd man is applying his analytical spirit to Time? Where Bergson saw an indestructible organization, he sees only a series of instants. It is the plurality of incommunicable moments that will finally account for the plurality of beings. What our author borrows from Hemingway is thus the discontinuity between the clipped phrases that imitate the discontinuity of time.

We are now in a better position to understand the form of his narrative. Each sentence is a present instant, but not an indecisive one that spreads like a stain to the following one. The sentence is sharp, distinct and self-contained. It is separated by a void from the following one, just as Descartes' instant is separated from the one that follows it. The world is destroyed and reborn from sentence to sentence. When the word makes its appearance it is a creation *ex nihilo*. The sentences in *The Outsider* are islands. We bounce from sentence to sentence, from void to void. It was in order to emphasize the isolation of each sentence unit that M. Camus chose to tell his story in the present perfect tense.[9] The simple past is the tense of continuity: "*Il se promena longtemps.*" These words refer us to a past perfect, to a future. The reality of the sentence is the verb, the act, with its transitive character and its transcendence. "*Il s'est promené longtemps*" conceals the verbality of the verb. The verb is split and broken in two.

On the one hand, we find a past participle which has lost all tran-scendence and which is as inert as a thing; and on the other, we find only the verb "être," which has merely a copulative sense and which joins the participle to the substantive as the attribute to the subject. The transitive character of the verb has vanished; the sentence has frozen. Its present reality becomes the noun. Instead of acting as a bridge between past and future, it is merely a small, isolated, self-sufficient substance.

If, in addition, you are careful to reduce it as much as possible to the main proposition, its internal structure attains a perfect simplicity. It gains thereby in cohesiveness. It becomes truly indivisible, an atom of time. The sentences are not, of course, arranged in relation to each other; they are simply juxtaposed. In particular, all causal links are avoided lest they introduce the germ of an explanation and an order other than that of pure succession. Consider the following passage: "She asked me, a moment later, if I loved her. *I answered that it didn't mean anything, but that I probably didn't love her. She seemed sad.* But while preparing lunch, for no reason at all she suddenly laughed in such a way that I kissed her. Just then, the noise of an argument broke out at Raymond's place." I have cited two sentences which most carefully conceal the causal link under the simple appearance of succession.

When it is absolutely necessary to allude to a preceding sentence, the author uses words like "and," "but," "then" and "just then," which evoke only disjunction, opposition or mere addition. The relations between these temporal units, like those established between objects by the neo-realists, are external. Reality appears on the scene without being introduced and then disappears without being destroyed. The world dissolves and is reborn with each pulsation of time. But we must not think it is self-generated. Any activity on its part would lead to a substitution by dangerous forces for the reassuring disorder of pure chance.

A nineteenth-century naturalist would have written "A bridge spanned the river." M. Camus will have none of this anthropomorphism. He says "Over the river was a bridge." This object thus immediately betrays its passiveness. It *is there* before us, plain and undifferentiated. "There were four negro men in the room . . . in front of the door was a lady I didn't know. . . . Beside her was the director. . . ." People used to say that Jules Renard would end by writing things like "The hen lays." M. Camus and many other contemporary writers would write "There is the hen and she lays." The reason is that they like things for their own sake and do not want to dilute them in the flux of duration. "There is water." Here we have a bit of eternity—passive, impenetrable, incommunicable and gleaming! What sensual delight, if only we could touch it! To the absurd man, this is the one and only good. And that is why the novelist prefers these short-lived little sparkles, each of which gives a bit of pleasure, to an organized narrative.

This is what enables M. Camus to think that in writing *The Outsider* he remains silent. His sentence does not belong to the universe of discourse. It has neither ramifications nor extensions nor internal structure. It might be defined, like Valéry's sylph, as

Neither seen nor known:
The time of a bare breast
Between two shifts.

It is very exactly measured by the time of a silent intuition. If this is so, can we speak of M. Camus' novel as something whole? All the sentences of his book are equal to each other, just as all the absurd man's experiences are equal. Each one sets up for itself and sweeps the others into the void. But, as a result, no single one of them detaches itself from the background of the others, except for the rare moments in which the author, abandoning these principles, becomes poetic.

The very dialogues are integrated into the narrative. Dialogue is the moment of explanation, of meaning, and to give it a place of honour would be to admit that meanings exist. M. Camus irons out the dialogue, summarizes it, renders it frequently as indirect discourse. He denies it any typographic privileges, so that a spoken phrase seems like any other happening. It flashes for an instant and then disappears, like heat lightning. Thus, when you start reading the book you feel as if you were listening to a monotonous, nasal, Arab chant rather than reading a novel. You may think that the novel is going to be like one of those tunes of which Courteline remarked that "they disappear, never to return" and stop all of a sudden. But the work gradually organizes itself before the reader's eyes and reveals its solid substructure.

There is not a single unnecessary detail, not one that is not returned to later on and used in the argument. And when we close the book, we realize that it could not have had any other ending. In this world that has been stripped of its causality and presented as absurd, the smallest incident has weight. There is no single one which does not help to lead the hero to crime and capital punishment. *The Outsider* is a classical work, an orderly work, composed about the absurd and against the absurd. Is this quite what the author was aiming at? I do not know. I am simply presenting the reader's opinion.

How are we to classify this clear, dry work, so carefully composed beneath its seeming disorder, so "human," so open, too, once you have the key? It cannot be called a story, for a story explains and co-ordinates as it narrates. It substitutes the order of causality for chronological sequence. M. Camus calls it a "novel." The novel, however, requires continuous duration, development and the manifest presence of the irreversibility of time. I would hesitate somewhat to use the term "novel" for this succession of inert present moments which allows us to see, from underneath, the mechanical economy of something deliberately staged. Or, if it is a novel, it is so in the sense that *Zadig* and *Candide* are novels. It might be regarded as a moralist's short novel, one with a discreet touch of satire and a series of ironic portraits,[10] a novel that, for all the influence of the German existentialists and the American novelists, remains, at bottom, very close to the tales of Voltaire.

NOTES

1. *The Myth of Sisyphus.*
2. *The Myth of Sisyphus.*
3. Quoted in *The Myth of Sisyphus.* Note also Brice Parain's theory of language and his conception of silence.
4. *The Outsider.*
5. *Ibid.*
6. *The Myth of Sisyphus.*
7. *Ibid.*
8. *The Outsider.*
9. The following passage dealing with M. Camus' use of tenses is not intelligible in translation. The simple past tense in French is almost never used in conversation; it is limited almost exclusively to written narration; the usual French equivalent of the English past is the present perfect. (Translator's note.)
10. Those of the pimp, the judge, the prosecuting attorney, etc.

THE TRIAL
(FRANZ KAFKA)

"The Trial"
by Erich Heller, in *Franz Kafka* (1974)

INTRODUCTION

In this chapter from his 1974 study of Kafka's fiction, Erich Heller explores how *The Trial* alienates readers by placing them in a relationship with the text that parallels Joseph K.'s predicament with the law. Joseph K.'s inability to penetrate the bureaucratic proceedings of the court, or even to learn his offense, mirrors the reader's experience of trying to discern meaning from Kafka's story. Both protagonist and reader, according to Heller, play a nightmarish game of interpretation as the narrative progresses, always "harbor[ing] its secret . . . [and] only occasionally allowing for those glimpses of illumination that blind rather than enlighten." By narrating the fantastic, the impossible, and the nightmarish as if they are real, Kafka renders a harrowing portrait of the alienation experienced when trying to understand a world that often does not make sense.

There is only one way to save oneself the trouble of interpreting *The Trial*: not to read it. Not reading it would be, moreover, the only

---

Heller, Erich. "The Trial." *Franz Kafka*. New York: Viking Press, 1974. 71–97.

available manner of fulfilling Kafka's wish that all his unpublished writings should be destroyed. For to take advantage of the contrary decision made by Max Brod and to read the book is to become an interpreter; and this in a much more radical sense than applies to all intelligent reading. Goethe, in the Preface to his *Theory of Colours*, says about any experience of the mind: "Looking at a thing gradually issues in contemplation, contemplation is thinking, thinking is establishing connections, and thus it is possible to say that every attentive glance which we cast on the world is an act of theorizing." For the same reason one may say that every attentive glance at a text is an act of interpreting. But this, Goethe adds, ought to be done with the consciousness that it *is* an interpretation, and therefore, "to use a daring word, with *irony*"—a quality oppressively absent from the minds of many literary commentators who go through their texts with the professional air of policemen searching for the "meaning" as if it were contraband or stolen property. Their findings more often than not tend to provoke the question: If *this* is what the author meant, why did he not say so?

In the case of Kafka, and *The Trial* in particular, the compulsion to interpret is at its most compelling, and is as great as the compulsion to continue reading once one has begun: the urgencies are identical. For Kafka's style—simple, lucid, and "real" in the sense of never leaving any doubt concerning the reality of that which is narrated, described, or meditated—does yet narrate, describe, or meditate the shockingly unbelievable. While it is in the nature of Biblical parables to *show* meaning, through concrete images, to those who might be unable to comprehend meaning presented in the abstract, Kafka's parables seem to insinuate meaninglessness through nonetheless irrefutably real and therefore suggestively meaningful configurations. "The most wondrous poetic sentences are those which make us see, with indisputable certainty and great clarity, the physically impossible: they are true descriptions through words," Hugo von Hofmannsthal said with regard to Novalis.[1] It might carry even greater conviction if it were applied to Kafka, perhaps with the rider that in his case the "physically impossible" makes us see not the miraculous, as sometimes happens with Novalis, but infinite expanses of meaninglessness endowed with whatever meaning its "true description through words" is capable of yielding.

Yes, it is so! is what Kafka's reader is made to feel, only to look up and add, "It cannot be." It is the most sensible vision of an insensible world that produces this dizzying simultaneity of Impossible! and Of course! That Gregor Samsa of "The Metamorphosis" wakes up one morning to find himself transformed into a giant insect is reported without the slightest vestige of the fuss usually accompanying the fantastic. Does the narrated event, therefore, persuade us to suspend our disbelief? Not in the least; but as if we watched an unheard-of natural phenomenon, we are forced to ask: What does it mean? Again like an unheard-of natural phenomenon, it defies any established intellectual order and familiar form of understanding, and thus arouses the kind of intellectual anxiety that greedily and compulsively reaches out for interpretations.

"The right perception of any matter and a misunderstanding of the same matter do not wholly exclude each other." This is what the priest in *The Trial* affirms—talmudistically to the point of caricature—concerning the flawed understanding which the doorkeeper in the legend "Before the Law" has of his duty (which consists in keeping watch at the gate leading to the interior of the Law). Of the many divergent opinions which interpreters of the legend have entertained, the priest says: "The text is unalterable, and the interpretations are often merely expressions of the despair engendered by this." Did Kafka make him say this, prophetically, also of his own texts and their future interpreters? The legend "Before the Law" is at the heart of the novel and harbors its secret in the way Kafka's best stories harbor their secrets: unyieldingly and only occasionally allowing for those glimpses of illumination that blind rather than enlighten.

Joseph K., high official of a Bank, mysteriously tried by a sordidly mysterious Court of Justice for a mysterious offense he is accused of having committed against a mysterious law, has been waiting in the Cathedral for an Italian businessman to whom he was to show the artistic monuments of the city. His waiting has been in vain. (With Kafka *all* waiting is futile, although it is also right to say of it what a character in the novel says: that it is not the waiting that is useless but only action; or, as the prophet Daniel pronounces: "Blessed is he that waiteth.") The guided tour of the Cathedral is not to take place. In any case, it would have been impossible to see the works of art inside the Cathedral for the darkness of the winter morning is growing ever darker and is finally impenetrable; the reader joins K. in wondering whether winter clouds are its sufficient cause. The blackness soon reveals its symbolic character when the priest (who turns out to be the Court's prison chaplain), angered by K.'s persistent defamatory remarks about the Court, shouts at him, "Can you not see two steps ahead of you?"

"You are Joseph K.," says the priest from his pulpit, and then warns him of the bad prospects of his trial. "Yet I am not guilty," K. once again maintains. This time he adds the question of whether guilt has any place at all in human affairs: "We are all human beings here, every one of us," implying: human beings with their inevitable failings. "True," replies the cleric, "but this is how the guilty tend to speak." When K. complains about the bias of the Court and once again about its corruption, the priest, descended from the pulpit, admonishes him not to misjudge the character of the Court—after the fashion of his misjudging the doorkeeper in the legend "Before the Law" which he now narrates.

The legend, which according to the priest is part of the prefatory explanations introducing the Law itself, tells of a man from the country who arrives at the entrance gate of the Law. There he encounters the doorkeeper. He asks to be admitted. The doorkeeper refuses: "Not now," he says. "Perhaps later?" asks the man. "It is possible," is the doorkeeper's reply, "but not now." There never will be "now." The man from the country is kept waiting forever. Having vainly entreated and even bribed the doorkeeper, and having become so familiar with him that he knows "even the fleas in his fur collar," he is, after years and years, about to die. He asks his final question:

> Everyone strives to attain the Law ... how does it come about, then, that in all these years no one has wanted to be admitted but me?" The doorkeeper recognizes that the man is approaching his end and in order to reach his hearing that fails, he bellows in his ear: "No one but you could gain admittance through this door, since this door was meant for you alone. I am now going to shut it."

The parable "Before the Law" is the only part of *The Trial* that Kafka, with infallible discrimination, published himself. Despite its familiarity, it has retained its terrible charm and shows all the characteristic features of Kafka's art at its most powerful—possessing, that is, the kind of power that is in the gentle wafting of the wind rather than in the thunderous storm, and is the more destructive for it. Parodying Biblical simplicity, *sancta simplicitas*, it expresses the most unholy complications of the intelligence and raises hellish questions in the key of the innocently unquestionable. Its humor is at the same time tender and cruel, teasing the mind with the semblance of light into losing itself in the utmost obscurity.

It may have been from sheer benevolent consideration for the reader that Kafka did not let the parable, as its own aesthetic will seems to demand, stand by itself. In *The Trial*, he supplemented it with pages of exegesis that encroach upon its sovereignty but for once forestall any interpretative maneuvers: the writer himself demonstrates their futility. For instance: Has the doorkeeper deceived the man from the country? Joseph K. feels immediately certain he has, but the priest exhorts him not to judge too rashly and above all not to venture outside the text; the text allows for no such condemnation of the doorkeeper; all that we come to know is that the man is not permitted to enter *now*, even though this particular entrance is meant only for him. It is not the doorkeeper's fault that the moment never comes which would redeem the supplicant as well as the very existence of the door. (Doors in Kafka's writings appear to be an architectural invention for the purpose of preventing people from entering.)

There is not the slightest hint to be found anywhere in the text that the doorkeeper—humble because he is only the lowest in the hierarchy of the Law, and yet powerful because he is, after all, in the Law's service—violates his commission by not admitting the man at that particular moment or at any particular time. It has to be assumed that he acts in accordance with the Law. Why should he act otherwise? From a capricious dislike of the man? On the contrary, it may be from kindness that—at least in the opinion of many learned interpreters—he goes beyond the call of duty by allowing the man to know that at some future time his request may be granted. Or is he corrupt in accepting gifts? The text does not support the conclusion that such acceptance is against the Law, although it would no doubt be against the Law if the doorkeeper let himself be seduced by bribes. Is there any reason for not believing him when, with the accent of Kafka's wit and the logic of the Hapsburg bureaucracy, he says that he only takes the man's presents to comfort the giver with the certainty that he has tried everything in his power? And so the exegetical dialogue between Joseph K. and the priest continues, leaving no pebble of interpretation unturned, and then throwing all of them away as worthless missiles, unfit to make so much as a dent in the armor of the mysterious futility. "The text is unalterable, and the interpretations are often merely expressions of the despair engendered by this."

Is there any fissure in it, undetected by Joseph K. and left unprotected by the priest? It seems there is not. We have heard the priest say that the correct comprehension of any matter *and* its misunderstanding are not entirely incompatible; and this paradox—like all good paradoxes, a splendid performance of the mind, induced by the castration of logic—was prompted by the observation that the doorkeeper was both right and wrong with regard to his office. In this respect he gives the impression of being simple-minded as well as conceited. True enough, his power is considerable, yet his manner suggests that he is unaware of the measure of his subordination. He conducts himself after the fashion of "great men" and does not seem to recognize that in some respects the man from the country might well be superior to him: he is free and has made the journey on his own volition, possessed as he is by the desire to come to know the Law. The doorkeeper, on the other hand, has long since accepted (if indeed it has not always been a matter of indifference to him) his lack of courage in not daring to face even the third of the many other doorkeepers on the way to the Law, not to mention the fact that he is bound by the Law to stay in the place assigned to him, while the man from the country is free to leave if he so wishes—like Joseph K. himself, from whom, in the parting words of the priest, "the Court wants nothing.... It receives you when you come and it dismisses you when you go." The doorkeeper does not even know the Law that he so obediently serves—just as the Whipper of the Court, in one of the most disquieting episodes in this disquieting book, cruelly and incorruptibly beats the "culprits" assigned to him without questioning the assignment, and responds to Joseph K.'s attempt to ransom the victim by saying: "I refuse to be bribed. I am commissioned to whip, and whip I shall" (an anticipation of that evil honesty and conscientiousness which later was to beget the most abhorrent deeds in the regions of Kafka's birthplace).

Compared even to the pitiable condition of the man from the country, shrunk and blind and deaf in the end, the doorkeeper is an obtuse creature. The story does not record that, with his eyes intact, he has ever seen what the man in his blindness perceives: the immense radiance streaming forth from the Law. Also, as some of the fictitious commentators of the legend believe, he may be deluded or be bragging or be cruelly determined to inflict grief and regret upon the man in his last moments when he tells him that now, in the hour of the man's death, he is going to shut the door that was meant only for him. Has he the power to do so? Has it not been said at the beginning of the parable that the entrance to the Law is always open? This "always" cannot possibly be affected by the death of the individual. Nevertheless, despite all his failings, the doorkeeper is, as the priest affirms, a servant of the Law and as such "beyond human judgment." Therefore it ought after all not be assumed that he is really inferior to the man from the country. To be enlisted by the Law, even as the lowest of doormen, is incomparably more than to live freely in the world; and to doubt this guardian's worthiness is to doubt the Law itself. Thus speaks the priest—not unlike K.'s lawyer, who advises him early in the novel that often it is better to be in chains than to be free. But at this point Joseph K. disagrees with the priest; if he were right, one would have to believe that everything the doorkeeper says is true; and has not the priest himself proved that this is impossible? No, the priest replies, one need not accept everything as true, "one must only accept it as necessary." K. calls this a "melancholy opinion": it holds that the order of the world is based upon a lie. This Joseph K. says "in conclusion," but Kafka sees to it that it is "not his final judgment." "The simple story had lost its clear outline, he wanted to put it out of his mind and the priest, who now showed great delicacy of feeling, suffered him to do so and accepted his comment in silence, although undoubtedly he did not agree with it."

Kafka's art of conclusively stating inconclusiveness is unsurpassed and probably insurpassable, and unbreachable seem the fortifications he builds to protect the mystery from the onslaughts of dogma, opinion, or conviction. Merely to protect the mystery from them? No, to deprive dogmas, opinions, and convictions of the air they need for breathing. And if they were as firm as rocks they would become like the sand of the desert, blown hither and thither by the wind and blinding even the most determined believer. Yet there is one certainty that is left untouched by the parable as well as by the whole book: the Law exists and Joseph K. must have most terribly offended it, for he is executed in the end with a double-edged—yes, double-edged—butcher's knife that is thrust into his heart and turned there twice. Three years before Kafka began to write *The Trial*, he had, on November 11, 1911, entered in his diary: "This morning, once again after a long time, I took pleasure in imagining that a knife was being turned in my heart," and as late as 1921 (October 20) he recorded a dream in which there was "... happiness ... in the fact that I welcomed so freely, with such conviction and such joy, the punishment when it came."[2] But there is no joy in *this* punishment; it comes to Joseph K. in a deserted quarry on the periphery of the city, while the casements of a window on the top floor of a neighboring house fly open and a human figure stretches his hands out toward the scene of horror. The questions, evoked by this apparition and presumably issuing from Joseph K.'s mind, might be taken to point toward a miscarriage of justice: who was the person at the window? "A friend? A good man? ... Someone who wanted to help? Was it one person only? Was it mankind?" The friendliest impulses of mankind, then, may well be working against the Court's administration of justice and may side with its unhappy victim. But, on the other hand, the gestures of the figure up there might be mere projections of K.'s will to live, rising up in vain against the secret logic of the case, this logic being unshakable—and yet, we read—"it cannot withstand a man who wants to go on living."

Alas, it can, and Joseph K. dies "like a dog!" These are his last words; and if the reader's terrified revulsion leaves him capable of reflecting, he might find them somewhat inappropriate. For this is not how dogs are killed. Rather does it resemble the matador's way of killing the bull; and although no perfect metaphor is perfectly fitting, we come a little closer to it by remembering the episode with the painter Titorelli, the amiable charlatan and lover of children, confidant of Court officials and their only licensed portraitist, who adorns his portraits of the judges with the allegorical figure of justice in a kind of personal union with the winged and dynamic goddess of victory. "Not a very good combination," says K. "Justice must stand still, or else the scales will waver, and a just verdict will become impossible." But still worse, after a few more strokes of Titorelli's crayon there emerges, dominating the previous image, the goddess of the hunt. But this is in blatant contradiction to what one of the warders, who come to arrest Joseph K., says of the Court: its officials "never go hunting for guilt in the populace but are drawn toward the guilty . . . and must send out us warders."

There is no end to such contradictions and ambiguities in *The Trial*. No end: the novel was doomed to remain a fragment and, as a novel, had to fail, even though Kafka did write the final chapter. As a conclusion to whatever might have been the whole work, it too is a failure, despite its superbly sustained, quietly sensational tone of narration, which is a little reminiscent of the last pages of Stendhal's *Le Rouge et le noir*. It fails in aesthetic and—which in this case is the same—ethical logic. For a nightmare will not become a novel even if it is pursued and elaborated through episode after episode. And an ending, unquestionable in its stark finality, is aesthetically and ethically offensive if it is supported only by a sequence of arbitrarily protractile scenes, all showing a presumed culprit who, not knowing the nature of his guilt, helplessly casts about for help; or the sordidness and corruption of the judiciary order (at least in its lower echelon, and we come to know only this); or the clownish irresponsibility of those who claim to be able to assist the accused in his desperate struggle for acquittal. What *is* his guilt? What *is* the Law?

It is the secret of Kafka's art almost to silence such questions. They are laughed out of court, as it were, by demons mischievously squatting in the empty spaces between the questions and the sought-for answers. Boorish curiosity in the company of tragic subtleties! And do such questions not miss the very point of *The Trial*? Yet, such is the mechanism of the moral and aesthetic sensibility that even the most accomplished description of a death sentence carried out with studied violence by two men looking like "tenth-rate old actors"—"What theatre are you playing at?" K. asks them—must affect us, in the absence of any answers to those questions, like the indiscretion of a sadistically bad dream told in public.

NOTES

1. Hugo von Hofmannsthal, *Aufzeichnungen* (Frankfurt am Main, 1959), p. 138.
2. The thought of dying in this manner must have obsessed Kafka's imagination. Even in his earliest story, "The Description

of a Struggle," written about 1904, the following thought suddenly breaks the peace of the "I"'s nocturnal walk with an apparently harmless companion. ". . . this is the time for the murder. I'll stay with him and slowly he'll draw the dagger—the handle of which he is already holding in his pocket—along his coat, and then plunge it into me. It's unlikely that he'll be surprised at the simplicity of it all—yet maybe he will, who knows? I won't scream, I'll just stare at him as long as my eyes can stand it."

WAITING FOR GODOT
(SAMUEL BECKETT)

"A World Without Solace . . . Nearly Almost Always: Alienation in Samuel Beckett's *Waiting for Godot*"
by Ken Betsalel,
University of North Carolina at Asheville

I had a friend named Art. For many years Art lived with a chronic heart condition he knew would kill him—eventually, it did. Art loved to tell stories, especially the kind of funny, bittersweet stories that got you to think about the meaning of life. At Art's funeral friends and family recounted how Art's stories kept them going in the face of loss. Art said he learned to tell stories from vaudeville comedians he heard as a young person; their timing was impeccable. In one story Art liked to tell, two bewildered old men crash into each other in a supermarket while looking for their wives. In Art's stories the logic of the familiar was upended by the unexpected punch line. Not all of Art's stories had moral purpose; some simply amused.

At Art's funeral, I began thinking about Samuel Beckett's *Waiting for Godot* (one of the most wickedly funny plays I know) and its theme of alienation. The play, like so many of the Laurel and Hardy movies that are its indirect models, employed burlesque elements in response to such exasperating travails as ill-fitting boots and loss of bladder control. The difference is that *Godot* couples lowbrow humor with highbrow musings delivered in the disguised voices of poets pretending to be tramps. As Estragon says, "Isn't that obvious?" (9a).

The opening scene in *Godot*, when Estragon (a.k.a. Gogo, alias Adam—read Oliver Hardy) sits on a low mound like a circus clown trying to pry his boot off, presents a puzzle the play never resolves: Are Estragon's boots too small or his feet too big? For Beckett, it is a matter of probabilities—dumb luck, if you like (like his being born on Good Friday, April 13, 1906—is this a good omen or bad? For a superstitious Beckett this was mostly bad except when it wasn't)—and for some, that conundrum is absurdly funny!

Giving up in exhaustion, resting, and trying with both hands again, Estragon declares: "Nothing to be done." Vladimir, (a.k.a. Didi, mistakenly referred to by the boy in the play as Mr. Albert—read Stan Laurel) advances with "*short, stiff strides, legs wide apart*" (like the exaggerated footfalls of Charlie Chaplin) and responds, "I'm beginning to come round to that opinion. All my life I've tried to put it from me, saying, Vladimir, be reasonable, you haven't tried everything. And I resumed the struggle" (7a). What makes this opening scene both funny and tragic, thereby setting the tone for the play, is that both Estragon's and Vladimir's words appear to be philosophically exaggerated responses to a gag-like setup—the difficulty of repeatedly trying to pry a boot off with both hands! The phrase *Nothing to be done* is an ironic and direct, if unconscious, response to (or parody of?) V.I. Lenin's call to armed struggle and Communist Party discipline in his famous pamphlet published on the eve of the Russian Revolution, *What Is to Be Done? Godot* may be many things, but a message play for the establishment of a workers' utopia, let alone a liberal democracy, it is not. Consider Vladimir's lines in act 2: "We wait. We are bored. *(He throws his hand up.)* No, don't protest, we are bored to death, there's no denying it. Good. A diversion comes along and what do we do? We let it go to waste. Come, let's get to work! *(He advances towards the heap, stops in his stride.)* In an instant all will vanish and we'll be alone once more, in the midst of nothingness!" (52a). In one sense, *Godot* can be considered a deeply conservative, as it were, *conserving* work of theater that is profoundly antipolitical or apolitical, to say the least. Or is it? (Some critics even accuse such works of subtextually advocating a quietism or antihope ideology known as nihilism or middle-class apathy.) We will come to that question later.

While *Waiting for Godot* may read like serious stuff, the play is billed as a "tragicomedy" (the shared letter "c" that combines the two words suggests somehow that the comedy begins where the tragic

ends). Unlike Euripides's *Antigone* or Shakespeare's *Hamlet*, there are
no suicides in *Godot*—except, of course, the two comically feigned
attempts by Estragon and Vladimir in acts 1 and 2—or in any of
Beckett's work, with the possible exception of Old Boy in *Murphy*,
who, as C.J. Ackerley and S.E. Gontarski point out, only "cuts his
throat for a necessary reason: it is a cut-throat razor." *Godot* consists
"only" of witty, ironic banter, word games (at times sad and remorseful),
puns, and lyrical-sounding soliloquies that serve as poetic setups for
yet another round of pricks and kicks, all ending in a final pratfall—or
nearly so. Remember the penultimate scene in *Godot*?

> Estragon: "Why don't we hang ourselves?" [The tragic setup]
> Vladimir: "With what?" [The slightly more intellectual but no
> more effectual one] Estragon: "You haven't got a bit of rope?"
> Vladimir: "No." Estragon: "Then we can't." *(Silence)* [Notice
> the flat, comic deadpan—once again, heightening the setup;
> the timing here is impeccable.] Vladimir: "Let's go." [The
> crescendo—comic relief? Hardly.] Estragon: "Wait, there's my
> belt." [Once again, the setup—the expectation is that this time
> they will do it!] Vladimir: "It's too short." [A cowardly retreat?]
> Estragon: "You could hang on to my legs." [We have heard that
> before, or something close to it, in act 1.] Vladimir: "And who'd
> hang on to mine?" [Again, the satiric employment of reason?]
> Estragon: "True." Vladimir: "Show all the same." [Meaning
> let's see your belt; hand it over.] *(Estragon loosens the cord that
> holds up his trousers which, much too big for him, fall about his
> ankles. They look at the cord.)*

With Estragon's pants falling now to his ankles, exposing his boxer
shorts and knobby legs, this is nothing less than pure burlesque—the
pratfall! This nearly perfect slapstick scene, which goes on for another
twenty-two lines, nearly prevented *Godot* from opening in London
in 1955 due to the Lord Chamberlain's concerns about indecency—
never mind what some critics saw as the underlying tone of pessimism
in the play regarding the future of mankind! (The Lord Chamberlain's
office until 1968 acted as a kind of *ex officio* state censor.)

Godot could only be performed in England, Deirdre Bair points
out, after certain words deemed offensive were changed and the scene
with Estragon's exposed bottom was altered. It is instructive to compare

this faux-suicide scene, and the equally satirical suicide contemplation
by Estragon and Vladimir in act 1, with the original Laurel and Hardy
film *The Flying Deuces* (1937), in which a brokenhearted Hardy (Ollie,
the heavy one) comically attempts to engineer a suicide by throwing
himself and his reluctant partner, Laurel (Stan, the thin one), into the
Seine in Paris by using a length of rope fashioned around their waists
and tied to a block of cement. Like Estragon and Vladimir, the pair
does not get far, due to a combination of incompetence and bad luck
(depending on how you look at it!).

> Stan: Well, goodbye Ollie.
> Ollie: Goodbye, Stan.
> Stan: Good luck.
> Ollie: Hey! Where are you going!
> Stan: Well, I don't want to get my name dragged into this.
> Ollie: (Tying rope around Stan's waist)
> Stan: What's that for?
> Ollie: When I count to three, we will both jump in.
> Stan: What do I have to do with it! I am not the one in love.
> Ollie: So that's the kind of guy you are.
>> After all I have done for you, you will let me jump in there
>> alone.
>> Do you realize you will just go off living by yourself?
>> People will stare at you and wonder what you are.
>> I won't be here to tell them.
>> There will be no one to protect you.
> Stan: I never thought of that. I didn't mean to be disrespectful.
> Ollie: That's all right. We will let bygones be bygones.
>> This is going to be easier than you think!

In the closing pages of the earlier comic novel *Watt*, Beckett had
his protagonist of the same name play on the need to plant a "hardy
laurel," the pun being that nearly all laurels are hardy (Laurel and
Hardy, get it?) when planted in the right plot, including *Godot*'s.
Though Samuel Beckett and his friend and mentor James Joyce
were, in their own ways, very different stylists (one adds, where the
other subtracts), one of the challenges in reading Beckett's *Godot*,
which is like reading Joyce's *Ulysses* and *Finnegans Wake*, is to know
where words employed as symbols begin and end; of course, for

an adventurous and free-spirited reader that is always, or nearly always, part of the great charm and frustration in reading and rereading these works.

And yet to argue, as some scholars do, that *Waiting for Godot* has the comic pedigree of a funny bone that goes back beyond Laurel and Hardy, Charlie Chaplin, and Buster Keaton to the seventeenth-century commedia dell'arte or, further still, to the tradition of the Homeric bard himself is not to deny an underlying sense of loss that runs through the play like an exile longing for home or a Gnostic preacher predicting apocalyptic doom of mankind (remember that *Godot* is also billed as a tragedy). Just listen to these lines of sad resignation uttered by Pozzo ever so lyrically, yet somehow inauthentically (another word for alienated): "The tears of the world are a constant quantity. For each one who begins to weep somewhere else another stops. The same is true of the laugh. *(He laughs.)* Let us not then speak ill of our generation. It is not any unhappier than its predecessors. *(Pause.)* Let us not speak well of it either. *(Pause.)* Let us not speak of it at all. *(Pause judiciously.)* It is true the population has increased" (22a).

What makes *Godot* so sad—so tragic, if you like—is that all of the characters (even the boy in acts 1 and 2) are estranged and made strange—separated, indeed alienated—not only from one another, God, and nature (that poor tree!) but also from time itself (how old are these characters anyway?), a day of the week (does the "action" take place on Saturday, Sunday, Monday?), and everything they touch, think, feel, see, and even remember—or is it forget? It's hard to recall which, as "nothing" (no thing) really happens in a play in which the past itself is made foreign. Estragon: "I'm unhappy." Vladimir: "Not really! [Being ironic?] Since when?" Estragon: "I'd forgotten." Vladimir: "Extraordinary the tricks the memory plays!" (33a).

The very names Estragon and Vladimir suggest a kind of theater of allegory or antiallegory, where a character's name both means and doesn't mean anything. Estragon resonates in the Middle English word *estragen* or Middle French word *estrangier*, meaning stranger or one out of place (think of Albert Camus' novel *The Stranger*, the classic book of existential alienation, which Beckett greatly admired). Vladimir is a foreign-sounding Russian name, at least from an English or French perspective, with echoes in the Latin *validus*, meaning strong, valid, and truthful.

At one point, Estragon's desire to go barefoot and leave his boots to someone else leads to this curious exchange in which Estragon compares himself to the ultimate stranger—some consider him God—or as Karl Barth, the great Swiss theologian, phrased it, "the wholly other."

> Estragon: *(turning to look at the boots)* "I'm leaving them there. *(Pause.)* Another will come, just as ... as me, but with smaller feet, and they'll make him happy." Vladimir: "But you can't go barefoot!" Estragon: "Christ did." Vladimir: "Christ! What has Christ got to do with it? You're not going to compare yourself to Christ!" Estragon: "All my life I've compared myself to him." Vladimir: "But where he lived it was warm, it was dry!" Estragon: "Yes. And they crucified him quick." *(Silence.)* Vladimir: "We've nothing to do here." Estragon: "Nor anywhere else." (34b)

However, unlike medieval morality plays in which the personification of names and action are unambiguously intended to mean something (as when Everyman meets the Devil, Fellowship, Wealth, and Good Deeds along the road to salvation), our little wayfarers appear not so much lost as going nowhere (is this a state of purgatory?), while waiting for what feels like an eternity. "Nothing happens," Estragon cries out. "Nobody comes, nobody goes, it's awful!" (27b). That is not exactly so, as our heroes—or are they antiheroes?—run into Pozzo, whom Vladimir mistakenly identifies as Godot himself and Estragon incorrectly calls Bozzo. The name *Bozzo* sounds like Bozo, as in Bozo the Clown, a name that can be traced back to the medieval character Baso, the "dunce" in Saint Anselm of Canterbury's eleventh-century ontological dialogues that logically attempt to prove the existence of God. Pozzo is with his servant Lucky (some say "lackey"), whose very being personifies the unlucky, as he is led by his master's rope tied around his bruised and bloodied neck. Lucky's fortune appears to change for neither better nor worse in the second act of *Godot*, when, though "struck dumb," he silently leads his blind and shaken master in the uncertain direction of home. Such is the picture of human despair—pure alienation if it was not so darkly comic to some.

As for the name *Godot* itself, scholar Martin Esslin, who has interviewed Beckett, contends that while it may sound like the word *God* in English (in French—the original language of the play—the word for God is *Dieu*, all of which adds to the mystery of Godot), it was not the playwright's intention to "mean" God. In fact, Beckett has quipped, "If by Godot I meant God, I would say God and not Godot." Beckett told Roger Blin, the theater director who also played the role of Pozzo in *En attendant Godot* (Waiting for Godot) on January 5, 1953, that the name Godot finds its origin in *godit-tots* (masculine) and *godasses* (feminine), French colloquial words for boot. Could God be a boot? More on that later.

The eminent theater critic Eric Bentley made the link between Godot and a character named Godeau in a Balzac novel, a character who never shows up though he's central to the plot. Over the years, Beckett's reply to the question of Godot's identity became, "If I knew, I wouldn't have written the play!" The playwright was either alienated from the meaning of his own work or he was allowing others the freedom to discover the meaning of the play on their own (according to some critics and scholars, a nearly impossible task).

The boy in the play appears to be just an unnamed boy who tends his goats, though his reliability and that of his (possibly twin?) brother as messengers might be questioned; after all, in act 2 the boy cannot recall whether it was he or his brother (who raises sheep and is now sick) who was sent the day before by Godot. When questioned by Vladimir, the boy does "think" (rather than know) that Godot has a white beard and he appeared quite certain that "He does nothing, Sir" (59a). Beckett wanted the boy to be played like an angel (the Greek word *angelos* means messenger). All of this adds to the strange distance and almost ethereal quality of this scene and the play itself.

But where does all of the separation and alienation in *Waiting for Godot* come from? Is it in the bones of the play itself? How much of it derives from the playwright's philosophy of life (if it can be found)? How much of the alienation in *Godot* is a product of the times in which the play was written? How much of the perception of alienation in *Godot* resides in the audiences' and critics' interpretations of a kind of theatrical Rorschach test? These are difficult questions to answer, and that adds to the allure, mystery, and alienation of *Godot*, which might never be completely understood or reckoned with.

In many ways *Godot* is like an alienated young person, neither understanding nor understood, who nevertheless has important, albeit troubling things to say and is therefore worthy of serious respect and attention. We might not like what *Godot* has to say, but it behooves us to listen. What, then, does alienation reveal in *Waiting for Godot*? While *Godot* is a work of art made up of many disparate parts and conflicting fragments and is not a systematic work of philosophy or a political-science thesis, three lessons might be gleaned.

First of these is that language matters and, despite our best efforts, we might not always say what we mean to, especially when forced to explain ourselves to others (because we are thinking and doubting animals). Consider Lucky's "thinking" speech—"think, pig!" as Pozzo commands (28a). What appears to be pure gibberish is actually a reasoned, or overly reasoned, attempt to "establish beyond all doubt" the nature of human existence. Absurd, you say, and yet we are compelled to do so, or something like it, every day.

Secondly, the problem of being human begins at birth. This is a pessimistic view; it might be an overly simplistic view, but it is true: At our birth, until science proves otherwise, we are animals destined like all others for death. As Pozzo puts it near the end of the play: "Have you not done tormenting me with your accursed time! It's abominable! . . . They give birth astride of a grave, the light gleams an instant, then it's night once more" (57b). This dark passage appears to be confirmed soon after by Vladimir: "Astride of a grave and a difficult birth. Down in the hole, lingeringly, the grave-digger puts on the forceps. We have time to grow old. The air is full of our cries" (58a-b). What can all this alienation possibly teach us?

Finally, the real question the play asks is not so much how we are going to explain our lives away (is it character or temperament, fate or free will?) as we wait, for who knows what, in an endless game. The real question is: What do we do about it? How are we going to live our lives? How do we use the freedom that our alienation from everything and everyone makes possible? In that sense, alienation in *Godot* is a great teacher, for alienation reveals the perennial questions of what, who, where, and how we are going to be in the world. Not as a thing, but as a person, will we make excuses for ourselves and blame others, or as Vladimir comically puts it, "There's man all over for you, blaming on his boots [or God, Godot, you name it] the faults of his feet" (8a).

To answer a question posed earlier in this essay, *Godot*, from one perspective, is a profoundly political (though not partisan) play, for it asks the audience, collectively and individually, what kind of choices we are going to make for ourselves and for society. *Waiting for Godot* leaves us without a place to hide, and while the world may be almost always without solace, we are condemned to choose, whether we like it or not, how to live our lives.

It is perhaps because *Godot* is so tragically comic at presenting the human condition of alienation and loss that it has so often been performed with great insight before audiences in difficult circumstances, be they inmates in a maximum-security prison such as San Quentin, besieged residents of Sarajevo at the height of the Bosnian war, or residents of the Ninth Ward in New Orleans after Hurricane Katrina (for two thoughtful reviews of the production, see the *New York Times*, "Beckett's Tramps, Waterlogged While They Wait," June 3, 2006, Page B10; and "A Broken City. A Tree. Evening," December 2, 2007, A&L Page 1). Sometimes there is nothing more cathartic and healthy than laughing amid despair.

"A client is mad with a tailor for taking so long making a pair of trousers," so roughly goes a story of Beckett's, according to his biographer and friend James Knowlson in an essay aimed at defending modern art against its critics and more conventional ways of painting. "Do you know, it only took God seven days to make the entire world." "Yes," said the tailor, "and look at the world—just wait till you see your pants!"

My friend Art would have loved that story, as all good things are worth struggling with and waiting for.

BIBLIOGRAPHY

Ackerley, C.J. and S.E. Gontarski. *The Grove Companion to Samuel Beckett: A Reader's Guide to His Works, Life and Thought*. New York: Grove Press, 2004.

Bair, Deirdre. *Samuel Beckett: A Biography*. New York: Simon and Schuster, 1978.

Beckett, Samuel. *Waiting for Godot: A Tragicomedy in Two Acts*. New York: Grove Press, 1954.

Bloom, Harold, ed. *Modern Critical Interpretations: Samuel Beckett's Waiting for Godot*. New York: Chelsea House, 1987.

Cohn, Ruby. *Casebook on Waiting for Godot*. New York: Grove Press, 1967.

———. *Samuel Beckett: The Comic Gamut*. New Brunswick, N.J.: Rutgers University Press, 1962.

Esslin, Martin. *The Theatre of the Absurd*. New York: Doubleday, 1961.

Kenner, Hugh. *A Reader's Guide to Samuel Beckett*. New York: Farrar, Straus and Giroux, 1973.

Knowlson, James, and Elizabeth Knowlson. *Beckett Remembering: Remembering Beckett*. New York: Arcade, 2006.

Knowlson, James. *Damned to Fame: The Life of Samuel Beckett*. New York: Grove Press, 1996.

THE WASTE LAND
(THOMAS STEARNS ELIOT)

"'Each in His Prison': Damnation and Alienation in *The Waste Land*"
by Matthew J. Bolton,
Loyola School

The Waste Land is a poem of the city, and like a city it is crowded with
people of all classes and types. Marie, Madame Sosostris, Stetson,
the childless couple, the prolific parents Lil and Albert, the gossipy
publican, the typist, the clerk, Tiresias, and other nameless speakers
walk the streets or preside over the parlors and public rooms of
Eliot's unreal city. Yet, despite living near others, these urbanites
are profoundly alone. Their attempts to reach out to one another
through words or actions are doomed, because the pervasive sense of
alienation that characterizes the interactions among these characters
is rooted not in social conditions but in spiritual ones. It is not the
city but consciousness itself that forms a prison of the mind, closing
one off from one's fellows. As a nameless speaker, alluding to lines
from the penultimate canto of Dante's *Inferno*, says in the poem's
fifth part:

> I have heard the key
> Turn in the door once and turn once only
> We think of the key, each in his prison
> Thinking of the key.

This image and a series of other allusions to the *Inferno* equate the spiritual condition of modern man with that of the lost souls who crowd the outer bounds of hell or suffer in its inner circles. The fragmentary conversations and fractured confessions of *The Waste Land* might be read as a series of attempts to turn the key that will allow the modern, alienated individual to be released from his infernal prison to find communion with God, nature, and others.

Nowhere in *The Waste Land* is one more alone than in a crowd. Consider the businessmen who plod through the streets of London in the first part of the poem "The Burial of the Dead":

> A crowd flowed over London Bridge, so many,
> I had not thought death had undone so many.
> Sighs, short and infrequent, were exhaled,
> And each man fixed his eyes before his feet.

The second line is again from Dante, whose pilgrim figure marvels to see how many dead souls throng the gates of hell. By alluding to this passage from the *Inferno*, Eliot equates the London commuters with those souls who lived their lives "with no blame and no praise" and who therefore have been admitted to neither hell nor heaven. As Dante's guide Virgil says of the lost souls outside hell: "This blind life they lead is so abject / It makes them envy every other fate" (Canto 3). The Londoners, too, lead a blind life. Where Dante the pilgrim ends each book of the *Commedia* by turning his eyes upward to the stars—and in the *Paradiso* to see the face of God—the denizens of the unreal city look down at their own feet. They have lost their capacity to recognize not only God and nature but also one another.

It is ironic that this daily commute is made within sight and sound of one of the city's oldest churches. The crowd "flowed up the hill and down King William Street, / To where Saint Mary Woolnoth kept the hours / With a dead sound on the final stroke of nine." Once, the church bells would have called the faithful together to pray as a community. Now they are only a "dead sound" by which to set one's watch, for what was once a religious congregation has become a faithless crowd. The reader who comes to the poem with a cursory knowledge of Eliot's biography will recognize the poet among these lost souls, for during the time that he wrote *The Waste Land*, he worked in London at Lloyds Bank. Like Dante Alighieri, Eliot has divided himself between the pilgrim who traverses a wasted land and the poet who describes it.

Nor is this the only place in *The Waste Land* where crowds are equated with the lost souls of the *Inferno*. Madame Sosostris, plying her cards, says, "I see crowds of people, walking round in a ring." It is a haunting image that combines the children's songs that would later appear in Eliot's "The Hollow Men" ("Here we go round the prickly pear / prickly pear prickly pear") with the circles of hell that Dante describes. A crowd appears again in Part V of *The Waste Land*, "What the Thunder Said," where a Dante figure asks his Virgil:

> What is that sound high in the air
> Murmur of maternal lamentation
> Who are those hooded hordes swarming
> Over endless plains, stumbling in cracked earth
> Ringed by the flat horizon only

In a pattern that is typical of *The Waste Land*, a scene alluded to in the beginning of the poem becomes explicit by its end. If the earlier crowd scene was a vision of London informed by an allusion to Dante's hell, this later scene is a vision of hell itself. It is as if the poem is dreaming: The images and materials of its earlier passages have reordered themselves according to the subconscious logic of a nightmare.

The hoods that these men wear likewise suggest a grotesque reworking of the earlier crowd scene. In London "each man fixed his eyes before his feet," but here in this infernal world each man's eyes are fixed for him by a hood that both hides his individual identity and restricts his gaze. This garb might be read as an example of the *contrapasso*, the technique in the *Commedia* whereby the form of one's punishment in the afterlife is logically related to the sins one committed. Those who chose to be blind and anonymous in life now must be so in the afterlife. Indeed, they have lost their very humanity, for the gerund "swarming" not only encodes the wasps and hornets that sting the lost souls in the vestibule of Dante's hell but also casts the hordes of men in the language used to describe bees, flies, and similar insects. An element from later in the *Inferno* seems to inform the image of the hooded hordes: the lead-lined "cloaks with hoods pulled low covering the eyes" that the hypocrites wear in Canto 23. This reference is driven home by the Dante-like narrator's direct address to the reader

taken from Charles Baudelaire's *Les fleurs du mal* at the close of Part
I of the poem: "You! Hypocrite lecteur!—mon semblable, mon frère!"
The reader is told that he, like the narrator, goes through life hooded.
Narrator and reader alike resemble a "frère," or hooded, religious
brother. The glimpse into the abyss at the hooded hordes of "What the
Thunder Said" amplifies the earlier image of a crowd of businessmen
by suggesting that the modern human condition is a spiritual hell, and
the closing words of the narrator in "The Burial of the Dead" place
Eliot and his readers among these swarms of lost souls.

The men who swarm in "hooded hordes" have lost their individuality without gaining any sense of communion. Though they stumble
along together, each is profoundly alone. The hoods that blinker
their gazes suggest not only the garb of Dante's hypocrites but also
a quotation from philosopher F.H. Bradley that Eliot included in his
endnotes to the poem:

> My external sensations are no less private to myself than are
> my thoughts or my feelings. In either case, my experience falls
> within my own circle, a circle closed on the outside; and, with
> all its elements alike, every sphere is opaque to the others which
> surround it. . . . [T]he whole world for each is peculiar and
> private to that soul.

The idea that each individual moves through a world that is entirely
of his or her own creation is terrifying. To believe it is to teeter on
the edge of solipsism. For if each person's experience of the world
constitutes an opaque sphere, then there is no way to determine the
thoughts or feelings of another and no way to verify that another
has thoughts and feelings in the first place. Furthermore, since the
external sensations are likewise "peculiar and private," the people
around one might be moving through a world that is entirely
different from one's own.

Eliot had written his Harvard doctoral dissertation on Bradley a
few years before starting on *The Waste Land*, and he knew the now-
obscure philosopher well. The lines that he quotes in the endnotes do
not represent a central tenet of Bradley's philosophy. Rather, the solip-
sistic model that Bradley describes is one of several possible scenarios
that he presents but ultimately rejects. The vision of man as profoundly
and insolubly separated from his fellow man is as much Eliot's

preoccupation as it is Bradley's. Eliot selects a passage from Bradley that speaks to his own concerns, a model that renders consciousness itself as both the obscuring hood and the eyes the hood obscures, the walls of the prison cell and the prisoner they confine.

The denizens of the unreal city repeatedly try to break through the opaque walls that separate them from their fellows. In the London crowd scene, Eliot's narrator uses a Dantean device to single out a man he recognizes and address him directly:

> There I saw one I knew, and stopped him, crying: "Stetson!
> "You who were with me in the ships at Mylae!
> "That corpse you planted last year in your garden,
> "Has it begun to sprout? Will it bloom this year?

The speaker seems to know this wayfarer by name, calling him Stetson. Yet since the name Stetson also refers to a hat, there is something generic about the address. Has the speaker recognized a face or an accessory, an individual man or a universal type? Readers of Joyce's *Ulysses* may see a parallel with the unidentified, silent figure who appears at Paddy Dignam's funeral: the man in the macintosh, who will later be referred to simply as Macintosh. The next line furthers this sense of generic rather than specific identification. Mylae is the scene of a battle not from World War I but from the First Punic War. The anachronism renders the exchange timeless and unreal, a layering of postwar London, Dante's infernal circles, and the places and events of the classical world. The speaker's questions, too, are strange: They are urgent but unreal, like the fading thoughts as one wakes from a dream. The poet-pilgrim calls across the crowd to Stetson—who may be someone he knows or may be someone he only imagines he knows—but never tells the reader whether Stetson replied.

The poem echoes with such unanswered questions and unheard cries, for Eliot exploits the formal constraints of the poetic monologue to present only one side of any given exchange. Just as Stetson does not answer the speaker who singles him out, so the husband of Part II, "A Game of Chess," remains silent in the face of his querulous wife's questions:

> My nerves are bad to-night. Yes, bad. Stay with me.
> "Speak to me. Why do you never speak. Speak.

"What are you thinking of? What thinking? What?
"I never know what you are thinking. Think.

The repetitive, obsessive quality of her diction (as in the second line:
"speak . . . speak . . . speak . . .") attests to her nervous condition. Yet her
observation is no less profound for being neurotic. She, like Bradley,
sees the horror in being cut off from the feelings and perceptions of
the people who are closest to her. Her horror might be compounded
if she knew just how dark her husband's thoughts are: "I think we are
in rat's alley, / Where the dead men lost their bones." He, too, inhabits
a personal hell. Marriage, an institution intended to unite two people,
has brought only further division.

     Lest one conclude that spiritually deadening marriages are
suffered only by the middle or upper classes, "A Game of Chess"
contrasts the trials of this well-off couple with those of a lower-class
one. In a London pub, a gossipy publican relays the advice she gave her
friend Lil on keeping the affections of her husband, Albert, who will
be returning from the war. Where the neurotic couple is presumably
childless, Lil has many children. Her counselor says, "She's had five
already, and nearly died of young George."

     If marriage has compromised the nerves of the first wife, it has
compromised Lil's very body. The publican reminds Lil of this: "You
ought to be ashamed, I said, to look so antique / (And her only thirty-
one)." Albert has noticed the change as well and has given his wife
money to get a set of false teeth: "You have them all out, Lil, and get a
nice set, / He said, I swear, I can't bear to look at you." Finding herself
pregnant for a sixth time, however, Lil has used the denture money for
an abortion, which has further compromised her health. Lil laments:
"It's them pills I took, to bring it off . . . / The chemist said it would be
all right, but I've never been the same." It is a grotesque scenario, as if
O. Henry's 1906 short story "The Gift of the Magi," a sentimental tale
of the ironies of love and marriage, had been rewritten by an editorial
board of devils.

     Modern marriage is portrayed in *The Waste Land* as a fundamen-
tally alienating institution, but what of love, sex, or romance? Perhaps
in a city whose church bells issue a dead sound, one should seek
human contact outside the church. Yet the liaison of the typist and
the clerk in Part III, "The Fire Sermon," suggests that sex is as loveless
as marriage. As the Theban seer Tiresias watches, the clerk, a "young

man carbuncular," arrives at the typist's humble flat for a perfunctory dinner that is prelude to an even more perfunctory act of sex. In classical mythology, Tiresias was punished for interrupting the mating of two snakes, and in the typist's flat he now witnesses lovemaking that is just as cold-blooded. The typist and clerk have no sense of communion, the making of two into one. Because she is "bored and tired," the typist allows the clerk's "unreproved, if undesired" caresses. The clerk cares little about what the typist feels: "Exploring hands encounter no defence; / His vanity requires no response, / And makes a welcome of indifference."

In a poem that is full of voices, the typist and clerk say nothing to each other. The only direct quotation in the passage comes after the clerk has left, when the typist thinks, "Well now that's done: and I'm glad it's over." These closing words have all the listlessness of the "sighs, short and infrequent" of the morning commuters. Like the members of that crowd, she and the young man have done something worthy of "no blame and no praise." One cannot imagine them being damned for this passionless action, for what infernal *contrapasso* could be as banal and tedious as their sexual encounter itself? They have committed the same act as Paolo and Francesca, the mournful but passionate lovers who are doomed to ride the cold winds of the eighth circle, but they are not worthy of sharing their punishment. Dante's lovers are beautiful and damned; Eliot's are neither.

If sex is lifeless in the encounter between the typist and the clerk, elsewhere in the poem it will be equated with death itself. Toward the conclusion of Part III, a woman says: "Highbury bore me. Richmond and Kew / Undid me. By Richmond I raised my knees / Supine on the floor of a narrow canoe." The raised knees—a posture of sex and childbirth, of life itself—bring death instead. For the first sentence of the passage alludes to Dante's La Pia, who offers her own laconic epithet: "Siena made me, Maremma undid me." La Pia's "undoing" was at the hands of her husband, who murdered her in their home in Maremma. The nameless woman from Highbury's allusion to La Pia therefore collapses the distinction between the sacrament of marriage and sex outside of marriage. Neither arrangement allows two to become one.

In the unreal city, being with others only reinforces one's sense of being apart from others. Neither in a crowd nor in a marriage can one find communion. *Alienation,* a word derived from the Latin *alius, alienus* meaning "other," is fundamentally different from loneliness or solitude. The sensation arises from being physically close to—but spiritually distant from—other people. Might the alienated modern individual therefore leave the city and find solace and solitude in the natural world, as the English romantic poets and American transcendentalists did? Marie had said, in "The Burial of the Dead," "In the mountains, there you feel free." Perhaps a return to primal nature can free man from his modern condition.

Yet when one reaches the mountains in Part V of the poem, they offer neither communion nor solitude. Dry and lifeless, they are as wasted as the city:

> There is not even silence in the mountains
> But dry sterile thunder without rain
> There is not even solitude in the mountains
> But red sullen faces sneer and snarl
> From doors of mudcracked houses

Even here, man cannot escape from other men, and the sneers and snarls of the blighted country's inhabitants are no less alienating than the importunities of the city dwellers.

The mountains seem like a nightmarish version of the city itself, a phantasmagoric landscape where the elements of the earlier parts of the poem recombine in strange and disturbing ways. It is in Part V that a narrator glimpses the hooded hordes moving through an infernal landscape. Here, too, the argument of the neurotic married couple seems to play itself out again in the phantasmagoric passage beginning, "A woman drew her long black hair out tight, / And fiddled whisper music on those strings." And in this final part of *The Waste Land* an allusion from the *Inferno* speaks most directly to the hell of spiritual imprisonment: "*Dayadhvam:* I have heard the key / Turn in the door and turn once only." In Canto 33, the line is spoken by Count Ugolino, who, along with his sons, was imprisoned in the "Tower of Hunger," where they all eventually starved to death. Now he spends eternity locked in the ice of the frozen lake of hell, gnawing on the head of the archbishop who had him imprisoned. For Ugolino, physical confinement and starvation were only the beginning of his miseries.

Ironically, Eliot's haunting and beautiful rendering of Ugolino's line, and the echoes that follow it ("We think of the key, each in his prison / Thinking of the key, each confirms a prison / Only at nightfall. . . .") rests on a mistranslation of Dante's text. Eliot, who had a good reading knowledge of Italian, had studied the *Commedia* in its original language at Harvard. Here as elsewhere in his endnotes he includes the fragments of Dante's original text that he has reworked: "ed io sentii chiavar l'uscio di sotto / all'orribile torre." Yet Eliot, as he later admitted in one of three essays he wrote on Dante, was no Italian scholar. In translating Ugolino's line, he renders *chiavar* as "to lock" or "to turn the key." This makes sense if one is familiar with the modern Italian word *chiave*, meaning "key." Yet "key" is a newer meaning of the word; in Dante's time a *chiave* was a nail, and a better translation of *chiavar* would be "to nail up." Translator Mark Musa renders Ugolino's line this way: "Then from below I heard them driving nails into the dreadful tower's door." Nailing a door shut suggests a finality that turning a key does not, and Ugolino, high above in his tower, might just as well be hearing the nails driven into his own coffin and those of his sons.

Yet *The Waste Land* profits from Eliot's misreading of Ugolino's line, for the poem closes with the suggestion that the key that turned in the door might turn again. Even in the bleak environs of the modern city or the dry mountains, Ugolino's complaint assumes a more hopeful note than it holds in the *Inferno*, where the damned souls have no hope of ransom. This promise of release from the prison of the self is reinforced by the Sanskrit word that begins the line: "*Dayadhvam*: I have heard the key." For the thunder has begun to speak, its primal monosyllabic "da" suggesting a series of divine injunctions: "datta, dayadhvam, damyata" (give, sympathize, control). These commands, perhaps, are the keys that the alienated people of the city have been seeking. At Harvard, Eliot had studied not only the Italian of Dante's *Commedia* but also the Sanskrit of the Hindu Upanishads. "What the Thunder Said" brings these two languages and religious traditions into dialogue with each other. A poem that has represented the alienated and banal condition of modern man by systematically invoking Christian imagery—and in particular the Dantean vision of lost and damned souls—now reaches back to a pre-Christian cosmology to present the means of escaping that condition.

BIBLIOGRAPHY

Eliot, T.S. *The Complete Poems and Plays: 1909-1950*. New York: Harcourt, Brace & World, 1962.

Musa, Mark (translator). *Dante's Inferno: The Indiana Critical Edition*. Bloomington and Indianapolis, Indiana: Indiana University Press, 1995.

"YOUNG GOODMAN BROWN"
(NATHANIEL HAWTHORNE)

"Hawthorne"
by Charles Wilkins Webber,
in *American Whig Review* (1846)

INTRODUCTION

Explaining the story of "Young Goodman Brown" for first-time readers in an early review (1846), Charles Wilkins Webber describes the ambiguity and the gray shades of meaning that create a sense of alienation for Goodman Brown as he puzzles over what is real and for the reader, who struggles to understand Hawthorne's many rich symbols. Whether this story is seen as a fall from grace or the movement from innocence to experience, Webber explains why Goodman Brown becomes isolated from his Puritan community and why readers might feel alienated by Hawthorne's tale. For we, like Goodman Brown, must interpret the many symbols we receive. Rather than find one moral, we encounter paradox, the alienating contradiction at the heart of life.

Webber, Charles Wilkins. "Hawthorne," *American Whig Review*, 4 (September 1846). 296–316.

Walter Scott and Fouque have been masters; while in poetry Coleridge has triumphed supremely in *Christabel*. Hawthorne equals either of them in skill—but his subjects do not possess the breadth or histrionic grandeur of Scott's. His style and treatment have not equaled, though they have approached, the airy grace and tenderness of "Undine;" or attained to the mysterious dread which creeps through music in unequaled *Christabel*. Yet we think his story of "Young Goodman Brown" will bear to be contrasted with anything of this kind that has been done. The subject of course wants many imposing elements—for it is merely an Allegory of simple New England Village Life—but as a tale of the supernatural it certainly is more exquisitely managed than anything we have seen in American Literature, at least! He wins our confidence at once, by his directness and perfect simplicity. We have no puerile announcement to begin with of "A Tale of the Super-natural"—like the Painter's "This is a Cow," over his picture of that animal. We are left to find this out for ourselves in the due and proper time. In the meanwhile we are kept in a most titillating condition of uncertainty. We see that

> Young Goodman Brown came forth, at sunset, into the street of Salem village, but put his head back, after crossing the threshold, to exchange a parting kiss with his young wife. And Faith, as the wife was aptly named, thrust her own pretty head into the street, letting the wind play with the pink ribbons of her cap, while she called to Goodman Brown.
>
> "Dearest heart," whispered she, softly and rather sadly, when her lips were close to his ear, "pr'ythee, put off your journey until sunrise, and sleep in your own bed to-night. A lone woman is troubled with such dreams and such thoughts, that she's afeard of herself, sometimes. Pray, tarry with me this night, dear husband, of all nights in the year!"
>
> "My love and my Faith," replied young Goodman Brown, "of all nights in the year, this one night must I tarry away from thee. My journey, as thou callest it, forth and back again, must needs be done 'twixt now and sunrise. What, my sweet, pretty wife, dost thou doubt me already, and we but three months married!"
>
> "Then, God bless you!" said Faith, with the pink ribbons, "and may you find all well, when you come back."

"Amen!" cried Goodman Brown. "Say thy prayers, dear Faith, and go to bed at dusk, and no harm will come to thee."

So they parted; and the young man pursued his way, until, being about to turn the corner by the meeting-house, he looked back, and saw the head of Faith still peeping after him, with a melancholy air, in spite of her pink ribbons.

"Poor little Faith!" thought he, for his heart smote him. "What a wretch am I, to leave her on such an errand! She talks of dreams, too. Methought, as she spoke, there was trouble in her face, as if a dream had warned her what work is to be done to-night. But, no, no! 'twould kill her to think it. Well; she's a blessed angel on earth; and after this one night, I'll cling to her skirts and follow her to Heaven."

What does this mean, Goodman? Are you gone forth to some pledged revel with the young friends of your Bachelorhood—concerning which you have not dared to speak to your Faith? Ah, Goodman, these are dangerous vows to keep, and we are sure when it is all over this will be the last!—no, the Goodman belongs to a staid generation, and lives in pious Salem village. It is not because he goes forth to such sinful doings that his conscience is smitten—that his "Amen" startles us with its deep, sad tone! ah no! The Goodman is a young Bridegroom—"but three months married," and his heart yearns in tenderness towards his fair, young Bride, thus to be left alone through "the silent watches" for the first time. It is only some business of deep moment which would have called him forth—but it is an honest business, and we will go with him in confidence down the dreary road through the gloomiest part of the forest. When he suddenly beholds "the figure of a man in grave and decent attire seated at the foot of an old tree," who arose and walked onward with him as if be had been expecting him, our vague apprehensions are relieved at once and we feel gratified that our sagacious appreciation is sustained by the decorous and unquestionable character of his companion. Even when we see that strange staff of his, which "bore the likeness of a great black snake so curiously wrought that it might be seen to twist and wriggle itself like a living serpent," our faith in his grave and evidently acute friend is only slightly shocked. And when as they talk on, he claims to have been an old friend of the Puritan Grandfather and Father of the Goodman, and to be on terms of intimacy with the deacons and selectmen, and even with the Governor and Council, we absolutely take him into our confidence—for how could he be intimate with such people and not be trustworthy? Nay, although he seems to have something of a bitter tongue in his head, we have become so propitiated that we absolutely feel indignant at the Goodman's perverse hesitation to accompany so proper a person. To what evil could the old friend of his Fathers lead him—and why should you distrust him, Goodman? When we see before them in the path the form of Goody Cloyse, "who had taught him his catechism in youth, and was still his moral and spiritual adviser jointly with the minister and Deacon Gookin," we are surprised, as the Goodman was, that she should be so far in the wilderness at nightfall—but we feel hurt for him that he should be so cowardly as to turn out from the path into the woods to avoid meeting his old and honored instructress. Conscience-smitten Goodman! what can it mean? and then to be so suspicious of your venerable companion as to shabbily play the eavesdropper upon him! But the scene which follows begins to enlighten us somewhat:

> Accordingly, the young man turned aside, but took care to watch his companion, who advanced softly along the road, until he had come within a staff's length of the old dame. She, meanwhile, was making the best of her way, with singular speed for so aged a woman, and mumbling some indistinct words, a prayer, doubtless, as she went. The traveller put forth his staff, and touched her withered neck with what seemed the serpent's tail.
>
> "The devil!" screamed the pious lady.
>
> "Then Goody Cloyse knows her old friend?" observed the traveller, confronting her, leaning on his writhing stick.
>
> "Ah, forsooth, and is it your worship, indeed?" cried the good dame. "Yea, truly is it, and in the very image of my old gossip, Goodman Brown, the grandfather of the silly fellow that now is. But, would your worship believe it? my broomstick hath strangely disappeared; stolen, as I suspect, by that unhanged witch, Goody Cory, and that, too, when I was all anointed with the juice of smallage, and cinque-foil, and wolf's bane"—
>
> "Mingled with fine wheat and the fat of a new-born babe," said the shape of old Goodman Brown.

"Ah, your worship knows the recipe," cried the old lady, cackling aloud. "So, as I was saying, being all ready for the meeting, and no horse to ride on, I made up my mind to foot it; for they tell me there is a nice young man to be taken into communion to-night. But now your good worship will lend me your arm, and we shall be there in a twinkling."

"That can hardly be," answered her friend. "I may not spare you my arm, Goody Cloyse, but here is my staff, if you will."

So saying, he threw it down at her feet, where, perhaps, it assumed life, being one of the rods which its owner had formerly lent to the Egyptian Magi. Of this fact, however, Goodman Brown *could not take cognizance*. He had cast up his eyes in astonishment, and looking down again, beheld neither Goody Cloyse nor the serpentine staff, but his fellow-traveller alone, who waited for him as calmly as if nothing had happened.

"That old woman taught me my catechism!" said the young man; and there was a world of meaning in this simple comment.

Ah, Goodman! Goodman! now we begin to tremble for thee. Didst thou see those green twigs wet with the evening dew wilt up beneath the touch of his finger? Thou art in awful company! How we tremble for him when he says stubbornly, "Friend, my mind is made up; not another step will I budge on this errand." God help thee to stand up to that resolve! His Tempter disappears. But then all the air and forest is filled with his delusions. The voices of Deacon Gookin and the old minister go by. They are jogging quietly on the same road. "Where can these holy men be journeying so deep in the heathen wilderness?" The young Goodman nearly drops with faintness! All going—but yet there is hope. "With Heaven above and Faith below I will yet stand firm against the devil," he cries. Stoutly said, thou brave Goodman! Then the accents of many of his town's-people both godly and ungodly are heard going by—still the Goodman would have been firm—but alas! the voice of a young woman uttering lamentations, and a bit of "*pink ribbon*" flutters lightly down the silent air! ah, it is terrible. "Faith! Faith! Faith!" the strong man screams, and what wonder that now he is maddened and rushes on. "My Faith is gone"—come, devil! for to thee is this world given!" He speeds through the forest which was peopled with frightful sounds—but there was no horror like that in his own breast—until he saw a red light before him and that weird altar of rock "surrounded by four blazing pines—their tops a flame, their stems untouched, like candles at an evening meeting" rose in view—and the great concourse—"a grave and dark-clad company" of those who had collected there to the Saturnalia of Hell.

> Among them, quivering to-and-fro, between gloom and splendor, appeared faces that would be seen, next day, at the council-board of the province, and others which, Sabbath after Sabbath, looked devoutly heavenward, and benignantly over the crowded pews, from the holiest pulpits in the land. Some affirm, that the lady of the governor was there. At least, there were high dames well known to her, and wives of honored husbands, and widows, a great multitude, and ancient maidens, all of excellent repute, and fair young girls, who trembled lest their mothers should espy them. Either the sudden gleams of light, flashing over the obscure field, bedazzled Goodman Brown, or he recognized a score of the church-members of Salem village, famous for their especial sanctity. Good old Deacon Gookin had arrived, and waited at the skirts of that venerable saint, his reverend pastor. But, irreverently consorting with these grave, reputable and pious people, these elders of the Church, these chaste dames and dewy virgins, there were men of dissolute lives and women of spotted fame, wretches given over to all mean and filthy vice, and suspected even of horrid crimes. It was strange to see, that the good shrank not from the wicked, nor were the sinners abashed by the saints. Scattered, also, among their pale-faced enemies, were the Indian priests, or powows, who had often scared their native forests with more hideous incantations than any known to English witchcraft.
>
> "But, where is Faith?" thought Goodman Brown; and, as hope came into his heart, he trembled.

Terrible picture! Sad! sad night for thee, Goodman, when with thy young eyes thou lookedst upon it! Dark! all in dark with an unutterable gloom—for that lurid light upon it is only darkness heated white with the fierce glow of Hell-hate. No delusion of a mooned melancholy hast thou now to cope with, Goodman! They are all real—real to thee—and even we can feel the hot breath of the thick, infestious air, wrestling with our Souls. It shall not be, though. We will not believe it all! Goodman! Goodman! it is a delusion! Think of thy Faith! And he asks where she is, and trembles with the hope that she may not be there. And that "dreadful anthem" they were singing to "a slow and solemn strain, such as the pious love, but joined to words which expressed all that our nature can conceive of sin, and darkly hinted at far more"—with its awful chorus of all the sounds of "the unconverted wilderness," which ushers in the coming of the Chief Priest, the master Fiend of all this multitude. The fire on the rock-altar forms an arch, and beneath it he appears, "bearing no slight similitude, both to garb and manners, to some grave divine of the New England Churches! "Bring forth the converts," rolls out in the volumed solemnity of his tones. "At the word" the Goodman obeys—drawn—but with deep loathing in his heart. The shape of his father beckons him on from amidst a wreath of smoke, while a woman waves him back; "Is it his mother?" Beautiful question! But ah, that veiled and slender female led forward between Goody Cloyse and "that rampant hag," who is to be queen of hell, Martha Carrier! who is she, Goodman? Is this last terrible bolt to fall? Is it *she*? The Goodman is meek now—the doubt is enough! He no longer "loathes"—how can he loathe or feel anything? He is dumb and numb, and all his life lies still. He is turned into a machine, and looks round when the Orator requires—and the greeting of the Fiend-worshipers which grimed darkly upon him out of the sheet of flame—was like any other sort of greeting—quite a formal thing! Now he listens to that measured discourse from him of "the sable form," in which the monstrous and maddening creed, that Evil is the only real actuality, while virtue, truth, all godliness and righteousness, are hollow sounding names—as a very proper sort of discourse! That they were all here whom he had reverenced from youth, he knew already—that it was a deception when he had deemed them holier than himself, he had seen—for they were all here in the worshiping assembly of the Devil. And that diabolical summary of secret crimes and promise of the gift to know and see all beings in their true life,—this was all consequential and moved him not—but that veiled figure? What cared he that "the fountain of all wicked arts" should be opened up to him? he had not leaned so much upon those others; he had leaned upon the truth of his Fathers; but most upon his "Faith." The two converts are told by *him*, (The Evil One,) "my children, look upon each other!" They did so, and "by the blaze of hell-kindled torches the wretched man beheld his Faith, and the wife her husband."

"'So, there ye stand, my children,' said the figure, in a deep and solemn tone, almost sad with its despairing awfulness, as if his once angelic nature could yet mourn for our miserable race. 'Depending upon one another's hearts, ye still hoped that virtue were not all a dream! now ye are undeceived!' Welcome! and welcome! "repeated the fiend-worshipers, in one cry of despair and triumph!" Thou stricken Goodman! out of the agony that *doubt* had stilled—this last dreadful consummation had almost quickened thy wrenched soul into one spasm of expiring strength, when that accursed baptism, "the Shape of Evil" was prepared to mark with the red fluid upon thy forehead, in token of thy initiation into the mysteries of Sin, startles thee up. The old Puritan in thee rouses to the rescue at last! That ancient hatred of "the mark of the Beast" has stung thee! "Faith! Faith! look up to Heaven, and resist the Wicked One!" It has been spoken! You are saved Goodman! And now, considered merely as an artistic effect, comes the most exquisitely perfect dream-waking we ever remember to have seen. "Hardly had he spoken, when he found himself amid calm night and solitude, listening to the roar of the wind which died heavily away through the forest. He staggered against the rock and felt it chill and damp, while a hanging twig *that had been all on fire*, besprinkled his cheek with the coldest dew!'"

It has been all unreal, Goodman, as that chill sprinkle from amidst thy dreamland flames has taught thee! but canst thou ever forget that awful Dream, thou granite man? It has been burned into the stern substance of thy hard life, with each particular line deepened like a furrow. Is there any caoutchouc in your nature, which can give up to the energy of hope and truth beneath, and smooth out those sharp cut seams? He shrank from the good minister's blessing as he came into the village, with a wild stare in his eye. He heard the Deacon Gookin at domestic worship, and he asked unconsciously, "What God doth the wizard pray to?" Goody Cloyse cathecised a little girl before her door, and he snatched her away as from the grasp of the fiend himself. He spies the head of Faith looking anxiously out of his own door, with the same "pink ribbons in her cap." Though she skips to meet him, in a fond ecstacy, and almost kisses him before the whole village, yet he looks even *her* in the face with a sad regard, and passes on without a greeting. Oh, Goodman! Goodman! for this last we could weep over thee, as one for whom there is no hope—for Hope died in thy soul last night; and as for sweet, gentle Faith, she too is dead for thee, thou darkened man!

"Had Goodman Brown fallen asleep in the forest, and only dreamed a wild dream of a witch meeting?" "Be it so if you will. But, alas! it was a dream of evil omen for young Goodman Brown. A stern, a sad, a darkly meditative and distrustful, if not a desperate, man did he become from the night of that fearful dream." He even "shrunk from the bosom of his Faith at midnight;" and how can we doubt that, though he lived to a good old age—when he died—although he had "children and grand-children, a goodly procession," yet they "carved no hopeful verse upon his tombstone." Alas! Goodman, thou hadst seen *too much*; and if when thy Faith came to meet thee, with her chirruping joy, thy lips had only been unfrozen as they met her holy kiss, the dreadful Dream would have vanished, leaving no curse behind, and no doubt would have rested on thy cheerless grave. Ye men whose lives are shaded, who look out with a dulled, melancholic vision which *cannot* pierce the clouds to the blue heaven, with its stars beyond, take warning from the Goodman's Dream; for the same vision which cannot see to Heaven peoples the dull earth-mists around it with a Hell of Fiends!

This story is only one of many, which equal it in all the attributes of Artistic effect, but few of which approach it in power. The singular skill with which our sympathy is kept "halting between two opinions"—by which we are compelled throughout to recognize the flesh and blood reality of Goodman Brown; and necessarily, to enter into all the actual relations of the man, is only surpassed by the terrible elaboration with which this human embodiment of Doubt is compelled, through awe and madness, to struggle with the beings—almost equally human—of a self-created Hell.

❧ *Acknowledgments* ❧

Bluefarb, Sam. "The Head, the Heart and the Conflict of Generations in Chaim Potok's *The Chosen." College Language Association Journal* (CLA), Vol. 14, No. 4 (June 1971). 402–9. Copyright 1971 by the College Language Association. Reprinted by permission.

Ellison, Ralph. "Richard Wright's Blues." *Shadow and Act.* New York: Random House, 1964. 77–94. (First published in *The Antioch Review* 5.2 [June 1945]:198–212) Copyright 1964 by Ralph Ellison. Reprinted by permission of the William Morris Agency.

Goethe, Johann Wolfgang von. "Book IV, Chapter XIII." *Wilhelm Meister's Apprenticeship and Travels.* Trans. Thomas Carlyle. Boston: Ticknor and Fields, 1865. 229–32.

Hawthorn, Jeremy. "Divided Selves." *Virginia Woolf's Mrs. Dalloway: A Study in Alienation.* London: Sussex University Press, 1975. 28–44. Copyright Jeremy Hawthorn 1975. Reprinted by permission.

Heller, Erich. "The Trial." *Franz Kafka.* New York: Viking Press, 1974. 71–97. Copyright 1974 by Erich Heller. Reprinted by permission.

Miyoshi, Masao. "Masks in the Mirror: The Eighteen-Nineties." *The Divided Self: A Perspective on the Literature of the Victorians.* New York: New York University Press, 1969. 289–340. Copyright 1969 by New York University. Reprinted by permission.

Mochulsky, Konstantin. "The Journal *Epoch, Notes from Underground."* *Dostoevsky: His Life and Work.* Trans. Michael A. Minihan. Princeton, N.J.: Princeton University Press, 1967. 242–69. Copyright 1967 by Princeton University Press. Reprinted by permission of Princeton University Press.

Olderman, Raymond M. "The Grail Knight Arrives." *Beyond the Waste Land: A Study of the American Novel in the Nineteen-Sixties.* New Haven: Yale

University Press, 1972. 35–51. Copyright 1972 by Yale University. Reprinted by permission.

Sartre, Jean-Paul. "Camus' *The Outsider*." *Literary and Philosophical Essays*. Trans. Annette Michelson. New York: Criterion, 1955. 26–44. Copyright 1955 by Criterion Books Inc.

Watt, Donald. "Burning Bright: *Fahrenheit 451* as Symbolic Dystopia." *Ray Bradbury*. Ed. Joseph Olander and M.H. Greenberg. New York: Taplinger, 1980. 195–213. Copyright 1980 by Martin Harry Greenberg and Joseph D. Olander. Reprinted by permission.

Webber, Charles Wilkins. "Hawthorne," *American Whig Review*, 4 (September 1846). 296–316.

Index